LINCOLN'S
MEN

Smithsonian Books

COLLINS
An Imprint of HarperCollins*Publishers*

LINCOLN'S MEN

THE PRESIDENT AND

HIS PRIVATE SECRETARIES

DANIEL MARK EPSTEIN

HarperCollins books may be purchased for educational, business, or sales promotional use. For information, please write: Special Markets Department, HarperCollins Publishers, 10 East 53rd Street, New York, NY 10022.

FIRST EDITION

Designed by Mia Risberg

Library of Congress Cataloging-in-Publication Data

Epstein, Daniel Mark.
Lincoln's men: the president and his private secretaries / Daniel Mark Epstein.—1st ed.
p. cm.
Includes bibliographical references and index.
ISBN-13: 978-0-06-156544-1   1. Lincoln, Abraham, 1809–1865—
Friends and associates.   2. Private secretaries—United States—
Biography.   3. Presidents—United States—Staff—Biography.
4. Lincoln, Abraham, 1809–1865.   5. Presidents—United States—
Biography.   6. United States—Politics and government—1861–1865.
I. Title.
E457.2.E69 2009
973.7092—dc22
2008038812

09 10 11 12 13   OV/RRD   10 9 8 7 6 5 4 3 2 1

For Theodore John Epstein

CONTENTS

CHAPTER ONE

ILLINOIS PRELUDE

As the train pulled out of Springfield's Great Western Depot on the rainy morning of February 11, 1861, with president-elect Abraham Lincoln and his entourage bound for Washington, D.C., there were three young men aboard with exceptional promise: John Milton Hay, John George Nicolay, and Elmer Ephraim Ellsworth. Of the three friends, two would become the president's private secretaries during the most tempestuous era the nation had ever known; the third, Ellsworth, would briefly serve as the president-elect's head of security.

The twenty-three-year-old Ellsworth, an aspiring soldier, was so short that had it not been for his neat black mustache and whiskered underlip he might have been mistaken for one of the Lincolns' little boys. Though he was scarcely five feet in height, what Ellsworth lacked in stature he more than made up for in dignity and authority, having made himself famous—a public emblem—by a means altogether unique.

The son of a bankrupt tailor in the New York village of Malta, too poor and obscure to attend West Point, Ellsworth, through self-education and exercise, had made himself a drillmaster without peer in America. A born leader, in the late 1850s he organized companies of militia in Chicago that he outfitted in the loose scarlet trousers, blue jackets with gold braid, and jaunty red caps of the French Foreign Legion, calling them Zouaves after the soldiers who fought in the Crimean War. The men paid for their own uniforms. He trained them to do intricate military drills and manuals of arms. He lectured them on patriotism. On parade grounds in the major cities, Ellsworth and his Zouaves drew crowds and newsmen who raved about "the little colonel" and his superbly trained militiamen. They were equally impressed with Ellsworth's temperance, austerity, and code of honor. He refused to accept any pay for his services to his country, past or future.

Like many prodigies and early ripe composers and artists, Ellsworth was not long for this world. The nation was on the brink of war, folks sensed it, and Ellsworth was an avatar of courage and honor. He is a part of the history, essential to getting it under way, and also a victim of it, the first of many lives sacrificed to a cause at first only dimly understood. Lincoln met him during the winter of 1859–60 when Ellsworth came to study law in Springfield. After watching the Chicago Zouaves drill in a Springfield meadow in August 1860, the presidential candidate invited Ellsworth to remain in town and study law with him. Impressed with the soldier's zeal and intelligence, Lincoln sent him out, with John Hay, to stump for him in the election. He had served the candidate so well that when Lincoln was elected, in November, he invited Ellsworth to attend him as a bodyguard on the train to Washington, with a further prospect of getting him a position in the War Department.

TRAVELING ON THE TRAIN with Ellsworth was twenty-two-year-old John Hay. Hay was a poet, a smooth-faced, handsome fellow with a strong chin, long upper lip, and slightly protruding elfin ears that his wavy brown hair partly concealed. His dark eyes were deep-set, liquid, and his friends used to say you could see a mile into them. Only four inches taller than Ellsworth, Hay saw from his vantage point the soldier's "form, though slight,—exactly the Napoleonic size,—was very compact and commanding"; Ellsworth's sunny smile and deep, musical voice "instantly attracted attention; and his address . . . was sincere and courteous." Hay might as well have been describing his own winning smile and manner; it was not military skill or poetry that had won John Milton Hay his seat on the train to the capital—it was his eloquence and charm.

Hay also owed his place in Lincoln's retinue to the insistence of his best friend, the twenty-nine-year-old journalist John Nicolay. Standing next to the poet Hay and the soldier Ellsworth in the train's saloon car, Nicolay, at five feet ten inches and 120 pounds, looked like a gaunt giant, older than his years, with his receding hairline and dark goatee. He had served as Mr. Lincoln's personal secretary—at a salary of $75 per month—since June 7, 1860, soon after the Republicans nominated the "rail-splitter" to be their standard-bearer. He was Lincoln's door-keeper, his amanuensis, and his confidant. Born in Bavaria, the secretary had a low voice that still showed traces of a German accent. Orphaned at age fourteen and thrown upon his own resources—a vigorous mind in a frail body—the former printer's devil and editor had never wanted anything so much in his life as to serve the Republican nominee. Lincoln must have sensed this and, knowing Nicolay's politics as well as his past, knew he could count on the young man's loyalty and complete discretion.

Shortly after the election, on November 11, 1860, Nicolay wrote to his fiancée, Therena Bates, still living in Pittsfield, Illinois, where they had met as children.

> I can myself hardly realize that after having fought this slavery question for six years past and suffered so many defeats, I am at last rejoicing in a triumph which two years ago we hardly dared dream about. I remember very distinctly, how in 1854, soon after I had bought the Free Press Office [in Pittsfield], I went to Perry, with others, and heard Mr. Atkinson (the preacher) make the first anti-Nebraska speech which was made in Pike County in that campaign. Though I was fighting as something more than a private then, I should have thought it a wild dream to imagine

that in six years after I should find the victory so near the Commander in Chief.

It was "Nebraska," the bitter conflict over Stephen Douglas's Kansas-Nebraska Act—which repealed the Missouri Compromise and opened the new territories to the extension of slavery—that brought Nicolay and Lincoln together. Nicolay, as a crusading editor of the *Free Press,* and Lincoln, as an ambitious politician, denounced Douglas's idea of "popular sovereignty," the very idea that settlers in the territories might choose to allow slavery if they pleased.

On October 27, 1856, Lincoln had showed up at a free-soil meeting in Pittsfield. Nicolay, as a member of the Republican committee there that invited speakers, had hoped that Senator Lyman Trumbull, a Democrat, or the Honorable Abraham Lincoln would attend. He could hardly believe his good fortune when he watched, from a crowded shop, as the Democrat Trumbull welcomed the newly arrived Republican, Lincoln, and the two politicians warmly embraced on the street. Men of conflicting parties, they were united by the cause of freedom. Somewhat later in the day, Lincoln ran into a friend, the educator John Shastid, and asked him where he might find "an honest printer." Shastid led Mr. Lincoln to the east side of the square, where he found John Nicolay in the offices of the *Free Press.*

Charmed by the "kindly smile, the earnest eyes, the hearty grip" of the forty-seven-year-old lawyer, Nicolay was eager to hear Lincoln's speech that evening. And he reported the enormous success and turnout at the free-soil rally, "at least twice as large as the late [Stephen] Douglas demonstration." From then on, he would never neglect an opportunity to write about Lincoln's progress. As Nicolay recalled years later, the orator "held him spellbound and cemented his devotion."

And Lincoln—for his part—was impressed with the idealistic journalist. Nicolay was growing restless in the village. In July of 1857, Lincoln helped raise $500 to subsidize Nicolay as an agent for the *Missouri Democrat,* a staunchly free-soil newspaper published in St. Louis, with orders for him to increase the newspaper's circulation in Illinois. Preferring journalism to sales, Nicolay wrote more columns than the paper desired while selling too few subscriptions. The financial panic of 1857, touched off by the failure of the Ohio Life Insurance and Trust Company, discouraged all business ventures, publishing included. By the end of the year, the publishers relieved him of his duties. He returned, wistfully, to Pittsfield.

John Nicolay was in love with the dark-eyed, raven-haired, petite Therena Bates, daughter of "Squire" Dorus Bates, a farmer and justice of the peace. As the publisher of a small-town weekly, Nicolay would never make enough money to support a family in style. So he decided to become a lawyer, both for the financial security the profession promised, and because the law would better prepare him to take part in the momentous political drama of his time.

Because no attorney in Pittsfield was eager to take on the gruff, uncompromising journalist as a student, Nicolay accepted an invitation to visit with a friend of Lincoln's in Springfield, Ozias M. Hatch, secretary of state for Illinois, who also happened to be related by marriage to the Bates family.

A few weeks later, Hatch offered the young man a clerkship in his office, with the understanding that he could study his law books there when he was not otherwise engaged.

So, after Christmas, Nicolay bid his fiancée farewell for the time being and moved to Springfield, about seventy miles east, across the Illinois River. There, while studying law in the state library at the capitol—of which Mr. Hatch was the custodian—Nicolay had a ringside seat at the State Conventions, meetings of the legislature, courts, and party caucuses taking place so near the secretary's statehouse office.

Fascinated by Lincoln, Nicolay took every opportunity to converse with the celebrated lawyer-politician. The man was "an assiduous student of election tables," Nicolay observed. These records were kept on a shelf in the office where he clerked, so he was called upon time and again to show Lincoln the latest returns or the record of past elections, which he clucked and chuckled over, or frowned upon as if they had released some unpleasant odor. If business was slow on a snowy winter afternoon, Nicolay and Lincoln would sit down to a game of chess. Lincoln played the game distractedly, while singing snatches of ballads, and providing much extraneous and droll commentary: *You hear about that man up in Tazewell has got up a patent on a milking machine? Now. The best milking machine is a calf. You inventors ought to turn your attention to a patent for getting the milk out of the calf.*

Banter of this sort was not lost on Nicolay. He had a good sense of humor. He also held a government patent on a printing machine so ingenious that the lawyers in Pittsfield said it was a waste of time for him to be studying law when he ought to pursue his vocation as an inventor. He had studied the law all the same, while keeping his hand in as a journalist, writing columns for the *Chicago Tribune* and Springfield's own *Illinois Journal.* During the Lincoln-Douglas debates in 1858, Nicolay prepared a circular that he titled *The Political Record of Stephen Douglas,* a partisan pamphlet exposing the inconsistencies and treacheries of the Little Giant's approach to slavery and the Constitution.

When time came to publish the record of the debates, in 1859, Lincoln asked Nicolay to deliver his own carefully assembled scrapbook to the publishers, Follett, Foster & Co., in Columbus, Ohio. And in February 1860, on a trip home to visit Therena Bates, Nicolay dropped by the office of the Pittsfield *Pike County Journal* to chat with the editor, Dan Bush, and sing the praises of Abraham Lincoln. Bush put a pen in his friend's hand and asked him to write down what he had said. On February 9, that paper published one of the first presidential endorsements of Lincoln, and the validation was in Nicolay's enthusiastic words.

Nicolay greatly desired to write Lincoln's official campaign biography. He was disappointed when he discovered that the job had been promised to a twenty-three-year-old Ohio poet with powerful connections—William Dean Howells, who was already publishing in the *Atlantic Monthly.* Turning to Ozias Hatch for comfort, he could hardly believe his ears when Hatch said, "Never mind. You are to be private secretary."

LINCOLN WAS ELECTED PRESIDENT on November 6, 1860; after that, the current of his Springfield mail began to rise to a torrent that Nicolay could not handle alone. So, on a Sunday morning in late November, he invited John Hay to Lincoln's office (rooms on loan from the governor) in the statehouse to help out. Hay was reading law, with little enthusiasm, in Stephen Logan's office nearby on the square, and writing poetry. He was only too happy to oblige John Nicolay. The friendship of these two men was a felicity blessed by a rare and perfect complement of temperaments and favored by geography. For fifty years, these busy fellows—both of whom would eventually serve in the diplomatic corps—were rarely separated for longer than a few months.

John Hay grew up in Warsaw, Illinois, a hamlet on the Mississippi, the fourth of six children born to Dr. Charles Hay and Helen Leonard. Dr. Hay, a prosperous physician, was schooled first as a classical scholar. He taught his son Greek and Latin, so that by the age of twelve John had read six books of Virgil. Wanting the best education for the boy, the doctor accepted his brother Milton's invitation to board John at his residence in Pittsfield, Illinois, while he attended a private classical school there.

At the age of thirteen, in 1851, Hay went to Pittsfield to study at John D. Thompson's school. It was there that the Irish headmaster introduced the precocious scholar to John Nicolay. Hay happened to be fluent in German, Nicolay's native language. In German and English, the boy and the nineteen-year-old printer commenced a conversation that would continue for a half a century, despite the disparity in their ages, education, and social class.

In less than a year, having learned all there was to be learned at Mr. Thompson's (neither John's classmates nor his teachers could keep up with him), Hay moved on to a prep school in Springfield, where he prepared to enter Brown University in the autumn of 1855. Nicolay longed to go to Brown with his friend, but he had neither the funds nor the academic foundation to attend such a college. The office of the *Free Press,* a paper that Nicolay now owned, would be his classroom, and the politically storm-tossed state of Illinois his university.

While Hay was translating Racine and Goethe, and mastering the art of versification, Nicolay was learning how to balance the books in a small business with a narrow profit margin. While the romantic poet was following in the footsteps of Edgar Allan Poe, smoking hashish and frequenting the literary salons of Providence, Rhode Island—including the candlelit parlor of Poe's former fiancée, the poet Sarah Helen Whitman—Nicolay was covering the Anti-Nebraska Convention in Bloomington, Illinois. There, before that fractious crowd of free-soilers, he heard Abraham Lincoln defend the cause of freedom with such dramatic fervor that no stenographer could look down to record it. This was the legendary speech that put Lincoln on the track for the presidency.

On the evening of October 27, 1856, when Nicolay met Lincoln and heard him address the Republican meeting in Pittsfield, John Hay was sitting in the dress circle of Forbes Theatre in Providence. Like other stargazers and theater fanatics of that time and place, he would not have given up his theater tickets for all the harpoons in Bedford. He had been haunting the playhouse for a week, neglecting his studies, for what was to be seen there was a precious embodiment of poetry and art in one small person.

Her name was Jean Margaret Davenport. At twenty-seven, she was already a legend on both sides of the Atlantic—the greatest actress of her generation and one of the most beautiful. Born in England, the child of a provincial actress and a theater manager, at the age of eight, Jean Davenport made her debut as Little Pickle in *The Spoiled Child*. Months later, she appeared, in false whiskers, in the title role of Shakespeare's *King Richard III,* scoring an enormous financial and critical success. In these roles, she toured the principal cities of England and Ireland before coming to the United States. Heralded as "the little Dramatic Prodigy," she was satirized as the real-life model for Ninetta Crummles, "the Infant Phenomenon" of Charles Dickens's *Nicholas Nickleby.*

Unlike other child stars, Jean Davenport defied the odds, flouting the judgment that such prodigies cannot grow into mature artists. At thirteen, she took three years of literary and dramatic study in France and Italy, and at sixteen she returned to the stage transformed, a brilliant classical actress whose performances as Shakespeare's Juliet ravished audiences with their deep emotion and subtlety.

Miss Davenport had come to Providence on October 21 to play Julia in J. S. Knowles's *The Hunchback*. For nine days she was held over by popular demand. As the climax of her spectacular run, she was appearing as the tragic "Coquette" in the scandalous *Camille,* which she herself had first adapted from the French of Dumas and introduced to New York audiences in 1853. Only the pathos evoked by sublime acting could have rescued the play from police raids and censorship. According to the winds of public opinion, Miss Davenport had either corrupted or refined the morals of the decade. John Hay had never seen anything like it. She was blinding. He was only eighteen, of course, but no one else had seen anything like this performance in Forbes Theatre, a woman stripped of artifice and much of her clothing, her deepest passions shamelessly on display. He was "starstruck," he admitted, smitten by the image the young actress projected, "such stuff as dreams are made on." Would he ever find such a woman in real life?

WHILE JOHN HAY DREAMED of literary fame and the love of fair women, John George Nicolay cranked his press for the cause of free men, free soil, and the principles of the newly formed Republican Party. He studied law in Springfield, where he observed, with keen interest, the political rise of Abraham Lincoln within the new party. When Nicolay found time, he visited his fiancée in Pittsfield, keeping the romance alive.

Hay was a sensational student. At Brown, at last he was in his element. His classmates elected him class poet; he was popular within the college community, and embraced by the high society of Providence. He pledged the fraternity Theta Delta Chi (motto: *Our Hearts Are United*) in 1857. It is hardly surprising that upon graduating in 1858, his eastern idyll ended, he did not want to go home.

Life in Warsaw, Illinois, plunged the young poet into a Gothic mood of despondency worthy of the author of "The Raven." He wrote to Nora Perry, a fellow poet friend in Providence:

> If you loved Providence as I do, you would congratulate yourself hourly upon your lot. The city . . . is shrined in my memory as a far-off, mystical Eden, where the women were lovely and spi-

rituelle, and the men were jolly and brave; where I used to haunt the rooms of the Athenaeum, made holy by the presence of the royal dead; where I used to pay furtive visits to Forbes' forbidden mysteries; where I used to eat Hasheesh and dream dreams. My life will not be utterly desolate while memory is left me . . .

In the spring, he wrote to Miss Perry, "I have wandered this winter in the valley of the shadow of death. All the universe, God, earth and heaven have been to me but vague and gloomy phantasms. I have conversed with wild imaginings in the gloom of the forests. . . . into every parlor my Daemon has pursued me."

Part of Hay's problem was that he was madly in love with his cousin, Annie Johnston, with whom he had been on terms of intense intimacy throughout his adolescence. Now, for reasons that he could not quite comprehend, she was beginning to distance herself from him. Equally distressing was the fact that he could not imagine a future for himself in the West, "a dreary waste of heartless materialism, where great and heroic qualities . . . bully their way up into the glare, but the flowers of existence inevitably droop and wither." He was writing poetry and giving lectures now and then, but he had to admit that these occupations would not enable him to pull his weight in the large family that had done so much for him. His parents were affectionate and forbearing, but they would not permit him to go on moping in Warsaw and pining for Annie, at their expense, much longer. They thought him too skeptical to go into the ministry and they did not want him to be a schoolteacher. Worried, Dr. Hay wrote again to his brother Milton. At last, yielding to the inevitable, the twenty-year-old graduate accepted his uncle Milton's invitation to read the law under his supervision. "They would spoil a first-class preacher to make a third-class lawyer of me," he quipped.

Bidding his darling Annie a sad farewell, in May of 1859, John Hay returned to Springfield, where Milton Hay had gone into business with Stephen Logan, Lincoln's former law partner. The poet was lukewarm about practicing law; he simply did not know what else to do with his life. And at least, in Springfield, there was John Nicolay, and the spectacle of the state government, and some semblance of society. Nicolay's intelligence, energy, and musical gifts—he played the piano and had "a sweet, true tenor voice"—had made him a welcome visitor in the best houses. And where Nicolay went, Hay soon followed. The friends spent delightful evenings in the Victorian mansion of Nicholas Ridgely, a banker with three pretty daughters.

Anna Ridgely was smitten with Hay. She described him as "a bright, handsome fellow . . . with good features, especially the eyes which were dark, lustrous brown; red cheeks and clear dark complexion; small, well-shaped hands which he had a habit of locking together interlacing the fingers, and carrying at arms length, which the girls thought particularly fetching." (There is no accounting then or now for what people might find particularly fetching . . .) "He also dressed appealingly, wearing a long loose overcoat, flying open, his hands thrust into the pockets . . . graceful and attractive, as he swung himself along the street . . ."

Anna's elegant parlor was the gathering place for young folks who loved music and literature, and dancing, and speaking French and German as well as they could, which—in the case of the two friends from the West—was very good indeed. Nicolay, tall and slender, was light on his feet, and a popular partner in the quadrille. Of the two men, Nicolay was happier, and no doubt a great comfort to his friend, who was still disappointed in love and frustrated in his career. Nicolay was doing what he wanted to do. He had been admitted to the Illinois bar in January 1859, wrote columns for several journals while clerking in the statehouse, and saw as much as he pleased of his fiancée. He relished his daily contact with the leading Republicans of Illinois, including the droll Mr. Lincoln.

Hay was still clinging to memories of cousin Annie, and mourning a paradise lost. On New Year's Day, 1860, he wrote to her: "While all the world of Springfield is exchanging New Year greetings, partaking of New Year hospitality, eating New Year salads and drinking New Year's coffee (nothing stronger) let me, secluding myself for a while from the world aforesaid, make my New Years call on you. Let me in the morning of the year remind you of my existence that I might not be forgotten . . ." His letter is given over to a catalog of his miseries, and hoping that she will avoid his sorry condition. He says he cannot make any more visits because "I am becoming dreadfully cross, ill-natured and morose."

He blames his surroundings, saying that in Warsaw he is half-civilized, but "when I leave there I become an absolute heathen. Is it because I have no mother here to tell me to cultivate the humanities?" In Springfield he has no friend like Annie. He longs for her, yet urges her to take advantage of her beauty and charm. "Gather your rose-buds while you may, Annie, for the heavens may not be always cloudless." Even if the means of gratification lie within reach, he counsels, one may lose the capacity for enjoyment. "Unhappy is the being," he moans, "upon whom falls that everlasting cloud of discontent." He begs her pardon for preaching a sermon, "But I am very discontented, and cannot help writing sadly and foolishly."

His mood went from bad to worse that spring, as he wrote to Annie on a Sunday evening, April 15: "I should occupy the still sad hours of gathering twilight and falling shadows in trying to place my own soul in relation to yours which has always been with me an emblem of whatever of high and loveable that my life has seen." He dreams of her nightly, but she has another beau. He admits that he does have friends, and good prospects, and that his misery may be his own doing. Yet "my lonesome hours are peopled with ghosts of dead possibilities," and the "voice of desires and ambitions whose vanities I see, but whose cry I cannot stifle. . . . Would it not have been better never to have known the conquests of mind and the possibilities of existence? Then we never could catch the fearful contagion . . . of ambition."

Hay's spiritual crisis was soon to be resolved by a lanky, disheveled lawyer-politician who spoke in ironic aphorisms and barnyard metaphors, who had scarcely attended school, but somehow had managed to reconcile *ambition* and *idealism*. He had written poems and served in the U.S. Congress; he had provided very well for his wife and children. Few would realize how ambitious he was until his idealism came to the fore;

no one would have known the extent of his idealism, his reverence for Virtue and Truth, if he had never given free rein to his ambition.

John Hay, as his love letters to Annie Johnston reveal, was primed to appreciate Lincoln from the moment of their first encounter. That was in September of 1859. Hay was studying at a desk upstairs from the general store at Fifth and Washington streets, facing the windows on the square, in the law office of his uncle Milton and Stephen Logan. Lincoln "came in the law office where I was reading, which adjoined his own, with a copy of *Harper's Magazine* in his hand, containing Senator Douglas's famous article on Popular Sovereignty. Entering in his pale linen coat, without salutation, he said: 'This will never do. He puts the moral element out of the question. It won't stay out.'" He meant, of course, that Douglas spoke of slavery in the new territories as if it had been a mere economic necessity or property right, putting aside any question of the "peculiar institution" as being right or wrong. Hay may have seen a glimmer of hope: a balance of practical ambition and virtue was at hand.

Honest Abe, with his stories, jokes, and passion for freedom, was a magnetic personality. Hay found him irresistible and endlessly fascinating. Skeptical of all persons and things that were not either highborn or sophisticated, Hay was nonetheless curious about this idealistic backwoods lawyer. Hay and one of the Ridgely girls heard Lincoln lecture in Cook's Hall. By May 5, 1860, he wrote to a college friend: "I am as yet innocent of politics. I occupy myself very pleasantly in thoroughly hating both sides, and abusing the peculiar tenets of the company I happen to be in, and when the company is divided, say, with Mercutio, 'a plague on both your Houses.' This position I expect to hold for a very long time unless Lincoln is nominated in Chicago."

Hay did not have long to wait. Two weeks later, Lincoln *was* nominated to be the Republican standard-bearer, and in that time of national crisis no man with a conscience could remain neutral. John Hay, whose best friend was Nicolay, and whose Uncle Milton was one of Lincoln's advisers, would align himself with the Republican Party, with the cause of freedom and the Union, and against secession and slavery. In the fog of his own transition from adolescence to adulthood, yielding up the untenable purity of his poetic ideal for a real life that might accommodate both poetry and practical affairs, he could not have known how much one man, Abraham Lincoln, would contribute to his blossoming. Lincoln would become Hay's most inspiring muse.

True to his word, after Lincoln's nomination, John Hay dropped the mask of neutrality. Caught up in the tide of enthusiasm for the Republican cause, he began writing articles endorsing Lincoln. With Elmer Ellsworth, he gave stump speeches for the candidate; and when Nicolay called for help with the mail, Hay put aside his law books and hurried to Lincoln's rooms in the statehouse. Despite the gloom we have seen in his letters, Hay was known for his "sunny disposition"; he actually radiated good spirits and sanguine humor. Lincoln soon took to him, with more warmth perhaps than he had taken to his older friend Nicolay, who had assumed, under the severe conditions of an orphaned youth, an attitude of premature seriousness.

AFTER LINCOLN'S ELECTION IN November 1860, Hay found himself in the inner circle of the president-elect's supporters and advisers. Working side by side with John Nicolay and Elmer Ellsworth; Jesse Dubois, the state auditor; Norman Judd, chairman of the Illinois Republican central committee; factotum Ward Hill Lamon; and Judge David Davis, Lincoln's campaign manager, he must have known that he was in the right place at the right time. Having served Lincoln, as had Nicolay and Ellsworth, he hoped that the president-elect would find a place for him in the new administration.

Hay was admitted to the bar on February 4, 1861. While Nicolay's paid employment on Lincoln's staff had been formalized in June 1860, Hay's position was still voluntary. Sometime during the winter of 1860–61, Nicolay recommended that Hay be hired as his assistant. Lincoln gave Nicolay a quizzical look and said, "We can't take all Illinois with us down to Washington," but then, relenting, he added cheerfully: "Well, let Hay come."

Like his friends Nicolay and Ellsworth, Hay had made himself indispensable to the president-elect in the months before the election. His salary was still a problem, for there was money in the federal budget for only one secretary. Lincoln offered to pay him something out of his own pocket until after the inauguration, when he might have some sort of government appointment. But the devoted uncle, Milton Hay, guaranteed to pay his nephew's expenses for six months, just as many parents of the time subsidized their sons' apprenticeships to blacksmiths and shipwrights. Lincoln had gathered the core of his team.

And so, along with Mr. Lincoln, his family, and two railway carriages of guards, political advisers, friends, and physicians, they set out on the winding, tumultuous tour that newsmen called a "journey through ovations" from Springfield to Washington. As the train moved through the damp fields along the Sangamon River, Nicolay transcribed the "Farewell Address" that Lincoln had delivered extempore a few minutes earlier. Lincoln had begun the task, but, overcome with emotion after writing "Here my children have been born, and one is buried," he tearfully handed the pencil to Nicolay to finish. Slowly the secretary took dictation. "I now leave, not knowing when, or whether ever, I may return, with a task before me greater than that which rested upon Washington."

Every man aboard that train was aware of the fearful task they were facing. A pamphlet of instructions went ahead to all the towns where stops were scheduled, with this paragraph foremost: "*First:* the President elect will under *no circumstances* attempt to pass through any crowd until such arrangements are made as will meet with the approval of Col. Ellsworth." Ellsworth was the titular head of security. The passions over slavery and states' rights that had animated Lincoln's debates with the Democrat Stephen Douglas in the senatorial election of 1858 had created what New York senator William Seward called an "irrepressible conflict" between North and South. Abolitionist John Brown's attack on the U.S. arsenal at Harper's Ferry in October 1859; his plan of fomenting a slave insurrection; his subsequent conviction for treason, and hanging—all these things made him a martyr in the eyes of abolitionists. While levelheaded Republicans such as Lincoln and Seward condemned the fanatic act of treason, southerners saw Brown as part of a Republican plot to create a long-dreaded slave revolt. Southern

radicals—especially wealthy plantation owners—began urging secession of slave states as the only means of preserving their economy and
way of life. Speaking in Kansas on December 3, 1859, Lincoln declared,
"So, if constitutionally we elect a President, and therefore you under-
take to destroy the Union, it will be our duty to deal with you as old
John Brown has been dealt with. We shall try to do our duty."

No sooner was Lincoln elected than South Carolina called a secession convention. On November 9, Lincoln was hanged in effigy at
Pensacola, Florida. On December 20, South Carolina passed an ordinance dissolving the Union "now subsisting between South Carolina
and other States." On January 9, 1861, Mississippi passed a similar ordinance, and within three weeks Florida, Alabama, Georgia, Louisiana,
and Texas followed suit. James Buchanan, the lame-duck president,
believing he lacked the power to coerce the rebellious states, did nothing. By this time, Fort Sumter, the federal installation in Charleston
Harbor, had become an offense to the southern states. When "negotia-
tors" from South Carolina demanded that the fort be evacuated, Buchanan refused. He had sent the troopship *Star of the West* to reinforce
Fort Sumter, and when a rebel battery fired upon the vessel, striking
the fore chains, the *Star of the West* was forced to return to New York.
Many had felt that the "the Rubicon has been crossed," that the first
shots of the Civil War had been fired.

On February 18, Jefferson Davis was inaugurated as president of
the Confederate States of America at the state capital in Montgomery,
Alabama. Lincoln's train passed through crowds rioting in Albany, desperate for words of comfort in the crisis, or some comment on the rebellion. Lincoln, addressing the New York legislature, said, "I do not
propose to enter into an explanation of any particular line of policy as to
our present difficulties . . . I deem it just . . . that I should see everything,
that I should hear everything, that I should have every light that can be
brought within my reach, in order that when I do so speak, I shall have
enjoyed every opportunity to take correct and true ground . . ."

As the presidential party arrived in Philadelphia and Harrisburg,
the adventure grew perilous. John Hay wrote to Annie Johnston,
saying how sorry he was that his last weeks in Springfield had been

"so dreadfully hurried." He had wanted so much to pay her "a final visit . . . nothing but necessity could have made me forgo it. I was too busy to grow very homesick. Work is the best recipe for fancies." This was certainly true in Hay's case. Gone from this note, and from most of his future letters, are the florid, looping, and self-pitying sentences of adolescence—they are replaced by a more straightforward, precise eloquence laced with irony.

> I write you just this line tonight to let you know why I was so long silent, and to assure you that I still think of you . . . Tomorrow we enter slave territory. Saturday evening according to our arrangements, we will be in Washington.

> There may be trouble in Baltimore. If so, we will not go to Washington, unless in long, narrow boxes. The telegraph will inform you of the result, long before this letter reaches you. If all is well, this letter will do no harm. If anything happens, you will remember that I was at the present date,
>
> Very affectionately,
> Your friend J.H.

Hay was not exaggerating. A plot had been discovered to derail the train outside of Baltimore and murder everyone aboard. That very night, detective Allan Pinkerton, the hulking Ward Hill Lamon—one of Lincoln's former law partners, now his preferred bodyguard—and the president-elect boarded a secret train bound straight for the capital with no stop in Baltimore. Meanwhile, Hay, Nicolay, Ellsworth, Mrs. Lincoln, and the rest rode the decoy presidential special that would meet, head-on, the furious mob in Baltimore. According to newspaper accounts of the time, the danger was real, and the party considered themselves fortunate to arrive in Washington safely the next day.

CHAPTER TWO

WASHINGTON, 1861

On the fifth of March, John Nicolay wrote his first letter to his fiancée on White House stationery: "Dear Therena, As you see from the heading of my letter, I am fairly installed in the 'White House.' We had a gratifying and glorious inauguration yesterday—a fine day, and a fine display and everything went off as nicely as it could have possibly been devised."

The president-elect had been carefully guarded. Threats of assassination had prompted General Winfield Scott (as lieutenant general, the highest-ranking officer in the army) to post green-coated sharpshooters on housetops along Pennsylvania Avenue, where the restless crowd would notice them. Batteries of artillery were stationed north and south of the Capitol as Lincoln made his carefully worded speech. The nation wanted comfort and reassurance, but these things did not mean the same to all. The southern people wanted a promise that the government would not endanger their property or their personal security. The citizens loyal to the Union wanted a pledge that the Union would be preserved. Some hoped the president would suggest a policy to abolish slavery, while others wished he would tolerate it.

His speech was mostly gentle and conciliatory, promising not to interfere with slavery where it existed, nor to appoint offensive radicals to fill federal offices in southern states. Lincoln's first draft of the "First Inaugural" had expressed his intentions to retake the federal forts that the Confederate states had seized. But the diplomatic William Seward, secretary of state designate, had persuaded him to avoid such provocative gestures, so the speech was simply forceful in its defense of the Union. "We cannot remove our respective sections from each other, nor build an impassable wall between them," he said, ending in poetry: "I am loath to close. We are not enemies, but friends. Though passion may have strained, it must not break our bonds of affection. The mystic chords of memory, stretching from every battle-field, and patriot grave, to every living heart and hearthstone, all over this broad land, will yet swell the chorus of the Union, when again touched, as surely they will be, by the better angels of our nature."

The president had hoped that the passage of a few calm weeks would convince the anxious Confederates that the federal government did not intend to go on the offense, or further disturb the fragile peace. Perhaps by springtime the "chorus of the Union" would swell again. But it was not to be. Nicolay later heard Lincoln tell his friend Orville Browning, ". . .the first thing that was handed me after I entered this room [his office], when I came from the inauguration was the letter from Maj. Anderson saying that their provisions would be exhausted before an expedition could be sent to their relief." There was bread enough for a month, pork for a few days longer, and coffee, beans, and rice to last forty days. General Winfield Scott, called upon for his opinion, gravely advised that the fort be surrendered; so did most of the newly appointed, uneasy members of the cabinet.

Letting Fort Sumter submit to the rebel siege would amount to a validation of secession, the dissolution of the Union. "All the troubles and anxieties of my life," Lincoln told Browning and Nicolay, "have not equaled those which intervened between this time and the fall of Sumter."

THE GLORIOUS AND GRATIFYING inauguration, the fanfare, parades, and speeches, the elegance of the inaugural ball, were triumphs for which Nicolay could claim some credit. One of his first duties as the president's private secretary was to act on state occasions as chief of protocol. Protocol is the strict observance of etiquette, and above all *precedence* in state functions—who must go first, second, and third through a doorway or in a procession, or in being presented to a duke or chargé d'affaires. Who is to be seated in which chair, and next to whom, at a state dinner for forty?

It is nearly inconceivable that a twenty-nine-year-old German-American, an ex-printer's devil who had seen no more ceremony than could be learned in western parlors and the rustic Springfield statehouse, would find himself saddled with such a burden. Many people did not approve. One Republican leader thought it absurd: "It wants a man of refinement and culture and thoroughly at home in fine society. He arranges the President's dinners and parties . . . a great deal depends on that appointment whether our republican [administration] will make itself ridiculous or not. The idea of Nicolay being fit for such a place . . ." Men like Massachusetts senator Charles Sumner, chairman of the Committee on Foreign Relations, and Charles Francis Adams, minister to England, were deeply concerned, knowing the importance of appearances in effective diplomacy. What these men did not understand is that Lincoln—having to choose only one private secretary—instinctively chose a man whose virtues were complete loyalty, honesty, and almost uncanny versatility, traits that John Hay also shared.

We will never know exactly how Nicolay mastered protocol in six days—the time it took the Lord to make heaven and earth—but with Hay's help, dog-eared manuals, and a few mossy State Department veterans, Nicolay made a go of it. He does not explain this in his letters or journals. Like so many amazing tasks that Nicolay and Hay accomplished, the arrangement of state occasions was executed because it had to be; and nobody could persuade these cocky young fellows that there was anything they could *not* do. This will come to seem more astonishing, as we watch their work load increase, and as the president relies more and more upon them for peculiar and exacting duties.

No doubt their confidence was swelled by their immediate status as confidants to the president-elect. They were courted, flattered, and sought after. No longer was Hay a mere volunteer. Four days after the inauguration, Lincoln had him appointed a clerk in the Department of the Interior, whence he was detailed to the White House as Nicolay's assistant at a salary of $1,600 a year. Two old friends found Hay in the bar of Willard's Hotel, the main watering hole for Republican politicians, generals, and lobbyists, just around the corner from the White House. As they approached him to offer their congratulations on his new appointment, Hay was leaning back languidly against the broad cigar case, drink in hand, arms stretched out on either side as if to signal that the wide world was his.

This was an age—unlike our own—when even the busiest of men sometimes stood still. They struck poses for the sake of effect. So did women, with hands on seductive hips, or the proud chin held high. Perhaps the photographers had taught them this trick with their rigorous demands for stillness. Hay had assumed a characteristic pose, at once nonchalant and assertive, a man-about-town air of superiority and rakish humor. He acknowledged his friends' good wishes not without grace, but with a lofty qualification: "Yes, I'm the keeper of the President's conscience."

In the arrogance of youth, on that winter day when the Lincoln administration was still a work in progress, the poet may have half-believed what he was saying. The professors of philosophy at Brown, and the great poets, had taught him that conscience did not thrive in the rough-and-tumble world of politics; and, in the words of Percy Shelley, "poets are the unacknowledged legislators of the world." At this juncture, John Hay was more aware of Mr. Lincoln's limits than of his genius. It would take Hay several months before he recognized in his chief a conscience so firm that few occasions could compromise it.

And if ever there were occasions fit to try a man's conscience it was during those weeks before the evacuation of Fort Sumter on April

14, 1861. A change of political parties always causes traffic and confusion in the White House, as officeholders, office seekers, and petitioners lobby the chief executive for appointments. At this time of crisis, some wanted positions in the new administration; others wanted to be removed honorably; others, out of favor, begged to keep their old jobs. It is in the interest of the president and his cabinet to see this process completed as quickly as possible, for there is much to be done in running a government, and qualified persons are required to do the work. But for every post, there are several hopefuls; for every hopeful, there may be half a dozen sponsors, including congressmen, senators, governors, and bankers eager to speak on an applicant's behalf. And the subtext of the conversation is always influence, the subtle emanation of power. Conscience must guard against influence, whether it is the conscience of the chief executive, pressured to choose a mediocre cabinet member in order to reward a man who has won him votes, or a private secretary, persuaded to make way for an old friend desiring a postmastership.

No president had ever found himself under the pressure of so great a volume of office seekers, malcontents, influence peddlers, salesmen, congressional counselors, and cranks as did Abraham Lincoln—the Republican president who succeeded the Democrat Buchanan during the secession crisis. Washington, D.C., like the surrounding states of Maryland and Virginia, was overwhelmingly southern in its way of life and its citizenry. Slavery was widespread, and Republicans were a novelty. Many men who had held government positions under two Democratic administrations wanted nothing to do with these new "black" Republicans. The old guard submitted their resignations by the hundreds, cleaned out their desks, sold their houses, and moved south.

It was as if Lincoln and his cabinet had not only to effect a transition in the federal government; they also had to grow a new executive branch from the ground up. And the main action—which involved thousands of men, hundreds of jobs, seven cabinet members, and one president—went on in a space of about eighteen hundred square feet, nearly half of which was the inner sanctum of the president and his private secretary. In those two rooms on the second floor of the White House, there was relative calm. The halls, vestibules, and waiting rooms outside were crammed with legislators, army officers, tourists, and others seeking the president's attention. There was a hubbub and a jam when it was not chaos.

Nicolay and Hay, with no more than a doorman to assist them, were charged with directing traffic in and out of Mr. Lincoln's office, and at that time no white man or woman was denied access to the president during his office hours.

READING OF SABOTEURS AND assassination plots, Therena Bates feared for Nicolay's safety. He wrote to her on a bright frosty Thursday, three days after the inauguration, to assure her that at present there was no danger to the president or anyone around him. "I consider myself quite as safe here as I used to be in the Free Press Office years ago. Since I commenced writing this I have again been called away to appease visitors who are importuning to see Mr. Lincoln so don't be surprised if I break off . . ."

He predicts that the toil "will be a severe tax on both my physical and mental energies . . ." but that within a few months, when the appointments have been made, the work will be tolerable.

"John Hay and I are both staying here in the White House. We have very pleasant offices, and a nice large bed room, though all of them sadly need new furniture and carpets." A cousin of Mrs. Lincoln quipped that the White House furniture looked like it had been brought in by President Washington. Nicolay and Hay took their meals around the corner at Willard's Hotel, across from the Treasury Building at Fifteenth and Pennsylvania Avenue. But their days and nights were spent at the White House, upstairs in the East Wing. Elmer Ellsworth had a room at Willard's, but he spent most of his nights at the White House, in the bedroom Robert Lincoln used during his occasional visits from college.

For the private secretaries, there was little privacy—they lived where they worked, at the nerve center of the worst political and human upheaval the nation had ever known. The crisis had no respect for the hours of the day or the days of the week, darkness or daylight. The men were always on call. Their chief, they soon discovered, had demonic stamina, the public was unrelenting, the politicians and newsmen merciless. Across the hall from Lincoln's office, Nicolay and Hay slept, and worked, and entertained one another and a few friends in the early hours of the morning, late at night, and on major holidays when even the president closed his door.

After a meal and whiskey at Willard's, and a five-minute walk in the lamplight around the unfinished Treasury Building, the secretaries neared the White House, passed through the Ionic columns of the north portico, and climbed the two flights of steps to the main level. Each had a latchkey that fit the wide door into the huge downstairs vestibule, forty by fifty feet. Ahead of them was a screen of simple columns, imitation white marble, beyond which lay the Blue Room. As they entered, just to the left was an archway, and through it appeared the main staircase leading up to their rooms. The flight of stairs was wide and long, as the ceilings of the first story were well over twenty feet in height; this loftiness—despite the shabby furnishings—gave the mansion an air of grandeur.

At the top of the stairs, they passed through a door to the small office vestibule. Doors to the right led to the central hall and the West Wing, where the president's family lived. Straight ahead, opposite the stairs, a doorway led south to a formal office reception room, a cubicle fifteen feet square with horsehair chairs and sofas, a Brussels carpet, heavy draperies on the long window, and a fireplace on the left. This room, like the others, was also lofty, with fourteen-foot ceilings. At this hour, it was eerily silent.

They approached their quarters through the vestibule archway to the left and three steps down, through the rectangular office waiting room. This was really the extension of the central hall toward the east end of the house, forty-two feet long by sixteen feet wide, and illuminated by a single tall window in the east wall. The vestibule and the office waiting room were the main concourse for the business compartments of the Executive Mansion.

The four large rooms north and south of the waiting area with its chairs along the walls were architecturally symmetrical mirror images. The archway to the waiting room led to the door to the president's office on the right. Across from it stood the door to Nicolay and Hay's bedroom. Those rooms were of exactly the same size and configuration, thirty-five feet long by twenty-seven feet wide, each with a fireplace in the center of the west wall and two tall windows looking—from Lincoln's office—south to the Potomac and—from the secretaries' bedroom—out over the curved carriageway and the North Lawn. The other two rooms that opened off the waiting room, which faced each other through doors that were usually open, were Nicolay's office, adjoining the president's, and Hay's office, adjoining his bedroom. These rooms were half the size of the others but still commodious, thirty-five feet by fifteen, with fireplaces in the exterior walls at the end of the house, and high windows on either side of the chimneys that welcomed the light of the rising sun.

The floor plan was not designed for business efficiency, privacy, or flow of traffic. During the first weeks of the administration, Lincoln was at his desk as early as 6:00 a.m. An hour or so later, he and his secretaries could hear the rumbling of the crowd below, gathering on the steps and in the porte cochere outside the mansion. The doorkeeper would open the main entrance to the vestibule after eight o'clock, and the men and women eager to see the president would press through the doors toward the stairway without ceremony. A disorderly jam of hundreds of petitioners would quickly fill the office reception room, the office vestibule, and the long "hall" waiting room outside Lincoln's office. There was an effort on the part of the doorkeeper, a little Irishman named Edward McManus, to direct dignitaries such as senators, congressmen, cabinet members, and diplomats with appointments to the formal reception room across the upstairs vestibule so they need not rub shoulders with tradesmen and petty clerks in the waiting room. But democracy and sheer volume discourage privilege, and the mass of men pressed into the three public areas upstairs promiscuously, or sat or stood where they could while newcomers formed a double line upon the staircase.

Once the door to the White House was open, it stayed open to everyone until nightfall, when the last petitioner was rooted out of the mansion. Meanwhile, it was bedlam upstairs and down, as no part of the house was off limits to the public except the family rooms to the west—and even these were sometimes invaded.

It was Nicolay's responsibility to arrange appointments, consulting with the president between meetings concerning who, of the hundreds waiting, should be received next. And it was Hay's obligation to help out, gathering men's cards and letters of introduction, urging them to be patient. Cabinet members—Secretary of the Treasury Salmon Chase, Secretary of the Navy Gideon Welles, Secretary of State William Seward—would be expected and swiftly admitted to the inner sanctum. Congressmen and senators, unless they were men of extraordinary importance like Charles Sumner, head of the Senate Committee on Foreign Relations, usually had better luck approaching the office two or three at a time. The president received "delegations" from California, Indiana, Maine, Ohio, and other states with little more of an agenda than to remind him of their existence and good wishes. These would crowd into his office and read him a greeting. He would thank them, shake hands all around, measure his height with the tallest, back to back, and then show them to the near door where they entered. Nicolay would return from the far room holding a sheaf of introductory letters.

During the first weeks of the administration, many men and women waited all day long to see the president, and in that close space patience wore thin. The president's door stood in the direct line of fire of the office vestibule and the waiting room, while the secretaries' offices lay at the far end of the hall. The configuration should have been reversed so that visitors would have to pass Hay and Nicolay in order to get to the president. Instead, the secretaries were continually required to leave their offices—push against the oncoming crowd while begging for patience and civility—to greet or placate an office seeker or an impatient senator. Finding the president's door impassable, bold men would storm into Nicolay's office adjacent. They would assail Hay, coming and going. Some days the secretaries spent less time at their desks than on the battleground outside the president's door.

IN THE CROWD ON the steps one March morning, John Nicolay saw a familiar face, an uncommonly handsome, square-jawed fellow of twenty-six with wide-set, merry eyes and a light mustache. This was William Osborn Stoddard. "The stairs," Stoddard recalled, "were a sweltering jam but an usher at the top was managing to receive cards in some inscrutable manner. He obtained mine and it went in and in a few minutes Nicolay came to the banisters to shout my name while three or four eager patriots tugged at his coat tails. I hollered back."

Nicolay knew Stoddard from his days in the newspaper business, when the two journalists had been covering Illinois politics. Later, during Lincoln's campaign, Nicolay had become familiar with the writer for the *Central Illinois Gazette* (West Urbana) who had praised the candidate in many of his columns. Now, over the hubbub on the stairs, he asked Stoddard—somewhat superfluously—if he wanted to see the president. Not to be cowed by the secretary's officious tone, Stoddard cheerfully replied that he didn't, which must have surprised the rest of the company on the stairs, who laughed at his perversity. But Stoddard knew what he wanted. He once described himself as being happily free of humility.

"Tell the President I am here, according to orders," he ordered. "That's all. He'll know what to do. I won't bother him." This reply pleased the secretary, and Mr. Lincoln, too, who no doubt wished that several hundred more would follow the young man's example. Stoddard made his way against the tide of petitioners down the stairs and out the door, into the spring air. "It was only a few days before I received notice of my coming appointment as Secretary to sign Land Patents," he recalled. That was the first step in the process that would lead to Stoddard's becoming assistant to Nicolay and Hay, as Lincoln's third secretary.

Stoddard had been captivated by Abraham Lincoln, the man as well as his principles, since April 27, 1859, when the lawyer visited the offices of the *Gazette* in West Urbana to get acquainted with the staff and to discuss the field of presidential candidates. Although he modestly declined to be considered, the *Gazette,* a week later, noting his visit, said, "Few men can make an hour pass away more agreeably," and that should "he ever condescend to occupy the White House . . . he has established a character and reputation of sufficient strength and purity to withstand the disreputable and corrupting influences of that locality." In brief, the editors, including Stoddard, endorsed Lincoln as the best man for the job, whether or not he was running.

The fledgling journalist would never forget that first meeting with Mr. Lincoln. He later recalled that the fifty-year-old lawyer greeted him as "cordially as though we had known each other for a long time. There was no strangeness about him. He knew men on the instant." This echoes a judgment that Nicolay and Hay expressed in their biography of the great man: "Mr. Lincoln possessed a quick intuition of human nature and of the strength or weakness of individual character." It would be one of Stoddard's greatest life lessons—as it was for Hay and Nicolay—to have his character measured, now and again, by Mr. Lincoln.

Soon after the election, Stoddard expressed his desire to join the White House staff. Lincoln told him to write him a letter on the subject, and he would see to it. Months passed. When he had heard no response, Stoddard wrote to Lincoln's law partner, William Herndon: ". . . it is not unnatural that I should become a little nervous and desire to know what the indications are . . ." He understood that his "request was bold, even presumptuous. Very likely, also, others with greater ability . . ." were clamoring for the same position.

Knowing Lincoln only slightly, Stoddard was well aware that the president-elect would "have doubts as to my fitness for a post of so much responsibility, and hesitate about according to me the degree of confidence which a man must place in his 'private secretary.'" These uncertainties are revealing, reflections of a young man who doubted himself and perhaps wisely glimpsed his own weaknesses. Lincoln was indeed beset with applications, and Stoddard was on the short list, but at last John Nicolay was chosen, a man who never for a moment doubted his qualifications, chief among these being his ability to inspire Lincoln's confidence. Stoddard admitted that Nicolay was better qualified for the job, being "older, more experienced, harder, had a worse temper, and was decidedly German in his manner of telling men what he thought of them." Stoddard said that Nicolay could say no about as disagreeably as any man he ever knew. That was a useful skill in a world where so many men would not readily take no for an answer.

But the qualification for which everyone respected secretary Nicolay "was his devotion to the President and his incorruptible honesty Lincoln-ward. He measured all things and all men by their relations to the President . . . For this, and more," Stoddard wrote, "he deserves the thanks of all who loved Mr. Lincoln, even if at times they had reason to grumble at 'the bulldog in the ante-room.'" Hay, with his gracious manners, had his useful qualifications, as did Stoddard, as we shall see. But in that time of social confusion and political treachery it was selfless fealty Mr. Lincoln required, and he knew that Nicolay would offer it because the orphan's life had promulgated a need in him to give himself up, for a time. Hay had the healthy narcissism of the young poet; Stoddard was an adventurer and soldier of fortune; Nicolay was, for a time, an acolyte.

STODDARD, "THE THIRD SECRETARY," was raised in upstate New York, in the little town of Homer, in a family of Baptists and abolitionists. His father was a bookseller whose business failed in the 1840s; his beloved mother was an avid reader. After watching her die slowly of tuberculosis, Stoddard left home for the University of Rochester, which he attended for three years before heavy debts forced him to withdraw. He decided to try his hand at farming, bought land in central Illinois, and worked it for more than a year with his sister Kate. Bad weather on the prairie, unruly livestock, and finally a "bilious fever" put him off farming, whereupon he turned to the offices of the *Gazette* and became a reporter.

In February of 1861, remembering the president-elect's encouragement, Stoddard headed for Washington, where he observed office seekers "in untold and seedy looking multitudes. They roam the streets, seeking introductions, button-holing unfortunate great men." Stoddard was one of the lucky ones. As Lincoln had promised, he was soon granted a position in the Interior Department, signing Lincoln's name to land patents; and when land-office business dwindled in the summer, Stoddard was assigned to the White House to assist Nicolay and Hay with the mail.

The spoils system had prevailed since Andrew Jackson's election. Often an important office would go not to the best-qualified man, but to the one with the greatest clout among congressmen, cabinet members, or political bosses. During his first weeks in office, President Lincoln worked twelve hours a day against the pressure of the spoils system, to see to it that the best and most deserving men (in his opinion) got jobs. This was a chance for Stoddard, Hay, and Nicolay to witness the clash between ideals and expedience up close. Journalists north and south complained about this use of Lincoln's energies as war threatened, saying "grave affairs of State are to him of little moment in comparison with the distribution of rewards . . ." and such "confinement will ruin him if continued." Despite such warnings, on March 18, the *New York Tribune* reported that job applicants still monopolized the president's time.

Lincoln's order to Nicolay and Hay was "that all visitors shall be treated courteously and have a fair opportunity of communicating with him personally." This policy was considered hazardous to his health and equanimity, and his best friends urged him to give it up: Nicolay should screen applicants, and limit the president's office hours. Lincoln could have left the appointments up to cabinet members and concerned congressman, as many presidents had done. But he quickly learned that even the cabinet members as interested in the success of government as he was recommended men to "be appointed to responsible positions who were often physically, morally, and intellectually unfit for the place," as he confided to an old friend, paymaster Robert Wilson. "They [the cabinet members] knew," Lincoln continued, "and their importunities were urgent in proportion to the unfitness of the appointee." Lincoln told Wilson that he was so badgered with applications that "the only way that he could escape from them would be to take a rope and hang himself on one of the trees in the south lawn . . ." But he would not stand aside, for he knew that his position empowered him to be more objective than department heads, whose angry friends could then blame the president if he appointed a better man.

Nicolay and Hay described the scene upstairs at the White House:

> At any hour of the day one might see at the outer door and on the staircase, one line going, one coming. In the anteroom and in the broad corridor adjoining the President's office there was a restless and persistent crowd,—ten, twenty, sometimes fifty . . . each one in pursuit of one of the many crumbs of official patronage. They walked the floor; they talked in groups; they scowled at every arrival and blessed every departure; they wrangled with them for surreptitious chances; they crowded forward to get even as much as an instant's glance through the half-opened door into the Executive chamber. They besieged the Representatives and Senators who had privilege of precedence; they glared with envy at the Cabinet Ministers who by right and usage, pushed through the throng and walked unquestioned through the doors.
>
> At first, Lincoln bore it all with an admirable fortitude . . . [but] What with the Sumter discussion, the rebel negotiation, the diplomatic correspondence, he was subjected to a mental strain and irritation that made him feel like a prisoner. . . . He said he felt like a man letting lodgings at one end of his house, while the other end was on fire.

On March 10, Nicolay wrote to Therena Bates, begging her pardon that his letters were infrequent and hasty, but even on a Sunday he was obliged to work. The first great evening reception had taken place in the White House, and was widely regarded as the most successful ever. "For over two hours the crowd poured in as rapidly as the door would admit them, and many climbed into the windows . . . crinolines suffered, and at least fifty men" went home enraged "over the loss of hats and valuable overcoats" to another fifty men who preferred them to their own.

"I cannot yet form much of an idea how I shall like it here," he continued. "For two or three months the work will of course be pretty laborious. After that I expect to find some time for both recreation and study." He would indeed. The social season in Washington was rich, and he and Hay, as bright, eligible bachelors, immediately became luminaries in it. Nicolay seems to have kept quiet about his engagement. His letters to Therena, although occasionally tender, sometimes passionate, were not likely to allay jealousy, and sometimes seemed calculated to inflame it. Complaining of the slow mail from Pittsfield, he teases, "I shall have to make some of the Postmaster Generals look into that, unless in the meanwhile as you suggest I should run off with some beautiful and accomplished lady of the city. So far I have not discovered many of them. However, *nous verrons* . . ."

A week later, Nicolay's excuse for not writing to his fiancée is the party of the night before, "very pleasant or rather seemed to be so. Being strange to all but one or two of the ladies, I couldn't enjoy it, for I had to busy myself somewhat in getting acquainted—which is always work for me. The others however all seemed to be having a glorious time. They had music and danced as well as they could for the crowd, which was pretty dense." An enthusiastic dancer, Nicolay marveled over the distinctions between the eastern and western styles. Here in the capital there were no "callers," but they danced the same quadrilles over and over. They waltzed "without any apparent attention to time or grace. . . . There were a number of really pretty girls at the party," but he admits he did not have much of a chance "to judge much more than their looks."

"You cannot appreciate how much I would give for a quiet evening with you," he says in closing. Therena wanted greater proof of his devotion, and she soon received it—an apologetic but genuine love letter the next week.

If I had not been for years educating myself to be a mere bundle of quiet and imperturbability . . . I should sit down tonight and write you a real love letter—full of all the pathos and passion of which young men or rather boys in the foolish frenzy of their first love are guilty. . . . I feel that nothing would give me so much happiness as to enjoy with you an evening of that good old-fashioned quietness, which like all the great and common blessings we never fully appreciate until we are without them.

Nicolay is writing on a Sunday, St. Patrick's Day, and he speaks of "the dissipation of last night." He has been in the capital less than a month but already is deeply disillusioned. "When I become disgusted with all the glaring faults, the hollowness and heartlessness of the great crowd of people of both sexes whom I meet and see, an almost irresistible longing comes over me to go back to the one shrine where I can go to worship truth and devotion . . . If I were to write a dozen pages I could not say more than that tonight. I could only find happiness with and through you."

IF THERE WAS ONE incorruptible man—neither hollow nor heartless—in the wicked city of Washington, it was that prodigy of military science and patriotism, the drillmaster Elmer Ellsworth, who had served as a guard on the train from Springfield with Nicolay, Hay, and the Lincolns. Ellsworth had impressed Lincoln, as he had impressed much of America, as a born commander of armies, an avatar of the martial spirit such as the world had not seen since Roland of Roncesvalles. If it were possible to be jealous of a friend, Hay might have envied Ellsworth. "His voice," said Hay, "deep and musical, instantly attracted attention, and his address, though not without soldierly brusqueness, was sincere and courteous. . . . He had great tact and executive talent, was a good mathematician . . . sketched well . . . to his friends he always seemed like a Paladin or Cavalier of the dead days of romance and beauty."

Ellsworth was treated like a member of the official family, staying at the White House as much as at Willard's, attending the inauguration, the ball afterward, and all the levees and receptions. The day after his inauguration, Lincoln asked the secretary of war to appoint "my friend, Elmer Ellsworth" chief clerk of the War Department. As he signed the letter, Ellsworth recalled, Lincoln "swung round in his chair, and said in a peculiarly deliberate manner: 'I've been thinking on the way, & since we've been here . . . that when I can see how the *land lays,* that I'd put you in the Army, somewhere.'" At present, Ellsworth replied, he would prefer that job in the War Department, where he could begin to establish a Bureau of the Militia; he aspired to take charge of that himself.

A militia is a volunteer regiment, locally mustered to serve in times of emergencies. Technically independent of the U.S. Army, a state militia elects its own officers and selects its firearms and uniforms. During times of war, the regiment serves under the supervision of U.S. Army commanders. A U.S. Bureau of Militia would be required to oversee and regulate the dozens of miscellaneous state militias that had sprung up all over the North and the West in 1860–61.

Since Lincoln had put his friend's name forward for that chief clerkship, Ellsworth had found himself caught up in a web of political intrigue, professional envy, and bureaucratic tangles that made his head spin and caused him to wonder if he might ever serve his country as he had desired. The month following his arrival in Washington was—according to John Hay—the worst of Ellsworth's life, "brightened only by the society of those he trusted most, and by the unvarying friendship and confidence of the President and his family." First, Simon Cameron, the secretary of war, refused Ellsworth the clerkship because he had promised it to someone else. So Ellsworth knocked on many doors to learn what it would take to create a Bureau of Militia and put him in charge of it. If Lincoln appointed him a major in the U.S. Army pay department (the only department in which his appointed rank could be higher than lieutenant), then the president could assign him the duty of inspector general of militia, and station him in Washington. Cameron agreed to propose such a plan to the president, and in mid-March the three met in Lincoln's office, with Major David Hunter and Captain John Pope of the Regular Army in attendance to offer advice.

The president agreed that this was a fine solution. So did Mrs. Lincoln, who high-handedly summoned the secretary of war and made Cameron promise that all would go as Ellsworth had hoped. "I have the positive promise of both Mr. Lincoln & Cameron to create the Bureau of Militia and make me chief of it," Ellsworth wrote his fiancée. But there were two obstacles, of which none of the parties seemed aware. First, the rank of major in the pay department was so highly coveted among West Point graduates that giving it to the twenty-three-year-old drillmaster would stir up antagonism against the new commander in chief. Second, the president lacked the lawful authority to create a Bureau of Militia.

It would take another month to sort this out. Meanwhile, Lincoln and Ellsworth had become objects of mean gossip and malicious journalism. The *Chicago Times* wrote: "Mr. Lincoln has requested Gen. Cameron to appoint Col. Ellsworth, of Chicago Zouave notoriety, to the fat office of Chief Clerk of the War Department. Oh, my! Calico Colonels are in the ascendant. And who is it, pray, that Mr. Lincoln is so anxious to put into a twenty-two-hundred dollars a year office? A mere adventurer; formerly the pompous Captain of the Chicago Zouave Cadets, who went into the show business and traveled all over the Union . . ." There were many more public outcries like this. When Ellsworth had heard enough of it, he told Cameron to forget about "the Majority."

"I told him I would do nothing to cause ill feeling toward Mr. L. or himself . . . the next best thing was to take a Lieutenancy—about $1,850 a year . . . & be ordered to duty at Washington . . ."

On March 11, the cabinet had decided to withdraw troops from Fort Sumter. It became a shadow dance of indecision. Two days later, the president was meeting privately with selected cabinet members to discuss provisioning the fort. On the fifteenth, Lincoln presented his plan for relieving Fort Sumter to the entire cabinet. But on the eighteenth, the president wrote a memorandum titled "Some considerations in Favor of Withdrawing the Troops from Fort Sumter," the same day he had written an order to establish a militia bureau with Ellsworth as inspector general. The next day, three forts in Texas surrendered to Confederate troops, and the USS *Isabella*, sailing to provision the fleet at Pensacola Bay, Florida, was seized at Mobile.

On March 20, Second Lieutenant Elmer Ellsworth of the First Dragoons lay in his bed in Willard's—so sick he thought he had smallpox—contemplating his next move, trying to figure out what he should do if war broke out.

Ellsworth was depressed and very ill, with a high fever and red spots all over his body. His hands trembled and his eyes were so weak he could scarcely see his writing paper as he struggled to write to his fiancée, Carrie Spafford: "I have been confined to my bed by the measles and inflammation of the chest. . . . I would have let you know but . . . I became so ill I could not write I supposed I had the Small Pox & of course I wrote to no one." His illness was further complicated by pneumonia. Delirious with fever, he had formed a plan. He would go to New York—he informed Carrie at the end of the month—where "I will call to see you as soon as I arrive." They would celebrate his twenty-fourth birthday together on April 11; then he would set about recruiting his regiment—a militia finer than any this country had ever seen.

Nicolay, whose health had never been better, had reasons to worry about it that month. Mr. Lincoln's boys had both gotten the measles—usually a childhood illness, but Ellsworth had caught it from Willie and Tad. On the twenty-third of March, even the president was under the weather. The next day, Nicolay tore open a letter from Therena written in someone else's hand, explaining that she had come down with the measles, and now her eyesight was so dim she could read and write only with difficulty. For weeks, Nicolay would feel "a constant anxiety" that his fiancée might go blind. For his part, he was able to assure her "so far the extra labor and fatigue to which I am subjected seems to have no immediate bad effects," although he longed for a time when he could write a letter in peace, "without being haunted continually by some one who 'wants to see the President *for only five minutes.*' At present this request meets me from almost every man woman and child I meet—whether it be by day or night—in the house or on the street . . ." He caught cold on the twenty-eighth, but recovered quickly.

On Easter Sunday, March 31, while the president worked with Captain Montgomery Meigs, an army engineer, and Lieutenant Colonel Erasmas Keyes to devise a secret plan to relieve Fort Pickens in Florida, Nicolay and Hay had a quiet day together. It was chilly but clear. They put on their coats, cloaks, and hats and took a long walk around "the City of Magnificent Distances"—Charles Dickens's expression for the straggling, muddy city of sixty thousand on the Potomac River.

Pierre L'Enfant designed Washington to radiate in avenues like the spokes of two wheels emanating from the Capitol building on the east side, and from the White House and the Treasury Building at the northwest end of Pennsylvania Avenue. The Patent Office and the Post Office stood together midway between these hubs, and two blocks north of Pennsylvania Avenue; City Hall lay midway between the Capitol and the Patent Office—as the crow flies. These were the only architectural sites of interest except the curious redbrick Gothic towers of the Smithsonian Institution, to the south. The museum, newly constructed, made the southernmost angle of a parallelogram one might draw on a map of the chief points of interest.

As the men started out on their stroll, they could see, in the local square around the White House, the nexus of buildings in which decisions would be made concerning war and peace. Two hundred yards west stood identical brick buildings, two stories in height, housing the War and Navy departments. At the same distance to the east was a small house for the State Department, adjoining the immense, unfinished Grecian colonnades and porticoes of the Treasury. Between the executive mansion and the Treasury Building stood the stables where the secretaries would soon keep their own horses. Across from the front portico of the White House lay Lafayette Square, and around the square stood most of the finest private homes in the capital.

Visible from the White House was the steeple of St. John's Episcopal Church, at the corner of H Street North and Sixteenth Street West, where many presidents had attended services. There were thirty-seven churches in Washington, their steeples far-flung, rising above the brick and wood-frame houses all over the city, their bells summoning the faithful to pray for peace. These houses of worship towered over dwellings and shops of varied construction: brick mansions and wood-frame "cottages" with wide yards and outbuildings, barns, privies, and sheds. There were ramshackle groceries, livery stables, and stationers, sellers of dry goods, yard goods, and saddles, shoemakers, candlemakers, jewelers, locksmiths, and apothecaries; and every block and corner had its saloon.

In a few hours, Nicolay and Hay could visit the scattered architectural wonders, starting from the steps of the colossal Treasury Building, then rounding the corner of Fifteenth Street and Pennsylvania Avenue, where Willard's Hotel stood in the next block to the north. Willard's was an immense six-story hostelry with 150 rooms. There was a writing chamber, a large reception room, a lady's parlor, three bars, a barbershop, a dining hall thirty by a hundred feet, and a lecture auditorium. This was the first of six prominent hotels situated on the "high side" of the Avenue between the Treasury and the Capitol, the others being Kirkwood House on Twelfth Street, Brown's and the National on Sixth, and the St. Charles and Washington hotels on Third. The major theaters, shops, headquarters of several newspapers, telegraph offices, and studios ranged along the north side. Mathew Brady had his photography studio above Thompson's saloon in a five-story iron-framed, colonnaded building at Sixth and Pennsylvania.

Pennsylvania Avenue ("the Avenue"), with its brick sidewalk, was the town's favored promenade. The street was lined with ailanthus trees, each protected by a whitewashed wooden box from dogs, pigs, horses, and other livestock that roamed the city. The white hotels and redbrick buildings of the north side contrasted sharply with the Avenue's south side, whose irregularly built wooden houses and shacks pressed against one another, and sprawled in a triangular rat-infested neighborhood that backed onto the fetid canal north of the Mall. From Thirteenth to Fifteenth streets down to the canal was a slum so poverty-ridden and violent it was called Murder Bay.

Midway on their walk east toward the Capitol, the secretaries passed the Hay Market at Ninth Street. This was the main supplier of produce, seafood, game, meats, and staples for the hotels, restaurants, and households of the city. On their right hand, the bell tower of the Central Guard House overlooked the scene; to the left was the marquee of the bawdy Canterbury Music Hall, where the young men would find entertainment of an earthy sort not to be compared to the elegant dramas at Grover's Theatre. The market, usually crowded with wagons laden with fruits, vegetables, and caged chickens, bustling with vendors and shoppers, was quiet on Easter Sunday, the stalls boarded and padlocked, or canvas covered.

Straight ahead of the sightseers, on a hill surrounded by an iron-fenced park and some small farms, arose the unfinished dome of the Capitol. A crane angled above the wooden scaffolding from which the artisans lowered the cast-iron columns into place. The capital—with its avenues named for states, such as Ohio, Louisiana, Maryland, Maine, Illinois, Vermont—was a symbol of the Republic. The Capitol dome and the elaborate new wings and porticoes were a more concentrated form of the symbol, and the decision to finish the houses of legislature was a vote of confidence in the experiment of democracy.

On that Easter Sunday of 1861, as Nicolay and Hay surveyed the project—the gleaming marble wings stretched out on either side, incomplete, without steps; the blocks and scraps of marble scattered; iron plates, beams, keystones, capitals, and columns strewn here and there—it took a leap of faith to think that either the symbol or the Republic it symbolized would ever come together. The porticoes alone required a hundred Corinthian columns for their completion. So far, only three had been set in place.

Soon all three of the secretaries, William Stoddard included, would know the thrill of delivering the president's messages to the storied halls of the legislature—in this august and imperfect building. And for a brief time, their friend, Colonel Ellsworth, would bivouac his militia in the Hall of the House of Representatives.

Retracing their steps down Pennsylvania Avenue to the market, they could walk north on the only other brick-paved street in the city,

Seventh Street, which led to the Post Office and the Patent Office, two marble buildings facing each other between E and G streets, in a four-block square between Seventh and Ninth. The Post Office was considered the finest example of Italian palatial in America. The secretaries had little business there, but a good deal to do in the Patent Office, the larger Doric building to the north, a U-shaped structure more than 400 feet long, 275 feet deep, and nearly 75 feet in height. It was divided into three stories of rooms, the first two stories given to various bureaus. Until the Treasury Building could be completed, the Patent Office— the second-largest building in Washington—housed the Department of the Interior, which included the General Land Office, Stoddard's employer, the bureaus of Pensions and Indian Affairs, and the Department of the Interior proper, of which John Hay was, technically, an employee. The "model room" showcased tools and inventions, and took up the entire third floor. (It was soon to become a military hospital.) There were two fountains in the courtyard where workers in the departments could take their breaks on hot summer days.

Church bells were ringing. There were half a dozen churches between the Patent Office and Willard's, including St. Patrick's, the Methodist Protestant, Fourth Presbyterian, Epiphany, and Grace Island, all celebrating the resurrection of Our Lord.

It had been a good day for walking, and the young men had worked up a hearty appetite. Willard's, where they boarded, would have a feast in the public dining room downstairs, a huge hall without carpets or any furniture other than plain wooden tables and chairs. As they entered the room, they could hear the rumble of hundreds of conversations and the harsh screeching of chairs as the waiters shoved them back and forth over the floor.

The secretaries lifted their glasses in celebration of a small victory in their daily struggle to bring order and sanity to the Executive Office: they had at last persuaded the president to limit his business hours. He would receive visitors from ten o'clock in the morning until three o'clock in the afternoon. At least, that is what he promised.

———∽∽∽∽∽———

CHAPTER THREE

WAR

There were a few fine days at the beginning of April, when the peach trees blossomed and the grass grew green in the parks. Then it rained for a week and a half, turning the streets to rivers of yellow water, mud, and sewage, swelling the canal that ran along the north boundary of the Mall.

Nicolay took advantage of a quiet moment to write a letter to Therena, telling her that the president's new schedule had relieved them greatly, "and given us time at least to eat and sleep," but that "the crowd however hangs on with wonderful perseverance." It had been five weeks since the inauguration, but he had no idea when the mob of office-seekers would slacken. He mentions all the talk of war, "which the newspapers and the gossiping public insist is near at hand," but he sees no likelihood of it. Perhaps "a little brush at Charleston or Pensacola is quite possible but that any general hostilities will result from it I have not the least fear."

Four days later, on April 11, 1861, he reassured her, writing, "Don't get alarmed at the 'rumors of wars' which you hear from this direction," and adding that the danger of an attack on the capital was no more than idle gossip. Nicolay is echoing his boss, who later would prove a master at remaining calm when most people around him were panicked. In the same letter, Nicolay mentioned that a regiment of a thousand men had been mustered into service in the District in the last twenty-four hours, and that last night as he and John Hay were returning from downtown to the White House, they were—for the first time—challenged by a sentinel.

At 4:30 a.m. on April 12, the Confederate guns began bombarding Fort Sumter.

WAR HAD BROKEN OUT—DESPITE Nicolay's reassurances—and the events of the next few weeks were so surprising and dramatic that they rapidly defined the characters of the men at the center of the action.

William Stoddard, recently sworn in as an assistant to John Hay, let himself in to the White House with his latchkey early in the morning. He climbed the stairs and found the president alone, emerging from the oval library. "He was bent until he almost appeared to stoop," Stoddard recalled, "and he was looking straight before him, as if gazing at something in the distance or like a man who is listening intently."

"Good morning, Mr. Lincoln!"

The president stood still, looking down into Stoddard's face, but his expression did not change. "He may have been listening for the sound of guns in Charleston harbor," Stoddard guessed. He was alarmed by the deep circles under Lincoln's eyes, and the vacancy of their aspect.

"Why, Mr. Lincoln, you don't seem to know me!"

"Oh, yes, I do," he replied. "You are Stoddard. What is it?"

The new secretary wanted to ask a favor. "It's just this, Mr. Lincoln. I believe there is going to be fighting, pretty soon, right here, and I don't feel like sitting at a desk in the Patent Office, or here either, while any fight is going on." In his spare time, Stoddard had been drilling with an artillery company, the D.C. Rifles.

His face brightening, the president interrupted: "Well, well, why don't you go?"

The new secretary explained that he had just taken an oath to report to the president, and now it appeared that he would be asked to take a different oath "to obey somebody else. I don't see how I can manage them both without your permission."

"Go ahead!" the president exclaimed, straightening his back. "Swear in! Go wherever you are ordered to go."

Stoddard expressed his gratitude, and he was about to take his leave when Mr. Lincoln called him back. "Young man," he said gravely, pointing his finger, "go just where you're ordered. Do your duty. You won't lose anything by this!"

So the soldier of fortune, twenty-six-years of age, went off to serve the D.C. militia that guarded the Long Bridge over the Potomac and the palatial government buildings, and garrisoned redoubts at Tennally's Town and Edward's Ferry. He would not return to the White House for three months.

Stoddard's hero and role model that spring was not the staid and methodical Nicolay, or the debonair, ironical Hay; it was the quintessential soldier, Elmer Ellsworth. On April 14, Nicolay transcribed the president's proclamation calling up seventy-five thousand "militia of the several States of the Union," to be issued the next day. Fort Sumter had been evacuated. On April 15, Lincoln wrote a letter to Ellsworth that he was to use as a letter of credential or recommendation, stating that he, Lincoln, had "since the beginning of our acquaintance . . . had a very high estimate of your military talent. Accordingly I have been, and still am anxious for you to have the best position in the military which can be given you, consistent with justice." In brief, he would be obliged if the military authorities would place Ellsworth in a position that would be satisfactory to him. He knew the best place to begin was not Washington, but New York City.

Short on cash, Ellsworth turned to John Hay, who gave him all the money he had. Armed with the president's testimonial, Ellsworth boarded the next train to Manhattan. In this time of crisis there was not a minute to spare. His rendezvous with his sweetheart in Albany, his birthday celebration and dinner with Carrie, had to be canceled. He must try to raise a regiment of Zouaves at once, recruiting them from his friends in the Fire Department of New York. There he could expect enthusiastic support from the press. Arriving in Manhattan, Ellsworth walked downtown to 154 Nassau Street, to the office of Horace Greeley, editor of the *New York Tribune*. Showing him the president's letter, he detailed his plan of action. Charmed, Greeley published an interview with Ellsworth in a newspaper editorial, describing this young man "of an unusually fine physique, of frank and attractive manners and of great intelligence."

Ellsworth explained to the reporter: "I want the New York firemen, for there are no more effective men in the country, and none with whom I can do so much. They are sleeping on a volcano in Washington, and I want men who can go into a fight." The Washington militia was ill-trained and unreliable, full of southern sympathizers and spies who would turn against the Union at the first sign of weakness. The patriotic firefighters responded with overwhelming enthusiasm, and Ellsworth soon had more volunteers than he could enlist. By April 20, the New York papers were proud to report that the organization of the regiment of Fire Zouaves was well under way. The uniforms had been designed and ordered—not the flamboyant fezzes and baggy trousers, but standard army uniforms with a touch of scarlet in the shirts—and Ellsworth had been elected colonel by acclamation.

The New York legislature could not move quickly enough to fund Ellsworth's project; the money for guns and uniforms flowed from the purses of private citizens in Manhattan. Soon Ellsworth's eleven hundred recruits were drilling in Central Park to the applause of flag-waving throngs inflamed by talk of rebellion and war. John Hay called the colonel "the idol of the Bowery and the pet of the Avenue."

EACH MAN SHOWS HIS nature in a crisis; and such a crisis as this, the nation had never seen. Virginia, while it had not yet seceded, officially refused to comply with the president's call for militia. And on April 17, 1861, their State Convention adopted an ordinance of secession subject to a popular referendum on May 23. On the eighteenth, five companies of Pennsylvania troops arrived in the federal city. The day was cold

and windy. Hearths blazed, and the smell of wood smoke was in the
air. A citizen observed that "soldiers are now met with at every turn
and the drum and bugle are heard almost all the time from some quarter of the City." Lincoln agreed to quarter the "Frontier Guard," sixty
Kansas volunteers hastily organized by Senator James Henry Lane, in
the grand East Room of the White House—to Mrs. Lincoln's horror,
and to John Hay's amusement.

Hay's response to the tumultuous events of late April 1861 is most
peculiar and detached, as if what the poet was seeing and hearing was
too fantastic to be taken seriously—a hashish fugue. At first, he sounds
in his diary like an observer from another planet. Some folks later
claimed that Hay laughed his way through the war, but this was not
the case—although humor was his first line of defense against anxiety.
Of all the secretaries, John Hay, the youngest, would be most affected,
truly transformed by his White House years. And the greatest change
came in that first year.

On April 18, Hay, brimming with impressions, began a diary that
would become, arguably, the most important and eloquent source of information about Abraham Lincoln during the Civil War—apart from
Lincoln's own writings. And on the same day—or, more precisely, late
in the evening of that day—John Hay fell in love.

The weather was cold and clear, the moon in its first quarter. If Hay
was looking for portents, a brilliant comet appeared in the constellation of Draco, near the zenith. There were ominous signs of a more
mundane sort. Mails were suspended and the telegraph cut off, as secessionists north of the capital threatened the troops marching south.
All day long, a crowd of men had been lining up outside the war department, mostly local companies enlisting: the Potomac Light Guard
of Georgetown—Captain Boyd, three lieutenants, four corporals, one
musician and fifty foot soldiers were sworn in—as were the Jackson
Guards, twice the size of the Potomac outfit, with a quartermaster, two
musicians, and five sergeants, all blustering, singing, sounding drums
and bugles.

After a hectic day in the office, Hay considered attending the Washington Theatre down on Eleventh and C streets (the "wrong side" of

the Avenue) where the famous actor Joseph Jefferson was starring in the comedy *Babes in the Woods*. Now it was too late. The performance had already begun.

In a rare moment of leisure and reflection, he sat down at his desk and opened a new clothbound notebook with lined pages, and began: "The White House is turned into a barracks. Jim Lane marshaled his Kansas Warriors today at Willard's and placed them at the disposal of Maj. Hunter who turned them tonight into the East Room." Hay's writing desk stood directly above the immense room where the sixty warriors were now snoring, smoking, sipping whiskey, and cleaning their rifles. Although he calls them splendid, he never loses his sense of the ridiculous: "The Major has made me his aid, and I labored under some uncertainty as to whether I should speak to privates or not."

Of the day's business, Hay thought the most noteworthy development was a dispatch from several powerful New York merchants asking for warships, troops, and supplies to defend commerce in southern waters. This caused the president to summon the cabinet late in the afternoon; and after conferring, the secretary of state formally acknowledged the dispatch with one of his own, saying that the matter was under consideration. "All day the notes of preparation have been heard at the public buildings and the Armories," Hay wrote. "Every body seems to be expecting a Son or brother or 'young man' in the coming regiments."

The rest of Hay's first diary entry reveals that the most momentous event of his day occurred late at night, when the Lincolns and all but a few soldiers were asleep. The old doorkeeper, Edward McManus, crept upstairs and knocked on the secretary's door. He begged Hay's permission to present the card of a determined woman on a mission of the utmost importance. She and her lady companion would not be turned away, but they must see the president or his secretary at once. Nicolay was either out on the town or indisposed. So Hay took the card imprinted with the name Ann S. Stephens, upon which she had scribbled her note, "expressing a wish to see the President on matters concerning his personal safety." Mrs. Stephens could not be turned away without due courtesies. She was a distinguished woman, an editor, with Edgar Allan Poe, of *Graham's Magazine,* and later of her own ladies' magazine; she was also an author of popular fiction, including *Malaeska* (1860) the first "dime novel." The forty-eight-year-old cosmopolite was one of the most famous women in America. So Hay put on his coat, brushed his hair, and went downstairs to meet her.

In such weather, and at such a late hour, these two intrepid ladies would have been wrapped in cloaks and veiled bonnets, the better to conceal them from the stares of night watchmen, hackney drivers, drunks, and the soldiers that were now bivouacked in the room to their left, just beyond the stairs John Hay descended. McManus took him to his little room adjoining the corridor, and there he waited. Soon the doorkeeper ushered the visitors in.

Mrs. Stephens was tall and stout. Removing her bonnet, she uncovered a plain, broad face lambent with intelligence, and thick blonde hair streaked with gray. She took the hand Hay extended to her with her fingertips. The woman behind her, in contrast, was no taller than John Hay himself, dark-haired and dark-eyed, with delicate features perfectly formed but widely spaced, large eyes with long lashes, a firm chin, and slightly upturned nose—exquisite in profile. Mrs. Stephens introduced her little companion as Mrs. Lander. As she turned to face him, the delicately curved lips of the beautiful mouth reminded him of someone he might have known. Hay blinked—he could hardly believe his eyes.

It was Jean Margaret Davenport, the "Infant Phenomenon" actress who—five years earlier—had entranced theatergoers in Providence, New York, and San Francisco. Now, age thirty-one, she had recently retired from the stage to marry Colonel Frederick Lander, the famous explorer, civil engineer, and poet. Hay, not given to superlatives in expressing his personal feelings in his diary, makes an exception for Jean Davenport Lander: "I was infinitely delighted at this chance interview with the Medea, the Julia, the Mona Lisa of my stage struck salad days." Hay was not yet twenty-three, and he was more stagestruck than ever. Fortune like a tornado had swept him up out of the prairie, and had dropped him down into the one place on earth where this sort of miracle might happen. "Miraculous" is the word he chooses to describe the woman's beauty, but the word more aptly applies to the event itself—a man meeting the woman of his dreams in a circumstance where she has come to ask him for help.

In all the three and a half years of diary entries, there is no incident more curious than this nocturnal visit of the two famous women to the White House. Ladies of their age and class did not go out at that hour into the crime-ridden streets of Washington unescorted. Mrs. Lander lived far away on the other side of the Capitol. Where were their husbands? Mr. Stephens, we know, was very ill, and Colonel Lander was on a secret reconnaissance mission in the South. Yet could they not have enlisted the help of some gentleman friend to accompany them on such an urgent mission, or sent a courier with a detailed message? Signed by the two celebrities, it would not have been discarded. No, they had to go in person; they had to make an appearance, a *scene* for the benefit of John Hay, if not the president.

Ann Stephens, having made the introductions, having gained access for her illustrious friend, gave the floor to the great actress. Now it seemed that Mrs. Lander bore the burden of the terrible message. But she could hardly bring herself to set it down. She looked at John Hay with those enormous liquid eyes, looked away at the carpet, and gazed up at him again. She started to speak, stammered, twisted a handkerchief, and peered up at him, her head lowered, as if she had forgotten her lines. "After many hesitating and bashful trials, Mrs. Lander told the impulse that brought them."

A young gentleman she knew from Virginia, "long haired, swaggering, chivalrous of course . . . had come into town in great anxiety for a new saddle . . ." There she hesitated, pausing for an effect that was dramatic whether or not she intended it to be. She did not explain how or where she had met the southern knight (whom she did not name) or why he had so indiscreetly informed her "that he and half a dozen others including a daredevil guerilla from Richmond named Ficklin would do a thing within forty-eight hours that would ring through the world. Connecting this central fact with a multiplicity of attendant de-tails she concluded that the President was either to be assassinated or captured."

John Hay was astonished—not by the story, the likes of which he heard several times a week—but by Jean Lander's bearing, her bash-ful, halting presentation of the information in the throes of profound concern. This was not the proud Medea he had seen onstage, nor the shameless Camille. "She ended by renewing her protestations of ear-nest solicitude," Hay wrote, "mingled with fears of the impropriety of the step," and with good reason, as the odd visit, being both melodra-matic and disruptive, would be charged to the actress rather than the novelist. Mrs. Stephens would later become a friend of Mrs. Lincoln's. The glamorous Mrs. Lander would never again set foot in the house. At the moment, none of this concerned the secretary. Starstruck, be-witched, he marked the transformation of Jean Davenport.

"Lander has made her very womanly since he married her. Imagine Jean M. Davenport a blushing, hesitating wife."

Thanking the women for their concern and their diligence in coming to the White House so late at night to sound the alarm, he led them to the door. As they put on their cloaks and bonnets, he assured them that the president would be informed immediately of the threat, and bid them good evening.

Had it been anyone other than Jean Lander who had come calling, Hay probably would not have disturbed the president and his wife. But, true to his word, he went upstairs, and entering the office vestibule he passed through the double doors to the right and into the broad central hall that led to the family apartments. He passed the oval library on the left, the guest bedrooms and children's bedrooms on the right, and stopped at Lincoln's bedroom on the left.

He knocked on the door; Mr. Lincoln told him to come in.

"I went to the bedside of the Chief *couché*. I told him the yarn," Hay wrote, knowing that the president might have wondered why his secre-tary had troubled his rest with such a trifle.

"He quietly grinned."

THE NEXT MORNING, APRIL 19, Hay consulted Major David Hunter concerning White House security. Hunter, a powerfully built, balding man of fifty-nine with a drooping mustache, had been a guard aboard the train from Springfield. In Buffalo, he had protected the Lincolns from a mob that rushed the train, dislocating his shoulder in the melee. Destined for rapid military promotion in the field, he had already made himself essential to the Lincolns' peace of mind in the capital.

The gravity of military developments in the vicinity seems not to have dawned upon John Hay as quickly as it had upon Nicolay and the president. Keeping his own memorandum of events, Nicolay wrote that "Friday, April 19th 1861 is likely to become historic in the nation's annals. The 6th Regiment Mass[achusetts] Volunteer Militia in passing through the city of Baltimore, was assaulted by a mob, and finally in self-defense fired upon the mob in return." Nicolay and Lincoln received word from the governor of Maryland in the early afternoon "that a collision had occurred." Four soldiers and nine civilians had been killed in the streets around Camden Station, and the mayor of Baltimore wired the president, "send no troops here." Nicolay called it "the first bloodshed in this civil war," and wrote to Therena that "we are expecting more troops here by way of Baltimore, but are also fearful that the secessionists may at any hour cut the telegraph wires, tear up the railroad track, or burn the bridges." He also mentions rumors that a hostile army of fifteen hundred had gathered in Alexandria; a ship was seen unloading rebel soldiers on the Maryland side of the Potomac.

From all indications, the attack would come that night. The Federal garrison at Harper's Ferry, Virginia, had burned the U.S. armory there and fled, under threat of attack by the secessionists. This seemed to delight John Hay and Major Hunter, "as a deadly blow at the prosperity" of the southern traitors, who had coveted the armory. Anxious visitors filled the White House waiting rooms—congressmen, cabinet members, and militia officers all clamoring for the president's attention. For the time being, Nicolay would have to fend for himself. His friend Hay had gone downtown on a mission.

Making the most of his new prestige, Hay had arranged to call upon the stage actor Joseph Jefferson at his hotel. Thirty-two years of age, the comedian was already famous: roles in *Our American Cousin* at Laura Keene's theater in New York, and *Rip Van Winkle,* which he had adapted for the theater, had made him a star in his late twenties. Hay "found him more of a gentleman than I had expected. A very intellectual face, thin and eager with large intense blue eyes, the lines firm, and the hair darker than I had thought."

Jefferson had a good story to tell his visitor. When Joe was a child actor, on the road with his family of players, their engagement in Springfield was threatened by the city's entertainment tax. In the provinces in those days, theater was considered wicked, and the actors and actresses no better than vagabonds, as false and immoral as the roles they played onstage. While citizens could not lawfully ban show business, some town councils levied taxes on traveling companies so exorbitant they would be obliged to move on.

In Springfield, there lived a young lawyer who was very well liked, and who also happened to have a passion for stage plays—not that he'd seen many, but he'd read a few, especially the tragedies of Shakespeare. This lawyer went before the city fathers and spoke so eloquently on the high art of the theater, from the time of Thespis and the Greek tragedians to the golden age of Shakespeare and Marlowe, that the elders relented, suspended the tax, and the Jefferson troupe settled in for a long run.

The lawyer was Abraham Lincoln, who would spend many an hour reading Shakespeare aloud to John Hay.

But Hay had not come to visit the illustrious comedian in order to learn about theater history. He had other matters on his mind. In those days, everyone in the theater world knew everyone else—particularly at the top of the profession. So Joseph Jefferson, the same age as the "Infant Phenomenon," would be just the person to tell him all about Jean Margaret Lander.

She had been on tour in California in the autumn of 1860 when she met Colonel Lander, who was there on one of his explorations for the Department of the Interior. Dashing, gallant, an amateur poet, Lander wooed the renowned actress. They fell in love, and were married in San Francisco on October 13, in a blaze of publicity ("the marriage of Venus and Mars!"). Jean Davenport was quite wealthy, and the idea of her giving up the stage for home and hearth may have been as much her idea as her husband's. She could not remember when she had not worked, and basked in applause, and perhaps she had grown weary of it for a time. But six months after the honeymoon, she might have had second thoughts. There were rumors that Mrs. Lander had grown moody and high-handed with the colonel. As for him, the explorer, Indian fighter, and barroom brawler who had made five transcontinental explorations by the age of thirty-nine was as restless as ever. Although he had a genuine interest in the arts and amused himself for a while in developing Washington's art collections, as soon as war threatened, he was gone—on secret missions to the South, then to the most dangerous posts he could get assigned to him, in the West.

So, for the time being, Mrs. Lander was—as she would be for most of the Civil War—alone. She lived in a large, airy wood-frame house on B Street, looking out on the Capitol grounds to the north.

Taking his leave by thanking Joseph Jefferson for his hospitality, John Hay advanced up Pennsylvania Avenue to Capitol Hill, crossing Maryland Avenue and then New Jersey Avenue in rounding the Capitol Park with a view to dropping in on Mrs. Lander. Had he sent his card ahead? When would there have been time? He arrived at her door, and she invited him in. He was very handsome, in a boyish way, and knew exactly what charming things to say. Yes, he had seen her onstage, when he was a student, in Providence.

He had come, he explained, to hear her tell—now at her leisure, "just by way of a slant"—the story she had told in breathless haste the night before. It was, of course, a matter of the greatest importance, the president's security, and Mr. Lincoln had received the intelligence with gratitude. Now, if anything was left to be said, she must not leave out the least detail.

"I like Jean M. more and more . . . ," John Hay confides to his diary, and how much more we can never be certain. Someone has drawn a

line through this sentence in an effort to conceal Hay's feelings that is
less effective than other measures of the sort one can find throughout
the notebooks—furious cross-hatchings and ink spills, razor marks
at the gutter margins, entire seasons of inexplicable silence. Still, the
figure of Jean M. flickers through the pages of Hay's diary, as if it could
not be wiped out without burning the entire book.

WHEN HAY RETURNED TO the White House that afternoon, he was
awed by the crisis that the president and Nicolay had been struggling
to manage while he was calling on Jefferson and Lander. Lincoln had
issued a proclamation blockading the southern ports. At 3:30, a special
envoy from Baltimore's mayor delivered a letter insisting "that it is not
possible for more soldiers to pass through Baltimore unless they fight
their way every step." The president's wife was anxious. "I had to do
some very dexterous lying," Hay recalled, "to calm the awakened fears
of Mrs. Lincoln in regard to the assassination suspicion" that had been
aroused by the ladies' visit the night before. He might have altered Mrs.
Lander's tale of the long-haired Virginian and his guerrillas to make
it sound implausible; he could say with truth he had looked into the
matter that very day and found nothing in it.

"The organization of the militia, and the late arrivals of troops have
been making things seem quite warlike," Nicolay wrote, "but we have
been much more impressed with the conditions surrounding us by the
arrival this evening of Miss [Dorothea] Dix, who came to offer herself
and an army of nurses to the government gratuitously, for hospital service." Miss Dix, renowned for her work in asylums for the mentally ill,
had a clairvoyant sense of disaster. Her stern, elderly figure appearing
at the White House that evening was unsettling.

During the next week, there was intense anxiety that the feebly defended capital would be attacked. Nicolay complained that of five thousand men under arms in Washington, no more than two thousand were
reliable. He felt that the three thousand District militia were so full of
secessionists they might turn their guns on loyal Union troops at the

first sight of rebel invaders. Fretfully, the president and his staff awaited the arrival of regiments from New York, Rhode Island, Pennsylvania, and other states while negotiating with the recalcitrant Marylanders for the right of way. The cutting of telegraph lines by secessionists and interruption of the mails further intensified suspense, as the secretary of war and General Winfield Scott waited for news from the North in a virtual vacuum. It was with great relief that they received word from Elmer Ellsworth "that his regiment has been raised, accepted," and was ready to be assigned. "Much is hoped from the gallant Colonel's Bloodtubs. They would be worth their weight in Virginia Currency, at Fort McHenry tonight," Hay wrote. Exasperated, Lincoln told some Massachusetts volunteers on April 24, "I don't believe there is any North. The Seventh Regiment is a myth. R. Island is not known in our geography any longer. *You* are the only Northern realities."

The steamship *Baltic* transported Ellsworth's regiment of Fire Zouaves to Annapolis on April 29, and a special train delivered them to Washington the night of May 2. Hay noted that the president was greatly relieved, as there had been rumors "that the Firemen were cutting their way through Baltimore." Hay was on hand to greet his friend, "dressed like his men, red cap, red shirt, grey breeches, grey jacket." Ellsworth wore a sword, a heavy pistol, and a bowie knife in his belt with a heavy blade sixteen inches long, that might "go through a man's head from crown to chin as you would split an apple." At the moment, the weapons were not for the enemy, but to put fear into "the turbulent spirits under his command," Hay observed.

Hay went up to the Hall of the House of Representatives to see where the Zouaves were quartered, and described them as "a jolly, gay set of blackguards ... turbulent spirits" spoiling for a fight. After a week of nothing but parading and drilling, it would be all the colonel could do to keep them out of mischief. They chased imaginary rebels through the streets, frightening the ladies; they ordered expensive meals in restaurants, then told the owners to send the bill to the White House or Jeff Davis. Some set fire to a fence. One was accused of rape. But of the eleven hundred men, only six were sent home. The rest were behaving well enough. Ellsworth marched them past the White House where Mr. and Mrs. Lincoln, Tad, and Willie took delight in their intricate drilling.

TROOPS WERE ARRIVING BY the thousands every day, bivouacking in the Capitol and the Patent Office, and parading through the streets. On the morning of April 29, a clear, windy day after rain, John Hay dressed and went into Nicolay's office across the hall. At the south window stood Kansas senator Jim Lane, gaunt, uncombed, bewhiskered, wearing a rusty overcoat without a necktie or even a collar, his hair standing "fretful-porcupine-wise upon his crown." Holding a spyglass to his eye, he looked out over the wind-tossed trees, swearing sotto voce. Behind him was seated a slender gentleman, properly dressed and dapper, with long red hair, a carefully trimmed mustache, intense, bespectacled eyes, and delicate, intelligent features. This was the German-American Carl Schurz, thirty-two, a veteran of the German revolution, who had fled his homeland in 1849 after the coup failed. Schurz took up the Republican cause in the 1850s, bringing many German-American voters to Lincoln's camp. The president had assigned him to diplomatic duty in Madrid, but he was reluctant to leave the center of action in America. Hay found him an intriguing, romantic figure, "an orator, a soldier, a philosopher, an exiled patriot, a skilled musician" who played the piano beautifully in the Red Room at twilight, when he was not advising the president on military matters.

Senator Lane's stream of profanity addressed the Confederate flag whipping in the breeze over a roof across the river.

"Let me tell you," he growled, while keeping his eye on the telescope, "we have got to whip these scoundrels like hell, Carl Schurz. They did a good thing stoning our men at Baltimore & shooting away the flag at Sumter. It has set the great North a howling for blood and they'll have it."

"I heard," Schurz replied, in his soft German accent, "you preached a sermon to your men yesterday."

"No sir, this is not time for preaching." In Mexico, where he had fought with General Winfield Scott, there had been four ministers in Lane's regiment. Lane ordered them to stop preaching and take up card playing. "In a month or so they was the biggest devils & best fighters I had."

Carl Schurz told Hay that he had obtained three months' leave from his diplomatic duties to raise a cavalry regiment of German-Americans. The country had not seen such heartfelt saber rattling since the British arrived in Boston nearly a century before.

The bellicose tone of Hay's diary is characteristic of the widespread innocence of warfare, the rank ignorance of the horror that was to come. Visiting the Rhode Island regiment camped at the Department of the Interior, he remarks that "there was enough of breeding and honor to retone the society of the Gulf, and wealth enough to purchase the entire state of Florida . . . When men like these leave their horses, their women and their wine, harden their hands, eat crackers for dinner, wear a shirt for a week and never black their shoes,—all for a principle, it is hard to set any bounds to the possibilities of such an army. The good blood of the North must now be mingled with that of the South in battle, and the first fight will determine which is the redder."

On that date, April 30, 1861, it is fair to say that Hay had no idea what he was talking about, but he was about to learn before the end of June. He speaks of a "principle" for which the gallant aristocrats of Providence had left the comforts of hearth and home. But neither he nor John Nicolay precisely understood what that principle was until one morning a week later, when "the ancient" (as they sometimes called Mr. Lincoln) gave them an impromptu tutorial in his office. That room, with the maps covering the wall across from the grim portrait of Andrew Jackson, sometimes became an informal classroom.

Shortly after sunrise on May 7, Hay entered the president's office to relay intelligence that Ellsworth had just received concerning the moods and opinions of people in Illinois, as well as the news that he was planning to swear in the Zouaves that day. Hay also wanted to tell Mr. Lincoln of Senator Orville Browning's extravagant scheme for subjugating the South. Browning would "establish a black republic in lieu of the exterminated whites, and extend a protectorate over them, while they raised our cotton." Senator Browning had not meant his proposal as a joke.

Hay found Mr. Lincoln gazing out the south window at two U.S. Navy steamers puffing up the river, while resting the brass end of a telescope on the toe of his boot. Lincoln was lounging behind his desk in the far corner of the spacious chamber that he called his "workshop." Dividing the room lengthwise was the long table surrounded by twelve chairs where the cabinet convened. As Hay entered, to his right was the fireplace, and across from it, beneath the maps was a horsehair settee flanked by two button-and-roll upholstered armchairs.

"Some of our northerners seem bewildered and dazzled by the excitement of the hour," said Lincoln, his eyes twinkling, more amused than alarmed. John Nicolay entered from the door to his right with a sheaf of papers. "Doolittle [Republican senator from Wisconsin] seems to think that this war is to result in the entire abolition of slavery. . . ." And the old and venerable James Hamilton, son of Alexander, had been urging Mr. Lincoln to enlist slaves in the U.S. Army—a distant dream that Major Hunter would soon make a reality.

"The daily correspondence," Hay replied, "is thickly interspersed by such suggestions." Lincoln listened. Hay and Nicolay watched his features closely, knowing him well enough to sense when he was about to share his thoughts with them. This was such an hour, in the morning stillness, when the young men might be welcome to sit with Mr. Lincoln, pose questions, be questioned in turn, in the Socratic manner, and freely converse.

They were eager to hear him explain what he believed to be the meaning of the paroxysm that had seized the nation. Not until this moment, perhaps, was he fully prepared to articulate it. Lincoln had been working on a paper that was to be delivered to Congress on July 4, and he had been "engaged in constant thought upon the Message," which was to be "an exhaustive review of questions of the hour & of the future," Hay recalled.

"For my own part," Lincoln said, settling in, choosing his words carefully, "I consider the central idea pervading this struggle is the necessity that is upon us, of proving that popular government is not an absurdity. We must settle this question now, whether in a free government the minority have the right to break up the government whenever they choose." Over the bell-jarred mantel clock hung the illustrative image of Andrew Jackson, who had faced down South Carolina senator John C. Calhoun in 1832, during the famous "nullification controversy," when that state declared the federal tariff acts oppressive, and attempted to render them null and void. Jackson proclaimed nullification was rebellion and treason, and threatened to use the army to enforce the law.

"If we fail," the president continued, with a note of sadness, "it will go far to prove the incapability of the people to govern themselves." Looking far off in the distance, Lincoln allowed that final judgment might be suspended—in America's case—because of "a vast and far reaching disturbing element," slavery in other words, with which no other free nation would have to contend; but "that however is not for us to say . . . Taking the government as we found it we will see if the majority can preserve it." The way Nicolay heard this, as he noted later in the day, was: "Admit the right of a minority to secede at will, and the occasion for such secession would almost as likely be any other as the slavery question."

That was the day's lesson. The globes of the chandelier glowed faintly above them. As the morning light swept the shadows from the corners of the long room, the men pondered the important discourse, logical and legalistic on the face of it, but resting upon the mystical and sacred bedrock of brotherhood and union. Mr. Lincoln hated slavery, but he understood that this evil would perish under its own weight much sooner if the Union were preserved than if the slave states created their own government, their own laws and borders.

For this principle, the gentlemen of Rhode Island had left their wives and their wine, and the New York firemen had left their lager, hoses, and ladders to sail to Washington and practice field drills and the manual of arms. How many of these patriots understood what the president had just explained to his secretaries?

IN THE AFTERNOON, ON the East Front of the Capitol, Colonel Ellsworth called his soldiers into a square formation around him. John Hay was watching, and heard Ellsworth address his men. "A great speech," Hay wrote, with "more commonsense, dramatic power, tact, [and] energy . . ." than he'd heard in all the "spread-eagle" speeches in Congress. Ellsworth "spoke to them as men. Made them proud of their good name . . ." Other regiments were enlisting for thirty days, while the Fire Zouaves were enlisting "for the war."

"Now laddies," the little colonel announced, good-naturedly, "if any one of you wants to go home, he had better sneak around the back alleys, crawl over fences, and get out of sight before we see him." President Lincoln, in his stovepipe hat, and Tad, in a broad-brimmed straw, drove up in a carriage and got out. There, in the shade of the unfinished Capitol, General Irvin McDowell administered the oath of allegiance to the Fire Zouaves, and the eleven hundred men—firefighters only weeks earlier—became the Eleventh New York Infantry Regiment.

Two days later, on May 9, Mr. and Mrs. Lincoln, Hay, Nicolay, and others from the White House, spent "a very agreeable afternoon" at the Navy Yard with the New York volunteers. Their ranks included some excellent musicians who improvised a concert to which several hundred guests were invited. Lincoln requested "La Marseillaise." When the concert was over, Hay recalled, "we went down to the [USS] *Pensacola* and observed the shooting of the great Dahlgren gun . . . two ricochet shots were sent through the target and one plumper." Everyone was amazed that the deadly cannonball was clearly visible in flight. "The splendid course of the 11 inch shell . . . the lightning, the quick rebound & flight through the target with wild skips . . . the steady roll into the waves were scenes as novel and pleasant to me as to all the rest of the party. The President was delighted."

The citizens were giddy, intoxicated by the colorful preparations for war, and perhaps no man was more excited than William Stoddard. When he was not drilling with the D.C. Rifles, or on guard duty, Stoddard wrote news dispatches for the *New York Examiner.* On May 12, he wrote that in his opinion "an attack on Washington is contemplated, and that it will be made as soon as possible." He assured his readers that "all the heights surrounding and commanding the city, are being occupied and fortified," and singled out the Rhode Island men and Ellsworth's Fire Zouaves for special praise. Recently he had written with concern that Arlington Heights, the range of hills south of the Potomac near Alexandria, afforded "positions from which hostile cannon would hold the city at their mercy" and even "reduce it to a heap of ruins ..." Now he was more optimistic that arrangements had been made to seize these positions at the first signs of danger.

Ellsworth and his regiment had moved from their quarters in the Capitol to an open-air camp, a beautiful site on the near bank of the river that runs between Washington and Alexandria. That day, Nicolay and Hay rode out to visit the colonel, and Nicolay gathered "the first wild flowers I have had this spring," pink spring beauties, wild geraniums, and violets. He wrote to Therena: "I enclose some of them, to remind you as they have very vividly reminded me, of the old days." He had just received a letter in which she had begged him to burn all of her correspondence. "What on earth you want me to do that for I cannot imagine," he answered, demanding an explanation. No doubt she feared for his life, and did not want her love letters to survive him. We will never know, because he did, eventually, honor her request— making it impossible to know how she spent those years in Pittsfield without Nicolay.

A week later, on a quiet Sunday, Stoddard took a furlough in order to visit his friends in the White House. He let himself in with his latchkey and went upstairs. The rooms were almost deserted. The president had gone to church, Mrs. Lincoln had gone to Cambridge with her son Robert, and the secretaries were out for a stroll. Stoddard entered the office he shared with Hay, and on his desk found a stack of patents awaiting his signature. Hearing movement across the hall he walked over to Nicolay's office, where he was welcomed, with a shout, by Elmer Ellsworth.

It was Ellsworth's habit, several times a week, to go to the White House, chat with Hay and Nicolay, visit the president if he could, and collect his mail. Getting letters in and out of Washington had become difficult. He carried on an intense correspondence with his sweetheart, Carrie Spafford, up in New York, and, of course, the postmaster treated Nicolay's office with special deference.

So here was the drillmaster, now head of a New York regiment, reading his letters.

"Hullo, Ellsworth, are you here?"

"Yes, I'm all the President there is on hand this morning. I got away from camp to run over to see him and the boys." Ellsworth, Nicolay, and Hay would discuss politics and the war, tell jokes, and share their hopes and dreams. If Mr. Lincoln had a free moment, he would join them in Nicolay's office. Inevitably the conversation would turn upon the defiant image framed by the south window—the red and blue Stars and Bars of the Confederate flag, across the river, flying over the Marshall House hotel in Alexandria. This was an affront, an insult. Ellsworth, more than the others, wanted to do something about it. As Virginia had not yet ratified the order of secession by popular vote, the state was still in the Union. Virginians had been maddeningly evasive about their status. Until the popular vote to secede was cast, not a thing could be done about that flag, and the voting was not scheduled to occur until May 23. Everyone was waiting.

Today, Stoddard was particularly pleased to have a moment alone with Ellsworth, one of his heroes, so he might get a lesson or two in the art of combat. Ellsworth—as Hay had observed—was a superb fighter, who "could hold a rapier with De Villiers," the greatest swordsman of the day. Ellsworth had "a hand as true as steel, and an eye like a gerfalcon. He used to amuse himself by shooting ventilation holes through his window panes. Standing ten paces from the window, he could fire seven shots from his revolver and not shiver the glass beyond the circumference of a half-dollar." In the corner of Nicolay's room, somebody had left a carbine. Stoddard picked it up and passed it to the colonel, asking if he wouldn't mind demonstrating the manual of arms. "He went through the motions with mathematical precision; but when he came to 'make ready,' he had forgotten his proximity to the south window, and the muzzle of the piece went crashing through a pane of glass," as if to attack the rebel flag. Ellsworth, abashed, "shouldered arms," and the drill came to an end.

Hay arrived, and then Nicolay, wanting to know what had happened to the window. So Ellsworth and Stoddard, taking turns, embellished a wonderful tale, "told with masterly gravity, a yarn of a man hiding in the shrubbery," an assassin surely, who had taken one of them for the president and tried to shoot him. "Perhaps the yarn would have lasted longer if Ellsworth could have kept his face straight," Stoddard recalled, "but the fun ended and he and I went to our quarters to prepare for the invasion of Virginia."

When the news came on the evening of May 23, 1861, that Virginia had seceded, Ellsworth and his Zouaves were prepared. Alexandria must be taken immediately, and he had asked General Joseph Mansfield if his regiment might lead the charge.

In the light of a full moon, at midnight, when at last he was alone in his tent, Ellsworth wrote to Carrie Spafford.

> My own darling Kitty,
> My regiment is ordered to cross the river & move on
> Alexandria within six hours. We may meet with a warm
> reception & my darling among so many careless fellows
> one is some what likely to be hit.
> If anything should happen—Darling just accept
> this assurance, the only thing I can leave you—the
> highest happiness I looked for on earth was a union
> with you. . . . God bless you as you deserve and grant
> you a happy & useful life & us a union hereafter.
>
> > Truly your own,
> > Elmer

As the Federal troop steamers approached the Virginia shore, a few Confederate guards fired their rifles into the air and ran away. In the dawn light, the Zouaves went ashore. Ellsworth sent a company to pull up the railroad tracks to Richmond while he led a squadron to the town center, where they intended to cut the wires to the telegraph office. They met with no resistance, as the Confederate troops had retreated an hour earlier, under a flag of truce. Spying the Confederate flag still flying over the Marshall House—the banner that had provoked such anger and disgust as Mr. Lincoln, Hay, and Nicolay regarded it daily from the White House windows—Ellsworth said, "Boys, we must have that down before we return."

He entered the hotel with seven men—four corporals, a lieutenant, a chaplain, and a newspaper reporter. Posting three of the corporals on the first floor, Ellsworth led the rest of the party bounding up two flights of stairs to the attic. From there, he and the lieutenant climbed a ladder to the roof, where the flagstaff was planted. Handing the lieutenant his pistol, the colonel cut the halyard with a knife and brought down the immense flag.

Technically under a military cease-fire, the men had nothing to fear. They descended the staircase: Corporal Francis E. Brownell first; Ellsworth next, absorbed in the ritual of folding the flag; Edward House of the *New York Tribune;* then the lieutenant and the chaplain. At the first landing, James W. Jackson, the innkeeper, leaped out of a dark hall, aimed a double-barreled shotgun at Ellsworth, who was still too engrossed in folding the flag to notice, and discharged one barrel of slugs into the young man's breast. The reporter, whose hand had been resting on Ellsworth's shoulder, recalled: "He seemed to fall almost from my grasp. He was on the second or third step from the landing, and he dropped forward with that heavy, horrible, headlong weight which always comes of sudden death in this manner."

Corporal Brownell turned, raised his rifle, and shot Jackson in the middle of his face before thrusting a saber bayonet twice through his body.

CHAPTER FOUR

GRAVE
RESPONSIBILITIES

With all of its parades and marching bands and battle hymns, its gallantry and moral rhetoric, war has no reality apart from murder and mutilation, the grief of widows and mothers, friends and lovers left behind. Over his heart, Elmer Ellsworth wore a gold medallion inscribed with the Latin phrase *Non Nobis, Sed Pro Patria* (not for us, but for our country). The charge from the shotgun drove the medal deep into his breast.

As the men waiting on the docks of the Navy Yard saw the steamer *James Guy* approaching on the Potomac, they noted with dread that its ensign was flying at half-mast. They soon learned that the ship was delivering the dead body of Colonel Ellsworth. In a matter of minutes, the church bells began to toll and all of the city's flags were lowered to half-mast. A captain knocked on the White House door to inform the president and his family. Lincoln was in the library when the sad captain told the story of the colonel's death. Lincoln thanked the messenger, who left him alone.

The president looked out the window toward Alexandria, where there was no more sign of a Confederate flag in the sky. His back was to the door when two gentlemen were admitted on important business. He did not turn until they were nearly upon him, and then, extending his hand, he apologized that he was unable to speak. They thought that perhaps Mr. Lincoln was ill with a sore throat. But then he covered his face with his handkerchief and burst into tears. He walked up and down the room several times, struggling to compose himself, and at last invited the men to sit down with him.

"I will make no apology, gentlemen, for my weakness; but I knew poor Ellsworth well, and held him in great regard. Just as you entered the room, Captain Fox left me, after giving me the painful details of Ellsworth's unfortunate death. The event was so unexpected, and the recital so touching, that it quite unmanned me."

Ellsworth may have been prepared to die for his country—he said so many times—and it is said that in death his features were wonderfully peaceful and composed. But he was alone in this; his country and his friends, not to mention his fiancée and his parents, were unprepared for the untimely death of such a lovable man. John Hay wrote to his friend Hannah Angell, "When Ellsworth was murdered all my sunshine perished. I hope you may never know the dry, barren agony of soul that comes with the utter and hopeless loss of a great love." Nicolay informed Therena Bates: "I had supposed myself to have grown quite indifferent, and callous, and hard-hearted, until I heard of the sad fate of Col. Ellsworth . . . I have been quite unable to keep the tears out of my eyes whenever I thought, or heard, or read, about it. . . . I had known and seen him almost daily for more than six months past."

Mr. Lincoln wrote to Ellsworth's parents: "Our affliction here is scarcely less than your own . . . In the hope that it may be no intrusion upon the sacredness of your sorrow, I have ventured to address you this tribute to the memory of my young friend, and your brave and early fallen child. May God give you that consolation which is beyond all earthly power."

The day after the funeral—held in the East Room on May 25—

William Stoddard sat in Nicolay's office with Hay and Nicolay and some distinguished visitors. One was General Elias W. Leavenworth, whom Stoddard had known previously as mayor of Syracuse. It was a Sunday—exactly one week after the colonel had shown Stoddard the manual of arms. Leavenworth spoke of the great loss, and it was too much for Stoddard. "One glance at the window, with the fresh marks of the glazier's fingers on the pane, and another showed me that the General was in the same chair so lately occupied by the dead Colonel. . . . " Stoddard excused himself and quickly went out.

On May 31, the president announced that he would restrict his interviews to the most urgent business. The death of the Lincolns' friend Stephen Douglas three days later further curtailed the routine. "We had not become so hardened as we grew to be under the swift calamities that afterward trod so rapidly upon each other's heels," Stoddard recalled.

Later came the shock of the First Battle of Bull Run—on July 21, 1861—when Federal troops were routed and first heard the bloodcurdling sound of the rebel yell, and nearly four thousand men were killed and wounded; the Federal defeat at Ball's Bluff, Virginia, on October 21, 1861, where there were nine hundred Union casualties, and the Lincolns' friend Edward Baker was mowed down as he led a charge across the Potomac; the terrible Battle of Shiloh in April 1862, where nearly twenty thousand men were killed and wounded, North and South, and the Union victory was scarcely measurable. This is not a book of military history; it is concerned rather with the effect of war on a handful of men, civilians primarily, who were close witnesses of its higher administration and execution, and privy to rare intelligence of its progress and horrific results.

News came quickly to the secretaries—who lived in continual dismay that it came too slowly—and they were often the bearers of tidings, sad or satisfactory, almost never happy. On the afternoon of the First Battle of Bull Run, the president had gone out with his wife for a carriage ride to the Navy Yard, believing that his army had won the day. It was Nicolay and Hay who met him upon his return with the news that the Union army was retreating through Centreville, that the battle was lost, and they must prepare to save the capital.

"We told him," Nicolay recalled, "and he started off immediately," to the War Department. "John and I continued to sit at the windows, and could now distinctly hear heavy cannonading on the other side of the river."

IT WAS FORTUNATE THAT the rebels had not pressed their advantage. The day after Bull Run, July 22, thirty-five-year-old George McClellan was called to Washington to defend the city and train the Federal soldiers. Then came months of military preparation, military and political intrigue—a season of anxious waiting.

The president's stamina in handling interviews and meetings was prodigious. But the pressure in the waiting rooms, the trauma of Ellsworth's death, and the lack of privacy and relaxation had begun to tell upon the secretaries weeks before Bull Run. Nicolay had been the first to falter. When the Lincolns held their dinner for the diplomatic corps on June 4, Nicolay had to delegate the preparations to others. He had been given leave to go west for two weeks to visit his fiancée. He would not return until June 18.

William Stoddard was formally appointed to his White House assignment in July and called to his desk there in early August. This was fortunate, because after the Battle of Bull Run, Nicolay was exhausted, having been stricken with bilious fever. The day of the battle, he described his memory of the week past as "a jumble of blue-mass, calomel pills, seidlitz powders . . . the doctor found that I was very bilious, and has been at work all week trying to wake up my liver. . . ." On August 9, he set out for a resort in Long Branch, New Jersey.

John Hay was depressed. On August 12, he wrote to Hannah Angell, "I am dreadfully lonesome here." He was mourning Ellsworth; he was also lamenting the loss of his illusions. "Why don't the changing years which improve all things change me? My good is slipping from me, and evil is developing simply. . . . I am not improving company for a good Christian lady, on a rainy night."

Bear in mind that these bachelors were living not fifteen minutes walk away from some of the finest brothels in the East. This is not to say that such fastidious gentlemen as Hay, Nicolay, and Stoddard ever frequented such houses—there is no proof of it. On the other hand, given their youth, their freedom from family responsibilities, and the quantity of whiskey that they confessed to be consuming, it would be a statistical anomaly if one or another of them did not, now and again, visit a bordello for comfort and relaxation.

On August 15, Hay left to join Nicolay in Long Branch. Returning to the capital four days later, Hay wrote to his friend James A. Hamilton, "I am the unluckiest wretch that lives," and to Nicolay he wrote, "Nothing new. An immense crowd that boreth ever. Painters [house painters] who make God's air foul to the nostril. Rain, which makes a man moist and adhesive. Dust, which unwholesomely penetrates one's lungs. Washington, which makes one swear. There is not an item [of news]. We are waiting for your arrival to make one." Two days later, he wrote to the socialite Mrs. Charles Eames that if things did not improve, he was going to buy a cheap tombstone, write "Miserrimus" on it, and "betake myself to Prussic acid glacé." And on August 24, he wrote to Nicolay again to say he didn't mean to hurry him, but alas, "Dr. Pope's prediction has been realized. I am flat on my back with bilious fever. I had a gay old delirium yesterday, but am some better today. . . . There is no business in the office and Stoddard is here all the time. He can do as well as either of us. As soon as I get able, I shall leave."

Hay went to meet Nicolay in New York on August 28. Hay was bound for Illinois to see his mother, and to St. Louis to be the president's eyes and ears at Union headquarters in the West, but he wanted a word with Nicolay first. Hay was thin and pale. Nicolay had wished to extend his leave but saw that his friend needed it more. Besides, there was turmoil in the command of the Union forces of the West, under the imperious leadership of the ambitious General John C. Frémont, and Hay would know best how to disarm Frémont.

After arriving in Washington, Nicolay wrote to Therena at the end of August that Hay "himself had been sick and was compelled to leave. He is going to Illinois to stay three or four weeks. . . . From present appearances it will keep John and I both pretty busy to keep one *well* secretary here all the time. . . ."

By the late summer of 1861, a pattern of service had emerged for the secretaries that would continue for the next three years. One of the men would almost always be in Washington during the war. But for three years, Hay and Nicolay took turns on furlough, sometimes for weeks or months at a time. In their letters, they usually speak of these leaves of absence as holidays necessary to their mental and physical health.

It is true that both men suffered serious illnesses in the miasmic atmosphere of the swamp that bordered the White House grounds toward the river; so did Stoddard eventually. But the secretaries rarely left Washington for rest without an assignment somewhere in the vicinity of their destination, such as Hay's detour to St. Louis when he went to visit his family in Warsaw, 150 miles away. Nicolay's visits to Therena were often interrupted by long sojourns in Springfield, which must have been frustrating to the lovers, even though he had important business in the Illinois capital. The fact is that Hay and Nicolay—who both by now had Lincoln's complete confidence—were serving double duty as paper-and-ink secretaries and as emissaries. Their missions always required strict discretion, in some cases more than the State Department or the army could assure the president. They were so young (Hay, particularly, looked like he was eighteen) that they could move through a variety of social and military milieus unobtrusively. They were nonthreatening. As the president's aides, they had extraordinary access; as little-known clerks outside Washington, without high-sounding titles, they aroused few suspicions or jealousies. In a time when there was no Central Intelligence Agency, Nicolay and Hay often served as agents without portfolios.

Hay's detour to St. Louis in August was typical of Lincoln's delegation of assessment. The president had put General Frémont in command of the Union army's Department of the West, headquartered in St. Louis, in July. Frémont rented a mansion surrounded by gardens. He raised a flag on the roof, and recruited a guard of foreign officers in fancy dress uniforms. Soon Lincoln was hearing reports of highhanded treatment of local officials and army staff, and corruption in granting government contracts. While Confederate guerrillas were

wreaking havoc in Missouri, unchecked, there were rumors that Frémont had a grandiose plan to capture New Orleans. Some said he ate
opium. A Radical Republican and abolitionist, Frémont terrified the
slaveholders of the state.

On August 30, he declared martial law. Frémont said he would shoot
anyone bearing unauthorized arms, and proclaimed that the slaves in
the state were emancipated. This political decision far exceeded his authority as an army officer, embarrassing the president. Lincoln wrote
Frémont a confidential letter on September 2, asking that he modify
the proclamation to conform with acts of Congress that ensured that
property could not be confiscated without due judicial process. He also
kindly asked the general not to shoot citizens without asking him first.

Frémont refused. Lincoln sent Postmaster General Montgomery
Blair (an old ally of Frémont's), and Montgomery Meigs, his quartermaster general, to St. Louis to sound out Frémont in the matter. Frémont sent them packing. Then Lincoln sent Adjutant General Lorenzo
Thomas and Secretary of War Simon Cameron to St. Louis to see if
they could make progress, and evaluate the arrogant commander—to
determine if he was fit for his post. "He isolates himself," Lincoln concluded, on September 9, "& allows nobody to see him." While General
Thomas and the secretary of war might not see much of Frémont, the
president hoped that John Hay, with his renowned charm, would.

So, close upon the heels of the military and cabinet investigators,
during the week of September 15, Hay traveled to St. Louis, where he
"saw very much of Frémont and his wife. He was quiet earnest industri-
ous, imperious." This was the precise portrait of Frémont the president
needed. While Hay found more to admire than did Lincoln's other advisers, his arguments on Frémont's behalf did not win the day. The
president publicly revoked Frémont's proclamation, and began conferring with the cabinet and General Scott about Frémont's removal. In
mid-October, Lincoln sent Nicolay to Springfield to gather information about the matter. On October 21, Nicolay wrote to the president:
"I have taken some pains to learn the feeling here as to Frémont. The
universal opinion is that he has entirely failed, *and that he ought to be
removed . . .*"

Immediately upon receiving Nicolay's letter, the president relieved Frémont of command of the Department of the West, and replaced him with General David Hunter, Lincoln's loyal friend.

DURING THIS TIME, STODDARD wrote: "We live a strange life here, . . . in the very shadow of some great and terrible event, suspended over us by a thread as slender as that which of old upheld the impending danger of Damocles. We go about our accustomed duties with a cool, business-like manner," but now and then the sound of artillery practice, or the crack of a signal gun disturbs the precarious peace, the carpenter holds his hammer and the bookkeeper his pen, each man wondering, "Has it come, at last?"

War had come. The afternoon when Lincoln dismissed Frémont was on the day of Colonel Edward Baker's funeral. Baker was one of Lincoln's oldest friends from Springfield, where they had served as fellow Whigs in the legislature; the Lincolns had named a child after him. Elected to the U.S. Senate in 1860, Baker served there until the first adjournment. But that summer, after Bull Run, he could not resist the urge to lead men into battle, and joked about becoming—at age fifty—"a venerable martyr." He wrote his will and put his affairs in order before marching with the California Regiment along the Potomac River toward Confederate redoubts near Leesburg, Virginia. Leading a charge at Ball's Bluff, Virginia, where his troops were ambushed and surrounded, Baker was riddled with bullets. The embalming was accomplished with "great difficulty on account of the shattered condition of the corpse, which bore evidence of eight wounds."

Dr. Alfred Baker, brother of the slain hero, and his nephew, Lieutenant Edward B. Jerome, bore the news to the White House. The president and his wife and sons were devastated. Reading the orders from General Charles P. Stone found on Baker's person—"You will cross the river, take up a strong position, make a dash on Leesburg"—Lincoln cried, "Gentleman: my Baker was murdered." Stoddard wrote that officers must be more mindful of their orders. "Alas, for us all, that such and so valuable a life was so needlessly thrown away by its owner."

Nicolay had spoken of the frustration of being so near the fighting but not in it—which all of the young men felt in some measure. And yet they, like Baker, were worth far more to the Union alive than dead. In a revealing letter to his fiancée expressing this frustration, Nicolay comments upon a recent wedding in Pittsfield: "My theory and purpose, of this life is that of *approximation*, rather than perfect *attainment.*" He doesn't believe that bride or groom truly "wishes for happiness in that higher and aesthetic sense which grows out of a more perfect fitness, and which is purified by the fire of many ungratified aspirings." Unlike Baker and Ellsworth, different from the idealistic poet John Hay, the levelheaded, practical Teuton would settle for what was possible, sensible, and healthy. Perhaps he and Therena were not soul mates, ideal partners, but they would make a life together and a family; perhaps Nicolay would never win a medal for valor or die gloriously on the battlefield, but he would dutifully serve the president and the Union in dignified anonymity.

John Hay was growing as cynical of military heroism, and its contempt for human life, as was Stoddard. But for Hay, another sort of romanticism persisted. Never far from his thoughts was the bewitching voice and figure of Jean Davenport Lander. Now that her brave husband had returned to Washington as an aide to General McClellan, Hay saw more of him than of his wife. Frederick West Lander, thirty-nine, was six feet tall, broad-shouldered, and athletic. He had a high, noble forehead, a receding hairline, and wore a Vandyke beard. Trained as an artist and engineer, Lander was a Renaissance man famous in his thirties as a transcontinental surveyor, a poet, a painter, and a brawler. In March of 1859, he stood up to William McGraw, a freight contractor and pugilist who challenged him to a knockdown bare-knuckle match in the bar of Willard's Hotel, widely covered by the press. According to the *Evening Star,* the gladiators fought to a bloody draw, and both "left the scene of action terribly cut and disfigured." Weeks later, he lectured on fine arts at the Washington Art Association. Imagine Cyrano with a Roman nose. A Douglas Democrat, Lander refused Lincoln's offer to appoint him governor of the Nevada territory. Now he was on George

McClellan's staff, a brigadier general on the Upper Potomac, where Baker had gone to fight.

But Lander was dissatisfied. And Hay, with an eye on Mrs. Lander, was surprised by the brigadier general's show of exasperation in the presence of Lincoln and Seward. On October 10, 1861, Hay had been walking with the president and the secretary of state to McClellan's quarters in the War Department, and Lander fell in with them. "Lander was gasconading a little," Hay recalled, using the French term for boasting. "He said he would like a good place to die in with a corporal's guard, to set the nation right in the face of the world after the cowardly shame of Bull Run." Lincoln and the others could scarcely conceal their amusement until the swaggering general bid them good evening. As he walked away, the president wryly commented, "If he really wanted a job like that I could give it to him—Let him take his squad and go down behind Manassas [Virginia] and break up their railroad."

And Seward declared that "he disbelieved in personal courage as a civilized institution." He puffed on his cigar thoughtfully. He "had always acted on the opposite principle, admitting you are scared and assuming that the enemy is." Of course, the secretary of state added, if quarrels could be settled by his principles, all "would have been arranged satisfactorily and honorably before now." Hay was preoccupied with thoughts more personal than military. He must have wondered why the man who slept with Jean Margaret was so eager to leave home and risk his life leading men into battle on the front lines.

On a beautiful cool night, October 12, 1861, Hay walked with Mr. Lincoln across Lafayette Square to Seward's house. The moon was waning but shone brightly upon the white buildings as Lincoln showed Hay a telegram that had just arrived from General McClellan. It said "that the enemy was before him in force and would probably attack in the morning," Hay recalled, and "If they attack," the general added, "I shall beat them." At Seward's the conversation was far ranging, but it kept returning to General Lander's complaints. "Seward spoke of Lander's restlessness & griefs at inaction, his offered resignation—and resolve to go West and begin again—that watching the Potomac was not congenial, and other such. Seward told him to be of good cheer. Gen'l Scott was already fixing his orders for exactly the work he wanted to do."

The very next week, General Scott sent Lander twenty-five miles up the Potomac to serve Brigadier General Charles Stone on the same reconnaissance mission that claimed Edward Baker's life. After leading a platoon of soldiers across the river in frail skiffs, Lander took a Confederate bullet in his calf, at Edward's Ferry. The wound festered, but Lander would not stay home. McClellan was stricken with typhoid fever on December 30, and there was no adequate commander but Lander to block Stonewall Jackson's Confederates from swooping down upon the capital from western Maryland in January.

On New Year's Eve, General Lander wrote a curious and querulous letter to John Hay, asking him to lay it before the president, "at some leisure moment," and in honor of the late Senator Baker. In this letter, he protests that he has seen "weary emigrants and untrained mountaineers" win battles like Ball's Bluff, and that "our soldiers should be inspired to more confidence in themselves . . . by judicious promotions." In closing, Lander says he leaves the next day for the front near Hancock, Maryland, complaining that "the newspapers have so well apprised the enemy of our movements . . . I shall have great difficulties to encounter and few successes to chronicle." This premonitory letter was one of the last he would write.

In the bitter cold of January, General Lander led his men along the Potomac eighty miles northwest of Washington. Although greatly outnumbered, the Federal soldiers held off Stonewall Jackson's troops at Hancock on January 5. For two days, the rebels bombarded the town before giving up and retreating south to West Virginia.

Deathly ill from the infection in his leg, Lander maintained his outpost in the region. After Lincoln issued General War Order No. 1, calling for Federal troops to advance against the insurgent forces, Lander led a brilliant charge upon the enemy at Bloomery, West Virginia, on Valentine's Day. For this valiant action, he received a special letter of commendation from the War Department, but he had not long to enjoy it. The sepsis from the leg wound had caused delirium and "congestion of the brain." While preparing a new attack upon the rebels, Lander died on March 2, 1862. He was given a military hero's funeral in the home of Salmon Chase, whose daughter Kate was a friend of both John Hay and Mrs. Lander. The president, most of the cabinet members, and high-ranking generals attended the obsequies. The famous widow—who had been a bride for only sixteen months—received hundreds of condolence letters from all over the world. Among the letters so carefully kept is no letter from John Hay (whose diaries do not record the loss), and he was not observed among the mourners at the funeral.

IF LINCOLN'S SECRETARIES WANTED a model of marriage with all its challenges, stresses, and intermittent pleasures and sorrows, they had only to look toward the West Wing of the White House, where Mrs. Lincoln presided. According to William Stoddard, "Mrs. Lincoln is absolute mistress of all that part of the White House inside of the vestibule, on the first floor, and of all the upper floor west of the folding doors across the hall at the head of the stairs." He calls her authoritative and yet "ready to listen to argument . . . provided the arguments come from a recognized friend, for her personal antipathies are quick and strong, and at times they find hasty and resentful forms of expression."

A short, plump matron of forty-three with abundant auburn hair, a prim mouth, and wide-set, narrow eyes, Mrs. Lincoln, in the year since her husband had been elected, had adapted painfully to her change in station. Well-bred and well-educated in Lexington, Kentucky, the southern belle had lived most of her life in the upper strata of society in the provincial capital of Illinois, where few could look down upon her. Her volatile temper, snobbishness, and outspokenness on political subjects were tolerated there. Now, as mistress of the White House, she lived in a glare of publicity, subject to the scrutiny of journalists and sectors of the public who desired to discredit her, for political and personal reasons. By nature insecure, she became distrustful and suspicious. Her husband had little time for her. Mary overreacted to criticisms of her "western" rusticity by spending extravagantly on clothing and grandly refurbishing the White House. Her expenses, and her influence peddling on behalf of friends and relatives, had provoked gossip that was rising to the level of scandal by the winter of 1861–62.

While Nicolay was in Illinois in November of 1861, Hay wrote to him about Mrs. Lincoln's collusion with John Watt, the gardener, to divert White House funds from necessary budget lines to their own discretionary use. "Hell is to pay about Watt's affairs. I think the Tycoon [Lincoln] begins to suspect him. I wish he [Watt] could be struck with lightning."

Hay and Nicolay had begun to refer to Lincoln, affectionately, as the Tycoon, after hearing the funny-sounding word used to designate the shogun of Japan. Mrs. Lincoln they privately called "the hellcat" for her tantrums, and sometimes "Her Satanic Majesty" for her imperious and unprincipled ways. In this letter, Hay informs Nicolay that Watt has contrived to get two employees dismissed, and now "has his eye peeled for a pop at me, because I won't let Madame have our stationery fund," which amounted to $1,000 per year. "They have gone to New York together," Hay adds, on a shopping spree, presumably. What he does not mention is that there were rumors that Mrs. Lincoln's intimacy with the gardener exceeded the bounds of propriety.

The secretaries were at odds with "Madame" soon after taking up residence in the White House. All were rivals for Lincoln's attention, and there were days when the men saw more of her husband than Mary Lincoln did. Fortunately for all of them, William Stoddard had the wiles and good humor to win Mrs. Lincoln's trust and affection. It was probably to his advantage that he lived with his brother Henry and his sister Kate in a brownstone on Louisiana Avenue between the Centre Market and City Hall—known as "mortician's row" for all the embalmers in the neighborhood. So Stoddard did not invite the contempt that comes with familiarity under a shared roof.

His friendship with Mrs. Lincoln was sealed over the management of her mail. She got a great deal of it, not as much as Mr. Lincoln, but far more than she wished to read: letters from strangers begging favors, petitions, signed and anonymous letters of cajolery and abuse. Every morning, the mail arrived in leather sacks and was dumped upon Stoddard's desk, a large, "flat table desk full of capacious drawers for documents" that stood next to the hall door of John Hay's office. On either side of the north window were two rickety upright desks, "old and apparently somewhat infirm, over which John Hay claimed supervision," Stoddard recalled, although as long as Stoddard was there, Hay spent little time sitting down, as "his peculiar abilities quickly began to manifest themselves. He was a born diplomat," constantly in demand in the crowded, discordant halls and anterooms. The mail fell upon Stoddard's desk, and most days he sorted it.

One morning, after returning from a New York business trip a few months after he had joined the staff, Stoddard found that a lot of mail had arrived before him. "There on my table lay a heap of letters, all duly cut open but very few of them otherwise dealt with." He hung his coat and hat on the rack and sat down to work. In an hour, Hay came in, his usually bright countenance clouded by worry.

"Stod!" he exclaimed. "I'm in the worst kind of fix! You know how it is. Nicolay and I are out with Madame. She is down on both of us. Now! You were away, yesterday, and I tried to help you along on the mail. I had seen how you did it and so I turned a whole pile of them over on their backs and sliced them open . . ." He had done this without realizing that a dozen letters had been addressed to Mrs. Lincoln. Now he feared the worst.

"What shall I do about it?" Hay pleaded.

Stoddard was amused at Hay's melodrama. "Don't do anything . . . Shut up and say nothing about it. I'll take the letters and go down and see Mrs. Lincoln."

So Stoddard gathered up Mrs. Lincoln's mail and put on his frock coat and went down to the Red Room, the parlor where she usually received visitors. He asked Louis Burgdorf, one of the doormen, to send for Mrs. Lincoln, and took a seat in one of the plush red chairs. The furnishings were very fine: there were gilded cornices on the windows, gilded mirrors, and vases of ormolu. On the far side of the room stood a grand piano that Willie Lincoln played every day but Sunday. On the other side hung the famous portrait of George Washington that Dolley Madison had saved from burning by clipping it from the frame when the British soldiers had torched the mansion in 1814.

As Mrs. Lincoln entered the room and the dapper secretary rose to meet her, he beheld "a pleasant-looking woman . . . in fine health and spirits this morning." At the beginning of 1862, Mrs. Lincoln was in her prime as mistress of the White House, an eminence she had achieved by means that would disgrace her when discovered. She had refurbished the shabby mansion at a cost that would soon be a public embarrassment: she had falsified invoices, abetted graft; she had courted flatterers. To one of these she had leaked the president's State of the Union message, much to his embarrassment. She had amassed a queen's wardrobe by running up astronomical debts in her husband's name. At the moment, only the flattering effects were known, the grand appearances. Even now, she was planning a lavish private ball that would replace the customary free-for-all White House levee—one that would cause Mr. Lincoln and his secretaries no end of trouble.

"You sent word that you had a complaint to make to me," said the lady, inviting Stoddard to take a seat near hers. The gallant Stoddard, bidding her good morning, had the excellent manners to ask after her health, and the health of her good husband and children, before getting down to business.

"What is it?" inquired Mrs. Lincoln.

"This rascally paper-folder," he began, shaking his head, describing the dull-witted fictional character who was to blame for blundering and slashing into the mail. The envelopes had been lying face down on the table, "and he got them and . . . I caught him and choked him off before he had time to read them, but I'd like to know what I am to do about him?"

Mrs. Lincoln laughed at the secretary's yarn. Then she grew serious. "Mr. Stoddard, I want you, from this time onward, to open every letter and parcel that comes in the mail for me." She considered making an exception for her sister Elizabeth's letters, but then thought better of it. Since her husband's inauguration, she had been under suspicion for espionage. "They accuse me of correspondence with the rebels. I want them all read!"

She had seen enough pages of diatribes, tracts, profanity, and nonsense, and saw how the volume of it was growing. "Don't let a thing come to me that you've not first read yourself, and that you are not sure I would wish to see." When it became generally known that Stoddard was screening Mrs. Lincoln's incoming mail, this arrangement would help to shield Madame from charges of sedition. Stoddard recalled—with some resentment—"malicious people were afterwards able to speak of me as 'Mrs. Lincoln's secretary.'"

ALL THREE OF THE secretaries dealt with the mail, depending upon who was on duty, the volume of letters, and the importance of the communication. Military dispatches and other urgent messages came via the telegraph office in the War Department. Outgoing letters from the president were sometimes written by Nicolay and more often by Hay—sometimes so beautifully that experts puzzle over their authorship. For the sake of convenience, Hay learned to counterfeit Lincoln's signature so perfectly that a collector today, pointing with pride to a document signed by the sixteenth president, might in fact be admiring the forgery of his clever secretary.

All three shoveled, stacked, and waded in mail. It rose in paper tides in the forenoon and ebbed in rivulets to the president and the various departments and in streams that the maids bore in buckets and boxes to the furnaces in the basement in the winter and ash cans to be burned on the South Lawn in the summer, to quell mosquitoes. Of the three men, Stoddard probably handled the most incoming correspondence, and he recollects a great deal about the process. First thing in the morning, Louis Burgdorf, the president's messenger, would carry the leather and canvas sacks up the stairs and pour the mail onto Stoddard's desk.

Many newspapers arrived, gratis, from all over the country, with editorials marked, and stinging passages underlined. Although, Stoddard remarks, "We have to buy the newspapers we really need and read, like other people," there were dozens of obscure journals that wanted the president to know their opinions. When he first took office, Lincoln spent an hour every morning reading the papers, but as the halls grew crowded he had no time for this. And so he asked Hay and Stoddard to cut up "a daily brief made for him to look at." After two weeks, they noticed that he never once glanced at the synopsis, and so they gave up preparing it. Although Lincoln now and then read the *New York Times,* the *New York Tribune,* and the Washington papers—the *Star* and the *Chronicle*—it was more for diversion than for information. By 1862, he pointed out that he found nothing in the war correspondents' dispatches that he did not already know, and much that was inaccurate. On either side of Stoddard's chair was a large wicker wastebasket, and he began by tossing out newspapers.

Then there was the correspondence, official and private. At one time, Stoddard took pains "to strike an average of the daily arrivals, and was surprised to find that it was not far from 250." Some of these were bulky parcels of documents "related to business before one or the other of the departments," law cases, claims, patents, and so on. In his memoirs, Stoddard categorizes and describes the documents and correspondence, and how each piece must have been handled, so from him we get a picture of how all three of the aides spent much of their day.

In approximate order of importance, the following piles arose on the secretary's desk: applications for appointments to office everywhere, from postmaster in Cleveland to collector of the port of New York; pardon papers for soldiers imprisoned or sentenced to be shot; letters of advice and criticism from political allies and foes; and finally, letters of abuse, the musings of cranks and lunatics, and assassination threats. Early on, the three secretaries agreed that whenever an American citizen went crazy, the first thing he did was to take up a pen and write to the president. Among many examples, Stoddard mentions daily communications from "The Angel Gabriel" who wrote in red ink he claimed was blood, and appeared to have taken his inspiration from the cryptic book of Revelation. He also recalls long, elaborate, and quite well-written letters of counsel on political and military policy that were signed by the founding fathers, including John Hancock, George Washington, Benjamin Franklin, and Thomas Jefferson. The signatures were expertly forged, as if the author had traced them over a penny copy of the Declaration of Independence.

The secretaries kept a list, of course, of the names of the president's relatives and personal friends, such as Anson Henry, Joshua Speed, and Jesse Dubois, all of whom he had known since his Springfield days; these would be rescued promptly from the sludge and placed on Mr. Lincoln's desk. The letters concerning appointments had to "be examined with care, and some of them must be briefed [synopsized] before they are referred to the departments and bureaus with which the offices asked for are connected." In this business, and in the handling of "pardon papers," the secretaries exercised considerable and invisible power. Stoddard had this in mind when he later wrote that "there are seldom more than three members of the Cabinet who equal the Private Secretary in real power, and he must be a man of more than ordinary brains and integrity if he does not at times do mischief." Stoddard was not above occasional mischief. He was more vulnerable to temptation than his colleagues, and makes no secret of it in his memoirs. He tells a chilling story about the stack of pardon papers (whose "proper place, one would think, is in the War Office," where they would go eventually). Mr. Lincoln insisted on keeping pardon requests nearby in case some "mournful delegation" might appear to plead a case. Lincoln would pardon any case that he could, "and some people think he carries his mercy too far." Stoddard was one of these.

"There came, one day, a pile of influential petitions on behalf of a southwestern guerilla of the most cruel sort. He was unquestionably a red-handed murderer"; but for reasons Stoddard does not explain, the accused had strong defenders, including some loyal politicians, financiers, and generals. The next day these men came to see the president, and "spoke of the high character of the papers in the case . . ." They called for these papers, but, Stoddard recalls with passive vagueness, "they were not in my possession." Perhaps they had been duly transferred to the War Office? "Inquiry was made there but the papers could not be found. The delegation went its way and that application for pardon was hung up. So was the woman and child killer who was the most interested party in the case . . ."

No sooner had news of the execution reached the White House than Stoddard found the missing papers. "Just as well that one murderer has escaped being pardoned by Abraham Lincoln. Narrow escape too," said someone within the secretary's hearing. The fact that Stoddard had taken justice into his own hands and subverted due process did not trouble his conscience. The times called for desperate measures, and perhaps he had used his office to some advantage. "I think Mr. Lincoln did not more than look sidewise at me and I am sure he made no verbal commentary."

The president had to trust Stoddard, Nicolay, and Hay to help him separate the wheat from the chaff in a day's correspondence, of "applications for office, for contracts, for pardons, for pecuniary aid, for advice, for information, for autographs, voluminous letters of advice, political disquisitions, the rant and drivel of insanity, bitter abuse, foul obscenity, slanderous charges against public men, police and war information . . ." And Stoddard prided himself on his good judgment. "I seemed to myself to know exactly what he [Lincoln] would say about . . . the river of matter relating to appointments to office," and neither the president nor other officials ever found fault with him, "except in a few cases. . . . I believe," Stoddard concluded, "I really did do a number of helpful things for honest [men] . . . by my recommendations, and suppose they attributed it to that good man, Honest Abe."

Of course, the greatest mass of parcels and epistles belonged in those tall wicker wastebaskets that flanked Stoddard's desk. Letters flew into them as quickly as the secretary could make his decisions. He loved to tell the story about one morning when he was mercilessly deluged with impertinent, crazy, and abusive letters, and was busy slashing and tossing the mail into the baskets. Out of the corner of his eye he noticed a well-dressed elderly gentleman seated in a chair next to the chimneypiece, his walking stick rigid between his knees, frowning, watching him intently. The visitor had sent his card in to Mr. Lincoln, and was waiting to be called. The man's appearance suggested to Stoddard that, at home, this fellow was probably a judge, a college president, or maybe even a governor. "But he is not at home now," mused the secretary.

The distinguished caller was clearly upset by the way Stoddard was manhandling the mail. He shifted in his seat, grew red in the face;

finally he stamped his foot on the floor, exclaiming, "Is that the way you treat the president's mail? Mr. Lincoln does not know this! What would people say if they knew . . . ," he blustered. "Thrown into the waste-basket! What does Lincoln mean? Putting such an awful responsibility into the hands of a mere boy! A boy!"

Stoddard looked around him. He was twenty-seven years old. All the while he had seen the storm brewing, he had set aside a few "of the vilest scrawls that infamy could put on paper," including one from the Angel Gabriel written in blood. The gentleman rose from his chair and was pacing back and forth in indignation when Stoddard turned to him and, holding out the letters, mildly invited him to have a look.

"Please read these, sir, and give me your opinion." The gentleman took them and began reading. His eyes widened and his face grew redder still. His eye fell upon "stories of partisan bitterness and personal hatred . . . low, slanderous meannesses; of the coarsest, foulest vulgarity . . . the wildest, fiercest and the most obscene ravings of utter insanity . . ." At length, the old man threw them back on Stoddard's desk and, grunting, sank back in his chair. It took a moment before he could find his tongue.

"You are right, young man! He ought not to see a line of that stuff! Burn it, sir! Burn it! What devils these are!"

There were devils, and then there were also well-meaning cranks, whose letters sometimes provided the president with much-needed amusement. Stoddard read him a letter from an inventor in Tolono, Illinois, who said he had made "a cross-eyed gun, with two barrels, set at an angle so as to shoot in both directions." He claimed to know enough cross-eyed men to fill a regiment, and that he was cross-eyed enough himself to be their colonel. They would "march down the river and clean out both banks at once." Lincoln got a good laugh out of that.

By agreement of the White House guard and the president, the secretaries did not show Mr. Lincoln the assassination threats that arrived several times a week. These were forwarded to Ward Hill Lamon, marshal of the city of Washington. It was generally understood that no man serious in that endeavor would reduce his chances of success by warning the White House of it.

CHAPTER FIVE

TEAMWORK

The private secretaries often operated in the public eye. As chief of protocol, John Nicolay faced rare challenges. White House social events—public receptions and levees, more intimate "at homes," and formal state dinners—were frequent and sometimes elaborate. Nicolay, Hay, and Stoddard were expected to assist in making introductions at these functions. The cooperation of the executive departments, the military, and the diplomats during wartime all depended upon a high degree of social success in the Executive Mansion—and so did popular support.

A book of this scope cannot begin to chronicle those grand soirees catered by Chef Gautier, where thousands sipped champagne punch ladled from crystal bowls the size of washtubs, when rare varieties of flowers were shipped down from Bucat's in Philadelphia to adorn the tall porcelain vases, and the Marine Band played instrumentals from Verdi. The secretaries worked together with the Lincolns to make the White House a social haven in a crucial era of the Republic. They faced daunting crosscurrents, one of which was the novelty of a house of

Republicans entertaining violently opposed Democratic factions in a southern city.

Then there was the difficulty of the president's wife—her moods, prejudices, and jealousies, which the three young men cleverly managed. She was essential to the social enterprise, and could be splendid and effective; but, desperate for control, she was often stubborn, sometimes impulsive, and occasionally perverse. She may have courted scandal in her ways of refurbishing the White House, but now it was magnificent, and visiting dignitaries took note. She had incurred deep debts to New York clothiers that would embarrass her husband later, but now she dressed in the height of fashion, so that at least in this respect no society journalists would call her "provincial."

Early in 1862, Mrs. Lincoln made up her mind that she had had enough of the stuffy "state dinners" that had been the principal means of entertaining cabinet members, generals, heads of state, ambassadors, and leaders of Congress for a half century. She explained, first to her black dressmaker Elizabeth Keckley, and then to Mr. Lincoln, that the dinners were too costly; it would be more economical to scratch them from the program and instead give three large parties by invitation only. The real reason she disliked state dinners is that she had little control over the guest lists, and sometimes found herself out of her depth socially. She had cultivated a circle of admirers and sycophants who were not welcome at state dinners. For an entertainment that filled the East Room, she would have an allowance to invite whomever she pleased.

"Mother, I am afraid your plan will not work," said Mr. Lincoln.

"But it will work, if you will only determine that it *shall* work."

He explained to his wife that it was a violation of an old custom, to which she replied that this was wartime, and old customs might be put aside for the sake of economy, and moreover, "public receptions are more democratic than stupid state dinners. . . . There are a great many strangers in the city, foreigners and others . . . whom we cannot invite to our dinners." Against his better judgment, Lincoln let Mary have her way.

Nicolay knew immediately that this was a recipe for social turmoil, and wrote to Therena on February 2, 1862, that "Mrs. Lincoln has determined to make an innovation in the social customs of the White House," and had ordered seven hundred tickets for a party to be held on February 5. In the past, the only private entertainments that called for invitations were state dinners. Large receptions, such as the New Year's levee, were open to the public. "How it will work," Nicolay confided, skeptically, "remains yet to be seen. Half of the city is jubilant at being invited, while the other half is furious at being left out in the cold." He controlled the tickets and soon found himself at loggerheads with Mrs. Lincoln over the guest list.

Mrs. Lincoln abhorred Nicolay, who, gritting his teeth, struggled to conceal that the feeling was mutual. But the lady was too shrewd to be fooled. Even John Hay, with his boyish charm, could not get on with her or hide his dislike. Only the square-jawed, courtly Stoddard, who genuinely liked Mary Lincoln, got along with her well enough to reason with her, and now and again he would be called upon to intervene when she had disturbed the peace. This party by invitation was just such an occasion.

Stoddard recalled that "My Lady President's Ball" was quite formal, invitations having been "limited to certain species of men and women. Senators, Congressmen, Judges of the Supreme Court, members of the Cabinet." Generals, legislators, and diplomats and their wives would take up most of the space available in the reception rooms. But prominent men in Washington were besieged with requests for tickets from all over the Northeast, as if they were "free tickets to the Greatest Show on Earth." For every request granted by favoritism, there were dozens of people furious at being denied. "The first applicants to be disappointed and to get mad about it" were the journalists, who somehow imagined themselves to be sufficiently official or diplomatic to be entitled. Stoddard recalled that Hay and Nicolay mostly dealt with the newsmen, but insofar as he participated in the discussion, he "found all explanations in vain. A certain number, of course, could be admitted as 'reporters,' but when I mentioned that fact, the fat was all in the fire. In the language of one excited scribe, 'If we cannot come as gentlemen, we will not come at all!'" a comment that Stoddard—being a journalist—said was hard upon a "fellow who ceased to be a gentleman when he became a reporter."

He was at his desk one day raking mail when Hay rushed in from Nicolay's office across the hall, looking troubled. He said that Mrs. Lincoln was downstairs in the Red Room with two of her friends, former congressmen Caleb Lyon and General Daniel Sickles, both of New York. They had tickets, of course, and influence, and so they had asked for two more, one for Mr. George Wilkes, editor of the abolitionist *Spirit of the Times,* the other for an editor of the *New York Herald.* Both papers had been highly critical of the president's conservative approach to the slaves' plight.

Hay led Stoddard across the hall to Nicolay's office, where he found the senior secretary at his desk, his brow furrowed, in an advanced state of agitation.

"Stoddard!" he grumbled. "I can't do anything. It will make all sorts of trouble. She is determined to have her own way. . . . She wouldn't listen to me."

Nodding in appreciation of the difficulty, Stoddard asked for the tickets, and tried to reassure his friend that it might be resolved. He smoothed his hair, turned, and went down to the Red Room, where he said hello to Mrs. Lincoln. Seeing Sickles, an old friend, the secretary shook hands with him, and then was introduced to Caleb Lyon. Stoddard handed the tickets to Mrs. Lincoln, "which she had sent for under pernicious beguilement," he recalled. And his usually cheerful features could not, and would not, conceal his fury. "She could see that I was boiling over, wild mad about something," and when he drew her aside and asked if he might have a word with her, she excused herself and followed him into the Blue Room.

Stoddard was naturally histrionic, a man with dramatic instincts, one who struck poses. Now he pretended to be outraged, indignant almost to the point of being speechless, stammering mad.

"What is it, Mr. Stoddard?"

He confessed that he was about to throttle the visitors.

"Why? What for? What have they done?"

"Mrs. Lincoln, I suppose you have the right to *know*. They have demanded of Mr. Nicolay invitations for those two fellows . . . that have been abusing you, personally, and Mr. Lincoln, like pickpockets." He said it was better to give tickets to friends and not enemies, and that her inviting such enemies would offend her friends. Such logic appealed to Mrs. Lincoln, who tended to view the social world simply as a confrontation between her friends and foes.

"I wish you would put your foot down and stop it," he exclaimed, and soon had her singing right along with him. "They can't have the invitations—"

"Of course they can't!" she cried, as if she had known it all along, "I'll go right in and tell them so."

And so Mrs. Lincoln went back into the Red Room and told the two astonished ex-congressmen off, while Stoddard went upstairs to inform the other secretaries that the matter had been settled. They patted him on the back, eager to know how he had worked the miracle.

DESPITE THE FLEETING SUCCESS of Mrs. Lincoln's party on the fifth—which the president's critics attacked as a frivolity in wartime— February 1862 was the saddest month of the saddest year in the White House. While the leaders of government and high society mingled under the chandeliers of the East Room listening to the band play the overture from *Maniello,* dined on pheasant and venison, and sipped claret, the Lincolns' eleven-year-old son Willie lay deathly ill in a heavily draped bedroom upstairs. He had caught typhoid. After terrible fevers, dehydration, delirium, and pneumonia, he died on February 20. Cruel newsmen called this the judgment of a wrathful god upon Mrs. Lincoln's pride and extravagance.

On the day the boy died, Nicolay recalled that the routine had been attended to as usual, but the president appeared exhausted from his night vigils over Willie. "At about 5 o'clock this afternoon, I was lying half asleep on the sofa in my office, when his [Lincoln's] entrance aroused me. 'Well, Nicolay,' said he, choking with emotion, 'my boy is gone—he is actually gone!' and bursting into tears, turned and went into his own office." The family was helpless with grief. It was Nicolay's duty to arrange for the embalming, funeral, and burial of their favorite son. In this, he would have the assistance of Senator Orville Browning, the president's friend from Illinois, as well as Mrs. Browning, who would spend weeks attending Mrs. Lincoln and her younger son, Tad, who was also ill.

Mary Lincoln was inconsolable, hysterical, and would require opiates to subdue her. It is likely that she never recovered from this blow. Her mental balance, which had been precarious for several years, began an inexorable decline into madness. Although Lincoln tried to comfort her, and her sisters and close friends undertook to ease her grief, her instability and irascibility would be an increasing challenge to the president and his aides.

It is curious to see how little the secretaries had to say about the pathetic death of the Lincolns' son and the ensuing effects on the household. Perhaps, being bachelors, they had no personal gauges by which to measure the calamity. Mr. Lincoln resumed a deceptive composure that invited their admiration as much as their pity. Mrs. Lincoln immured herself in her dark bedroom. She had so alienated Nicolay and Hay, they probably thought of her as little as possible.

The day after Willie died, Nicolay briefly reported the event in his letter to Therena, saying that "his death was not altogether unexpected"; then he went on to say that "I have the gratification to inform you that I have got your brother Major and Robert Torrey appointed Second Lieutenants in the 13th Regiment of Infantry in the Regular Army." He needed to know the brother's full name for the Senate confirmation, and offered to recommend him for a place in the cavalry if he desired to ride.

Some of Nicolay's letters to Therena after Willie's death are quite pensive, introspective, as if his feelings about the misfortune were sublimated. When his fiancée wrote to ask him his opinion about her religious direction, he responded thoughtfully. "It is in my opinion, entirely an independent and individual responsibility ... You should permit, for example, neither myself, nor the Pope, nor [the Reverend] Mr. Carter to be your religious director." He urged her to guard her faith from "the magnetism or sympathetic impulse of personal surroundings ... ," and rather to hear all instruction "merely as so much *argument:* let nothing but your own mind and heart make up and render the *final judgment*."

Clearly he has been influenced by Lincoln's extraordinary example, the attitude of his boss and his mentor, a man of faith who subscribes to no creed, and belongs to no church. Lincoln does not look to the denominations of Christianity for his salvation or his solace. He has even paid a political price for his iconoclasm. Nicolay tells Therena to prepare herself to be disenchanted by the Church, for it cannot provide the support she might hope for. "Bitter as the conviction may prove, you will find that the boundary of the church, as well as the world outside, encircles all of human folly and weakness." With rare eloquence, he defines the true success of the faithful: "The Christian army never wins victories by battalions. It is individual strength, courage, heroism, that achieves its successes. ... it is only those who like Moses, climb *alone* up the mount of sacrifice, through the clouds of Creed, the thunders of Bigotry and the lightnings of Doubt, who shall see Divinity face to face with spiritual eye, and receive the true commandments."

There were few men of Nicolay's acquaintance who answered to that description, but one of them was in the office next door, grieving for his dead son.

Although John Hay wrote lengthy obituaries for other White House friends and Lincoln relatives, including Ellsworth and Baker, and years later, upon the death of Tad Lincoln, Hay makes no mention of Willie's death in his letters or journals. This brings to mind an unfortunate and tantalizing hole in the fabric of this history. Hay's diary, in many ways the most perceptive portrait of Lincoln and of the White House from April 1861 until December 1864, sputters to a halt in early December 1861; then—excepting a half-dozen undated jottings—it does not resume until April 1863. Close examination of the blue-lined notebooks reveals that at least one signature (eight pages) was razored out of the diary after November 13, 1861, and the nonsequential jumble of volumes strongly suggests that one or more have been altogether lost or destroyed.

That Hay's diary was censored for the sake of propriety, either by the writer himself or by his wife, Clara, has never been in doubt. In the 1960s, the scholar John Ettlinger masterfully rescued and transcribed many sections of the manuscript that had been inked out; other passages remain obscured, beyond salvation even by ultraviolet light; and if volumes are missing no one alive seems to know what has become of them.

It is a mystery that—evidence suggests—leads to the door of Mrs. Lander's "cottage," to which she had allowed John Hay access while her husband was gone to the wars, and after he died from his wound. Hay was, said one woman who visited the White House, the most attractive man she had seen in the city. And Jean Margaret Lander was one of the most captivating women in the world. That they were immediately drawn to each other even Hay's expurgated diary cannot conceal.

Hay's journalistic columns from this period have survived, but they contain no mention of Willie Lincoln's death or the grief in the White House. He writes of the war, and political intrigue. He praises the heroes of Fort Donelson, Tennessee, General Grant and General McClernand, who forced the unconditional surrender of the Confederate stronghold and twelve thousand rebel soldiers on the Cumberland River. He condemns the shameless opportunism of radical senator James Henry Lane of Kansas, who "used his position as a senator to have himself appointed a Brigadier General," only for political gain and prestige as an abolitionist. On February 21, Hay uses his column to praise the commander in chief for the recent military successes. "The welfare of the nation is in safe hands, when the Chief Magistrate has at once a genius in conception and a talent in execution that renders him at once independent of Generals and of politicians." He had begun as a humorous skeptic of the Illinois lawyer's executive gifts. Watching Lincoln for a year in office had made Hay a confirmed believer in his genius.

In Stoddard's column for the *New York Examiner,* we find only this comment on the president for March 3: "The President is looking somewhat better, the all-absorbing interest of this hour of action serving to draw his thoughts away from his bereavement." Every Thursday afternoon, at the hour of his child's death, Mr. Lincoln would shut himself up in the Prince of Wales Room, and think of Willie, and indulge his sorrow. He would emerge daubing his red eyes with his handkerchief, and return to work at his desk.

ON FEBRUARY 26, 1862, Nicolay celebrated his thirtieth birthday. He wrote to Therena on a rainy Wednesday: "Ten years ago, I was a printer's devil in Pittsfield, as you and I will long remember. Twenty years ago I was a school boy in St. Louis . . . thirty years ago I was born in the Flemish Palatinate of Bavaria." He laments the fact that much of the second decade of his life was wasted—through no fault of his own. Orphaned, unschooled, the boy that fortune spurned "might have gained much skill, knowledge and experience in that time, which I now sorely need." Now he was learning on the job in the most rigorous of classrooms—where men's fates hung upon his decisions—under the tutelage of incomparable masters. Mr. Lincoln knew, as we do, that the thirty-year-old former printer's devil had skill and knowledge equal to the challenges he faced in the White House. Yet John George Nicolay somehow tempered his confidence with a touching humility.

But by the spring of 1862, Nicolay was burned out. He missed Therena and wanted to breathe the air of the prairie and mountains.

The president gave him leave to go west on March 28, with specific orders. Nicolay would be gone for the entire month of April, but he would spend only a week in Pittsfield with his fiancée. First, he must go to Nashville on business for the Treasury Department. He went as a personal envoy to communicate instructions to the assistant treasurer, Allen A. Hall, concerning changes "made to facilitate commerce." Nicolay's duties in Nashville included intelligence gathering concerning the quantities of cotton and tobacco in the region, and when these would enter the markets. He must also assess the secessionist sentiment in Tennessee. "Still strongly predominant," he wrote, "and manifests itself continually in taunts and insults to federal soldiers and officials. . . . The rebels still hope that our army will have reverses and that the confederate troops will return and occupy and control not only this city but the State." Tennessee's allegiance was precarious, but Nicolay had the "decided impression, that if we win another important battle in the neighborhood . . . active secessionism in Tennessee will wilt and die out."

It was no coincidence that Lincoln sent Nicolay to Tennessee on the eve of what came to be known as the Battle of Shiloh. General Ulysses S. Grant and General Don Carlos Buell had more than fifty thousand Federal troops in western Tennessee, poised to invade Mississippi and take control of the Mississippi River. Forty thousand Confederate troops under General Albert Sidney Johnston assembled across the border in Corinth, to block the invaders. Their surprise attack on Grant's army at Pittsburg Landing, Tennessee, at dawn on April 6 resulted in the bloodiest battle of the war to date.

Nicolay had come up from Louisville via St. Louis to Springfield on April 7. He meant to board the train to Pittsfield—where Therena patiently waited—on April 9, when word of the great battle on the Tennessee River reached him. "As the governor and State officers are going down there, I have concluded to go with them," he wrote her. Leaving Springfield, he suspected that the rumors of casualties were exaggerated. But four days later, close to the battleground, he saw that the "battle reports support a dearly bought victory at Pittsburg Landing." He was Lincoln's scout in that remote corner of Tennessee, observing not only the horrible cost of the campaign to both sides but the stubbornness of the southern survivors, who "live in the Micawber-like hope that 'Secesh' will yet turn up triumphant, somewhere and somehow, when their political millennium will come," and they might "light their cigars with $5 Treasury notes and feast on jerked Yankee liver."

While Nicolay was gone, Hay and Stoddard struggled to keep the mail and the visitors moving efficiently through an Executive Mansion draped in mourning and continually embarrassed by Mary Lincoln's outbursts and demands. In Nicolay's absence, Hay bore the brunt of her animosity. For more than a month after Willie's death, she had remained secluded, attended by relatives from Springfield. Now she had begun to stir.

Lincoln was so consumed with military matters that he had tried to ignore the gossip and signs of trouble over Mrs. Lincoln's conduct during the past year. Only a week before Willie's death, the Senate Judiciary Committee had considered indicting Mrs. Lincoln on charges of sedition—supplying notes of the president's State of the Union address to a sycophantic journalist from the *New York Herald*. A week after the funeral, Senator Orville Browning informed Lincoln that his wife had colluded with the gardener John Watt to defraud the Treasury by submitting false invoices. Gossip over these affairs swirled around the White House even as Mrs. Lincoln lay grief stricken.

Whatever difficulty she caused, Hay tried to keep from the president. "The 'enemy' [Mrs. Lincoln] is still planning [a] Campaign in quiet," he wrote to Nicolay on March 31. "She is rapidly being reinforced from Springfield. A dozen Todds of the Edwards Breed [are] in the house." She had become such an impediment to their work, and so unpleasant, Hay and Nicolay began to refer to her and her hostility in military terms. She felt wronged in every way, slandered, cursed, and maligned. The culture of "sharp practices" by which she had survived her first year as mistress of the White House could not quickly be reformed. On April 4, Hay wrote Nicolay that Mrs. Lincoln had pressured him "to pay her the Steward's salary." This is one of a few scattered indications that Nicolay—and Hay in Nicolay's absence—held the purse strings for certain White House and family expenses. ("What did you do with the safe key?" he begs Nicolay. "I can't find it anywhere.")

One of Mrs. Lincoln's schemes for getting extra cash was to fire a steward or a maid and then expropriate his or her salary. They were short a steward, and Hay refused her. "I told her to kiss mine. Was I right?" Of course, he said no such vulgar thing to the president's wife, but Hay made it clear he would not be a party to any such double-dealing; and she would not forgive him for it. "The devil is abroad, having great wrath," Hay wrote the next day. "His daughter, the Hell-Cat [Mrs. Lincoln] sent Stackpole in to blackguard me about the feed of her horses." Thomas Stackpole was a night watchman who—after the dismissal of John Watt—carried on as Mrs. Lincoln's coconspirator in defrauding the Treasury. Stackpole was pressuring Hay to release funds for stable supplies so that he and Mrs. Lincoln might line their pockets with it. "She thinks there is cheating round the board and with that candor so charming in the young does not hesitate to say so. I declined opening communications on the subject," Hay explained. Mrs. Lincoln continued to badger him over the steward's salary. "There is no steward," Hay affirmed. "She thinks she will blackguard your angelic representative into giving it to her 'which I don't think she'll do it, Hallelujah!'"

The secretaries tried to protect the president from knowledge of this larceny while he was defending the capital, holding the cabinet together, and motivating the sluggish General George McClellan, commander of the Army of the Potomac. Lincoln did write John Hay a check for $1,002.19 on April 4, strengthening the hypothesis that the secretaries had a "slush fund" at their disposal, and that at the moment it was running low.

Five days later, Hay reported to Nicolay that "the little Napoleon [McClellan] sits trembling before the handful of men at Yorktown [Virginia] afraid either to fight or run. Stanton feels devilish about it." Secretary of War Edwin Stanton, who had replaced the controversial Simon Cameron in January, had visited the White House that morning to complain of McClellan's idleness. The general kept grumbling that his army was smaller than Stanton knew it to be. At last Lincoln, exasperated, told McClellan, "But you must act."

"Things go on here about as usual," Hay went on. "There is no fun at all. The Hellcat is getting more Hellcatical day by day. . . . I am getting along pretty well. I only work about 20 hours a day. I do all of your work & half of my own now you are away. Don't hurry yourself. We are getting on very well."

Lacking Nicolay's fluency in French—the language of diplomacy in those days—Hay and Stoddard hired a tutor, "a Professor Marix, a Russian Jew whose pronunciation had the St. Petersburg improvement upon the Parisian dialect," Stoddard recalled. "We really did pretty well with that matter." They also hired a dancing master that spring. He came to the office at odd hours to teach them the latest dance steps, "a kind of queer partnership," Stoddard called it, as they took turns leading and following, whirling around the echoing hallway as Professor Marini clapped time. "Hay may have afterwards become a good dancer but I never did, although I mastered shottisches, and broke down at waltzing." Sometimes they went out riding on two large bay horses on loan from the War Department; in this exercise, Stoddard was very accomplished and Hay was just learning.

AFTER SPENDING THE WEEK of April 15 in Pittsfield with Therena, Nicolay returned to the capital on the last day of the month.

As busy as they were, the three men who managed the executive office found time at night for barhopping, dance parties, and other entertainments. Nicolay's correspondence is full of descriptions of lively parties, particularly at the home of Mr. and Mrs. Charles Eames. He was counsel of the Department of the Navy, and his wife, Fanny—a witty, well-educated lady—was "at home" between eight and eleven on Sunday evenings, and some Tuesdays, at their house on the corner of Fourteenth and H streets. There, Hay and Nicolay could be sure to meet the most attractive women and fascinating men in the city. "Their parlor is really a sort of focal point in Washington society, where one meets the best people that come here . . . the brains of society—politicians, diplomats, authors and artists . . . titled foreigners, pretty women & c." The polyglot crowd spoke English, French, Spanish, and German. At one Tuesday gathering, the guest of honor was Lady Georgina Fane, daughter of the Earl of Westmorland, and the guests included Salmon Chase, Edward Bates, Mrs. Elizabeth Grimsley, and Senator Henry Wilson. He also mentions the poet and editor N. P.

Willis and Hay's friend Emmanuel Leutze, the painter—both close friends of Jean Margaret Lander, who was, in all likelihood, a frequent visitor in this house. The Eameses' and the Chases' were the most distinguished of several salons where Nicolay and Hay passed their time between working and sleeping.

Stoddard traveled in different circles. He had a taste for the rakish, the high rollers, the demimonde. Some of his best writing of the period describes the smoke-filled gambling dens along Pennsylvania Avenue, which he claimed to visit only as an observer; but his interest in the sporting life and high stakes was not merely clinical.

He was fascinated by economics, particularly that branch of it concerned with the monetary system, gold and silver coins and the way various paper currencies represent—or misrepresent—the hard money. He found that this dynamic resembled the operation of the faro tables and the roulette wheel. As he walked out on a cold winter evening, he studied the staggered columns of the unfinished Treasury Building, which "reminds one of the paper promises to pay which are flowing from it in a river." Some men were betting that those promises would not be kept, that bonds and banknotes would be devalued and become "as worthless as so much continental currency." When that occurred, the investors who were long on gold, or shorting the greenbacks, would be the richer for it. Those who had gambled on the paper stood to lose.

On the corner of Fifteenth Street and Pennsylvania Avenue, Stoddard noticed a group of men he identified as bitterly antagonistic "to anything or anybody coming from the White House," including himself, and so he crossed the muddy street to avoid them. He regarded in particular a tall man in a loose overcoat, wearing spectacles. While calling himself a Union man from Kentucky, he was, Stoddard knew, a spy with a commission in the Confederate army; but even Lafayette Baker, the head of the Washington detective service, could not get enough proof to arrest him. There was a "dark-haired, eagle nosed, brilliant-eyed, strikingly handsome man," who was a copperhead congressman, a well-known northerner who sympathized with the rebels, and another

two dandies Stoddard identified only as "sporting men." All were beautifully turned out. He notes that "the entire sporting fraternity here
leans toward secession. Its best patrons and victims, heretofore, have
been the reckless spendthrifts whose money was earned for them by
the unpaid toil of other men."

Why were they gathered on the corner under the streetlamp? The
men were either leaving, or about to enter a dark, windowless brick
building, "the famous gambling establishment known as Joe Hall's."
Like a mining town, Washington had long been a favorite resort of
gamblers because of the transient population of lawmakers, lobbyists,
and government workers—men loose from their families. There were
many legends concerning the gambling habits and card-playing predi-
lections of bygone statesmen, and now "all the vice and profligacy of
all the North and West and part of the South seem to be sewering into
this great frontier post and pay-station of the army."

Stoddard's desire—as well as his innate curiosity—to observe the
living legends led him through the door of Joe Hall's. Only gentlemen
were admitted there, those who could afford to gamble. While protesting that he was not really a sporting man, the secretary went directly
to the roulette table, where in a matter of minutes he lost $5. A day's
wages. That was the price of admission, his tuition fee. Too discreet
to identify the sporting men by name, he describes the gamblers by
class and profession. A rich Maryland planter, bent by his years, was
betting large sums at the faro table. He should have known better than
to squander money. But as he said to the congressman at his side, his
slaves were deserting him, and there was no power that would bring
them back. Maybe Lady Luck would be kind. Also at the faro table sat a
political leader and former friend of Daniel Webster who, only an hour
earlier, had sat for a long interview with Mr. Lincoln. Stoddard noted a
number of judges, well-known lawyers, and financiers. He saw almost
a dozen congressmen mingling with well-heeled lobbyists and contractors, northern businessmen, and some sightseers from the West. There
were also a few army officers on furlough.

In the smoke-filled room there were, according to the secretary,
"curious Washington traditions concerning the luck at cards, good

and bad, of the old-time party idols." One political leader Stoddard describes as "keen-visaged . . . near to Henry Clay," suggesting that Webster and Clay—the great men themselves—were not above a hand of high-stakes whist or euchre. This was part of the high life of the capital, in the old society as well as the new. If anything, gambling mania had increased since February 25, 1862, when the legal tender clause passed, and as greenbacks became more plentiful.

The lesson Stoddard brought home from Joe Hall's casino was that gambling is natural. The finest gentlemen have been known to enjoy it. He felt he could much better understand the problems that harass the president if he bore in mind "that he is dealing with an untellable mass of defective human nature." Stoddard wrote similar reports on the dance halls and drinking life of the city. He stops short of describing the bordellos.

Unlike the fastidious Hay and the virtuous Nicolay, William Stoddard is a worldly-wise, unabashed chronicler of the "untellable" human foibles—his own included. While not altogether corrupt, Stoddard was a man, like most, with weaknesses. He acknowledged them and labored mightily to overcome them without ever losing his sense of humor. We have little of Stoddard's correspondence, but a few revealing letters to his mentor, Martin Brewer Anderson, the president of the University of Rochester, have survived. In one letter dated March 11, 1862, Stoddard proudly informs Anderson that he is finally digging himself out of debt. "My property is small, to be sure, but I shall soon be able to look all men in the face and say that I owe nothing but kindness to any on earth." In several previous letters, he acknowledges his debt of gratitude to Anderson for his patience and moral guidance. "I know that on this I am sure of your sympathy, for you cannot have forgotten my old besetting sins of careless extravagance and rash speculation."

In 1862, Stoddard was twenty-seven years old. The specifics of the "sins of careless extravagance and rash speculation" that led him into debt while he was a wayward student of Professor Anderson's are unknown. But we do know from Stoddard's memoirs, and from a public scandal that caught up with him many years later, that the "old besetting sins" were not so old that they didn't have life in them still. He is quick to connect the games of chance in Joe Hall's, and the roulette wheels of the gambling dens along Pennsylvania Avenue, with the speculation in gold and greenbacks going forward in banking offices, counting rooms, and brokerages from Washington to New York to Chicago.

Stoddard was high-spirited, and—he would have us believe— no better or worse than other distinguished men of his time and place. Men like Daniel Webster and Henry Clay, congressmen, judges, and wealthy planters spent hours and greenbacks under the clattering whirl of the roulette wheel. And "almost every man who can discover means for doing so is gambling in stocks and gold." This game is fascinating, he says, because of "the sudden and unaccountable jumps and falls of what are called its prices, meaning the price of greenbacks. They are rather the pulsations of the public hope and fear concerning the national credit."

To put the case as simply as possible, the new greenbacks the government issued in 1862 were not backed by gold, but they were placed on a par value with bonds that were. The Union had not coin enough to pay its bills, so it issued the greenbacks to pay contractors and employers who took it upon faith that greenbacks would be redeemable or "as good as gold" sooner or later. It was patriotic to hold greenbacks. But even the truest patriot had himself and his family to feed. So rumors of a distant battle, another Union defeat or embarrassment, would set many citizens scrambling for gold and speculators selling the paper money short—or buying it in the belief a Union victory would send it soaring again.

The speculation that year was "running insanely wild in New York and other financial centers, and I formed an idea that it was almost true patriotism to be what was called a 'bear' in gold. I therefore went in, a little at first and then deeper . . . I had not the least idea that there was anything wrong in it for a fellow in my position . . ."

Stoddard had yet to learn some very important lessons about his position.

CHAPTER SIX

THE TYCOON AND LITTLE MAC

In February of 1862, the beautiful poet Julia Ward Howe, a friend of Hay's, published the stirring words to "The Battle Hymn of the Republic," set to the William Steffe tune "Glory, Glory, Hallelujah." This became the theme song of the growing Union army. Victor Hugo published *Les Misérables,* which all the secretaries read, and Daniel Butterfield, McClellan's chief of staff, composed "Taps," a bugle melody to be played at bedtime and at funerals. It was a year of suspense, as the vista of war opened wider and deeper than most people had foreseen.

There were two trials that faced the president daily, and his secretaries had much to learn from his management of them. One was his wife's grief over the death of Willie Lincoln; the other was the exasperating conduct of General George Brinton McClellan, commander of the Army of the Potomac. The mourning was mostly a private matter. After the funeral, Hay and Nicolay discreetly regarded the president's tender solicitude of Mrs. Lincoln, his growing stoicism as he measured out his hours of grieving and put aside his sorrow to finish the day's work. His work, on many days, was consumed with the Army of the Potomac and its puzzling commander.

After the Union defeat at the First Battle of Bull Run, back in July of 1861, Lincoln had put McClellan in command of the Federal forces in Washington and Virginia. Soon after the Federals lost at Ball's Bluff, Virginia in October, general-in-chief Scott resigned. Lincoln appointed McClellan commander in chief—a heady promotion for a thirty-five-year-old officer. McClellan was formidable, severe, with thick short hair parted on the side, wide-set eyes and strong features, a drooping mustache and tuft of beard. "The people call on me to save the country," he grandly wrote," I must save it, and cannot respect anything that is in the way."

He began by not respecting Mr. Lincoln. McClellan first regarded the president as a "rare bird," then he started referring to him as "the original gorilla," a curious evolution of species. Of course, neither Lincoln nor his young aides knew at first of this drollery, which evoked such mirth and guffawing in the barracks, and they had welcomed the new commander in person and in print.

Stoddard devoted a column in the *New York Examiner* to "Little Mac" in late October of 1861. "The demeanor of the young General whom the swift events of this war have called to so high a position . . . is singularly modest, unassuming, and therefore admirable. Seldom, indeed, have shoulders so youthful been called upon to assume a load so weighty." Can McClellan realize, Stoddard wondered, "that his actions will have a lasting influence on the fate of the greatest political experiment the ages have yet seen" and still sleep at night, and go to work the next day? If so, "it can only be because he feels within himself the strength necessary . . . May the God of Battles bless him."

Days later, John Hay echoed Stoddard in a column he regularly wrote for the *Missouri Republican*. He lauded the general, and defended him and the cabinet from critics who accused McClellan of being over-eager to attack, and the older men of restraining him. Hay calls this "a pet delusion of the aqua fortis [strong water] abolition journals . . . they see the General in their mind's eye as a prancing and high-mettled charger straining on the curb, and panting to be gone, while the laggard and imbecile Cabinet stand by in an agony of dread, fearing to hold and fearing to let go." Nonsense, Hay declares. There is perfect harmony between the general and the administration. McClellan lives with his pretty wife in a fine house across the park from the White House, a few doors down from Secretary of State Seward, and "The President and the Secretary of State . . . spend several evenings of every week in McClellan's private study, in friendly and intimate converse, discussing the campaign. . . . There was never a more perfect rapport between the civil and military authorities . . ."

Hay was present at many of these meetings, and thought well of McClellan at first. "The nation is fortunate in its new commander. It is seldom that a man so simple and so plain in his manners, so free from the ordinary tricks of popularity . . . attains a recognition so sudden and universal. The people repose entire confidence in McClellan. . . . Nobody in the country has called him a traitor or a coward because he has wished to be ready before moving." This was not exactly true. McClellan's delay was soon to become infamous, but Hay—like Stoddard—was learning to give men with such grave responsibilities the benefit of the doubt, and time, and patience. The secretaries' journalism (published pseudonymously) was often a reflection of Mr. Lincoln's point of view.

Not long after McClellan received this power and recognition, Hay witnessed a disturbing lapse of decorum on the general's part—what the secretary considered "a dreadful portent of evil to come." On a warm, fair evening in mid-November, Hay went with William Seward and President Lincoln to call upon McClellan at his home across the park. The moon, nearly full on the thirteenth, shone upon the dry, sparse leaves of the oaks and maples. The servant who welcomed them at the door said that General McClellan was at General Don Carlos Buell's house, where he had gone to attend Colonel Frank Wheaton's wedding. They should make themselves comfortable in the parlor and the general would return soon.

These three friends never lacked topics of conversation. Hay used to send his new poems to Seward, who admired them. During the past few days, Hay had spent a good deal of time in Lincoln's company while Mrs. Lincoln was away in New York. The night before, they had taken tea with Assistant Secretary of the Navy Gustavus Fox and his family, and two nights before they had been in this very room, discussing military strategy with the new commander.

When more than an hour had passed, the men began to grow restless and thirsty, checking their pocket watches. Finally they heard someone opening the door. It was McClellan, who evidently paid little attention to the porter in the hallway when he informed him that the president and the secretary of state had been awaiting him for some time. Passing the entrance to the parlor where his visitors were sitting, McClellan, in full parade dress, went clanking up the stairs. The guests were patient, knowing they had not been expected, and that every man has a right to compose himself before receiving company. They relaxed in their chairs, Seward puffing on his cigar, talking of this and that: the cotton trade, the presentation of foreign ministers, the disposition of military contracts. Another thirty minutes passed without a sign of McClellan. They called for the porter, as the clock on the mantle ticked, and asked him to remind the general that they were waiting.

The porter then informed them that the general had gone to bed.

Seward's reaction to this incivility is not recorded, but Hay was appalled. "I merely record this unparalleled insolence of epaulettes without comment," he writes, before commenting in his diary. He recognizes this as the first sign "of the threatened supremacy of the military authorities," a problem Lincoln would have to confront many times as general after general took high-handed actions. As they walked home in the moonlight, Hay tactfully inquired about the president's feelings concerning McClellan's behavior. "He [Mr. Lincoln] seemed not to have noticed it especially, saying it was better at this time not to be making points of etiquette & personal dignity."

There was much for a bright young man to learn in that time and place, but no lesson more valuable than the one Hay was now learning from Lincoln. "No man resolved to make the most of himself can spare time for personal contention," Lincoln once wrote to a captain reprimanded for dueling. "Yield larger things to which you can show no more than equal right; and yield lesser ones though clearly your own. Better give your path to a dog than be bitten by him in contesting for the right. Even killing the dog would not cure the bite."

IT IS NATURAL TO assume that the older man influenced his eager apprentices and more difficult to determine the extent to which the secretaries' opinions and sentiments affected their chief. They were passionate and articulate. The perspicacious Mr. Lincoln welcomed their counsel, and often relied upon their intelligence.

Little Mac's performance on Lafayette Square that night may not have fazed the president, but the general's rudeness on that occasion seems to have left John Hay permanently disillusioned. His journalism—public and private—swerves from columns of admiration and support of McClellan to irony and the faint praise that verges upon disrespect. Three weeks later, in a wide-ranging report for the *Republican* on the mood and current events in the capital, Hay repeatedly teases McClellan.

He begins with the good news that the citizens are putting off their aspect of distrust and dread, "and the city is growing as gay, as jolly and as dissolute as in the flush times that are gone." Willard's, where he and Nicolay took their meals in the enormous, clattering dining room, is "regaining its proud pre-eminence of being the most crowded, extortionate and uncomfortable" of hotels. Now on the Avenue one might see not only ambulances and soldiers, but also carriages and northern beauties in crinolines and bonnets. "There is the jingle of coin and the rattle of chips in the brilliantly lighted and grate-guarded dens," such as Joe Hall's, where Stoddard studied human folly and vice. Contractors "swarm at the hotels and on the sunny sidewalks; churches on Sunday are filled with bright silks and baggy broadcloth of this new-born shoddy aristocracy." Even the theater—the burned-cork fraternity of minstrels as well as the glamorous divas and tragedians of the classic roles—is reviving "since those evenings when Mrs. [Anna Cora] Mowatt charmed away the young heart ... and Jean Margaret Davenport left the stage disconsolate, to assume the role of First Lady in General Lander's household." Hay lumps McClellan with the minstrels, strippers, and sleight-of-hand artists, linking his name to that of Alexander Herrmann, a "boy wonder" magician who had recently come from Germany.

"But *faciles principes* as caterers for the public amusement stand McClellan and Herrmann," Hay writes. His use of the Latin for "easily foremost" hardly blunts the edge of his sarcasm. Three days earlier, Hay and Nicolay had driven six miles in a buggy through crowded roads to Munson's Hill, Virginia, to see the review of fifty thousand soldiers, General McClellan, his brigadier generals, and staff in parade dress, and the president and his cabinet members on horseback joining the cavalcade. Nicolay had remarked in a letter that the line seemed endless but "Like other things it too came to an end . . . I had tired myself out, lost my dinner, spoiled my pantaloons, and having got tangled in the road among a troop of cavalry had come pretty near getting our carriage broken to pieces—but I had seen the largest and most magnificent military review ever held on this continent."

The point Hay makes—so archly—is that McClellan's show is no more than sound and fury. "There has never been seen, since wars began to be fashionable on earth, such a brilliant succession of reviews . . . ten regiments, in their holiday clothes, wasted a splendid day *en grande tenue* [in full dress]. . . . There could have been no greater success, in this way, than that." The weather was fine; Brigadier General Irvin McDowell, showed that he knew how to order fighting men here and there ("in spite of the damaging memories of Stone Bridge"). There was such an audience as rarely inspires a cast of stars, Hay reports, harping on the theatrical simile: "The President, who like most long limbed men rides well; [Secretary of War] Cameron, who looks better on horseback than anywhere else; Seward, who looks better everywhere else than on horseback; Senators, and Governors, and postmasters, and reporters, and shoddy kings . . ." and glamorous women in sleek barouches.

"From noon till dusk the glittering battalions moved proudly by the reviewing party, an army large enough and brave enough to do anything, if they had for a leader a man of genius as well as energy, of inspiration as well as detail," Hay writes, abandoning subtlety. But the satirist is not done playing with General McClellan. He wants to get him in the same frame with the magician. "The war has been for a week a secondary topic of conversation in Washington. McClellan pales his ineffectual fires before Herrmann."

Now that there is a lull in the fighting, "the crowd rushes to see a man swallow rabbits, and turn a bandanna into a vase of goldfish, and tell you what you are thinking about, and whistle like a blackbird . . ." The night before, in the Blue Room of the Executive Mansion, a hundred dignitaries gathered to watch Herrmann, the eighteen-year-old "Great Prestidigitator," perform his transformations, vanishing acts, and miracles of clairvoyance. He turned to General McClellan. "Now think of a card, sir, but don't mention it!" The general followed orders, and thought. Herrmann handed him a pack of cards and asked him, in a heavy accent, if he would please find the card he had brought to mind. McClellan could not find it. He looked confused, even foolish, shuffling through the pack once more. The card was not there.

"Give *me* the pack," said Herrmann. The general handed it over, and the magician made a waterfall of the cards from his right hand to his left. The card that leaped to the top was the one that McClellan had thought of.

STODDARD RECALLED ANOTHER EVENING when the president, calling upon McClellan, asked the secretary to go along as "an attendant." The porter opened the door and invited them to be seated in an elegant reception room. The president was announced, and they waited. With every tick of the clock upon the mantel, Stoddard grew angrier, while Lincoln sat patiently, "like an applicant in an ante-room." At last, at the sound of approaching steps, the president arose, and so did his secretary.

"General McClellan is indeed a striking figure . . . ," Stoddard noted. "He is the impersonation of health and strength, and he is in the prime of early manhood. His uniform is faultless and his stars are brilliant, especially the middle of each strap. His face is full of intelligence, of will power, of self-assertion." Like the president, he was a born leader. He had been superbly educated, in sciences not accessible generally to men from the backwoods and the prairies, in law courts or political conventions. He clearly believed there should be no authority above him—certainly not in the realm of martial affairs.

And yet—beyond military matters—McClellan could not resist pressing his political opinions upon the president and the people. Stoddard watched the men converse, fascinated by the contrasts between them. "How will they ever agree?" he wonders. "They do not now, as they talk . . . for here are two generals widely at variance, not only as to plans of campaign, but also as to the extent and nature of their respective authorities . . . Here are also two political chiefs of two great parties into which the nation is dividing."

Stoddard was writing these impressions many years later, yet it is evident that he was aware, at age twenty-seven, of the rare opportunity he had been afforded to learn from this conflict of titans. "Keep your temper," he admonishes himself, "for the President does not seem to have any to keep . . . By keeping cool you will better understand the subtle process that is going on . . . You can perceive, as the conversational mist clears away, that the President has the deeper, stronger mind of the two . . . The great magic of the stronger will, the tougher fiber, the greater moral courage . . . are with Lincoln and are not with McClellan. . . ." The Constitution is also on Lincoln's side, and "the unanswerable logic of events, and he will surely win the long wrestling match."

"BY SOME STRANGE OPERATION of magic," McClellan informed his wife, Ellen, "I seem to have become the power of the land." But it was not *his* magic; and the heady power that had come to him so easily slipped from his fingers in the early months of 1862. At the end of January, Lincoln issued a general war order—superseding McClellan— that the army and the navy must move against the enemy by February 22. Lincoln wanted them to attack at Manassas. The general's grandiose scheme, which he did not share with the president, was to attack Richmond from the East, using both the army and the navy.

Nicolay, Hay, and Stoddard were sympathetic witnesses to Lincoln's exasperation with Little Mac, and if they did not fuel the embroilment, they did nothing to cool it. The only time Nicolay ever heard Lincoln curse in his presence was on the night of February 27, 1862, a week after Willie's death. At seven o'clock, Edwin Stanton, the new secretary of war, came into the office where the president was working with Nicolay and Stoddard, and shut the door behind him. Stanton was a grim-looking ex-Quaker with abundant black and silver whiskers and eyes that peered out accusingly from little gold spectacles. He had a long torso and short legs, so he preferred to be seen standing behind his high slant-top desk in the War Department. His visits to the White House were rare and intense.

This evening he had come to read the president two telegrams from General McClellan. The first dispatch boasted that a pontoon bridge had been assembled at Harper's Ferry; troops had advanced safely over the river into Virginia. The president grinned. "The next is not so good," said Stanton, turning the page. The second dispatch had to do with building a strategic bridge over the Potomac using canalboats. This would enable the great movement of troops, horses, and artillery to surge upon Winchester and Manassas in northern Virginia, as Lincoln had wanted. It cost a fortune to move so many boats up the canal toward Harper's Ferry. Somewhere north of Great Falls the pilots discovered that the lift lock on the canal was "too narrow to admit the passage of the canal boats through to the river." So they had to turn the boats around. The telegram that Stanton was reading conveyed McClellan's explanation of why he was revising his plan to move upon Winchester.

"What does this mean?" asked the president, frowning.

"It means," Stanton replied, "that it is a damned fizzle. It means that he doesn't intend to do anything."

"Why in hell didn't he *measure* first?" the president cried. Hearing the uproar, the secretary of state came in, and then General Randolph Marcy, who was McClellan's father-in-law and chief of staff, and they all listened to Lincoln rant and swear, wide-eyed at the wonder of it. Being unable to calm the chief executive, they swore right along with him.

"Why in hell and damnation, General Marcy," the president yelled, "couldn't the General have known whether a boat would go through that lock, before he spent a million of dollars getting them there? *I* am no engineer: but it seems to me that if I wished to know whether a boat would go through a *hole,* or a *lock,* common sense would teach me to go and measure it. I am almost despairing of these results," he said, by way of a decrescendo. "Everything seems to fail. The general impression is daily gaining ground that the General does not intend to do anything."

When General Marcy sheepishly tried to pacify the president, saying that no doubt McClellan would be able to explain the causes, Lincoln brushed Marcy off, still muttering as if he had been a buzzing insect. He dismissed him, once, and then again, and turned away to his desk. Stoddard witnessed this part of the scene and recalled that Lincoln, furious, picked up his pen and "wrote at about double his ordinary speed."

STODDARD'S JOURNALISM THAT MONTH includes several references to the president's "relieving General McClellan of a portion of his too cumbrous responsibilities . . . in the light of a quasi disgrace." Again, one might wonder just how much the secretaries were reflecting executive policy and how much they were anticipating it. After all, until March 1862, McClellan was still supreme commander.

Dramatic events that month soon made a prophet of Stoddard and confirmed Hay's opinion that McClellan had lost his magic. At 7:30 a.m. on March 8, the president summoned his sullen commander to the White House. McClellan had balked at Lincoln's insistence that thirty thousand soldiers be kept out of campaigns at all times to protect the capital. In the privacy of his office, Lincoln informed McClellan of a rumor going around that he, McClellan, planned to turn Washington and the Federal government over to the enemy.

Lincoln watched the general's handsome, immobile face carefully for a response. McClellan was indignant, protesting that he had no such treasonable plans. The president denied that he had any intent to accuse him—he was just reporting the rumor. But this was his way of letting McClellan know that he was losing his support. That afternoon, Lincoln issued General War Order No. 2: Under no circumstances would the city of Washington be left without forces that he, the president, saw fit to guard it.

That very day, the Confederate ironclad ship *Merrimac* destroyed two Federal warships at Hampton Roads, Virginia, and then turned its prow toward the capital, seemingly unstoppable. Nicolay was with the president the next morning when the dispatches came. Stanton rushed in, "very much excited, and walked up and down the room like a caged lion," Nicolay recalled. Lincoln summoned the secretary of the navy, the secretary of state, and several military officers along with General McClellan. "There was great flutter and excitement—the President being the coolest man of the party. There were . . . all sorts of expressions of fear." Perhaps the Confederate navy, in the wake of this monstrous ironclad, would attack New York or Philadelphia and hold one of those cities for ransom before moving on to Baltimore, or to Annapolis, where a flotilla of Federal troop transports had been gathered. And, of course, there was the terror that the invincible *Merrimac* and her murderous cohorts would sail up the Potomac and burn Washington.

Now we know that the catastrophe did not come to pass. The gallant sailors of the new Union ironclad, the turreted *Monitor,* drove the *Merrimac* back to Norfolk after the battle that marked the beginning of modern naval warfare. Yet the danger had been deeply felt. The northern coastal cities had been put on high alert. Timber rafts were spread out in the harbors and vessels were sunk in the channels to impede the invaders. General McClellan gave orders to move the troop ships in Annapolis out of danger. According to Hay, "Stanton was fearfully stampeded. He said they would capture our fleet, take Ft Monroe, be in Washington before night. The President thought it was a great bore . . ."

In the evening, Hay recalled, came news that McClellan's Army of the Potomac was marching south. Although they outnumbered the rebels, they had not gone to fight; they were simply occupying the abandoned Confederate camps before returning to Alexandria. To their embarrassment, the Union commanders discovered that there had been nothing more to guard in Manassas than "Quaker guns"—logs painted to look like cannons.

It was a bad week for McClellan. On the evening of March 11, Lincoln asked Hay if he could round up Mr. Stanton, Mr. Seward, and Mr. Chase. Seward appeared, puffing on his cigar, a compact, clean-shaven man with close-set, humorous eyes, a prominent nose, and thick white hair that did not quite cover his jug-handle ears. Why had Lincoln called him from his supper? The president offered him a seat. He proceeded to read him General War Order No. 3, leaving McClellan in command of the Army of the Potomac, but taking away the title of commander in chief, which had so ill-suited him. General Henry Halleck would take charge of the Department of the Mississippi, and General John C. Frémont would command the western armies. Seward approved. Lincoln said that the duty of relieving McClellan was painful, yet he "thought he was doing Gen. McC a very great kindness in permitting him to retain command of the Army of the Potomac, and giving him an opportunity to retrieve his errors," Hay recalled. Seward heartily agreed, growling about "the imbecility which had characterized the general's operations on the upper Potomac."

Stanton came in meanwhile, asthmatic, wheezing and blowing. Back when he had been the highest-paid lawyer in Washington—before giving up that career to serve his country—he had been close to McClellan, and even shared jokes with him about the president. But now, from the war department, Stanton took a dim view of the over-ranked general. He had suffered—with Lincoln—McClellan's continual delays and arrogance. Seward advised that Stanton issue the new order, as it would strengthen his position; he had been secretary of war only two months and needed public support. But Stanton objected to the order coming from his desk. He explained that his relations with the general now were so strained that friends—many of them powerful Democrats—might assume the demotion arose from personal animosity, and hold this against him. And so, Hay observed, "The President decided to take the responsibility." This was his usual course of action, no matter what impact it might have on his personal popularity.

The adjustment satisfied Mr. Lincoln for the time being. In late March of 1862, Stoddard observed that "the President has recovered much of his old equanimity and cheerfulness; and certainly no one who saw his constant and eager application to his arduous duties, would imagine for a moment that the man carried so large a load of private grief." Stoddard noticed that eight-year-old Tad was again up and about, but that he sorely missed his older brother Willie. Tad also missed his mother, who rarely emerged from her bedroom, so the child was seen at all hours of the day and night playing in his father's office. When Tad fell asleep on the floor or on a couch, Lincoln would carry him off to bed, and return to the maps and war strategy.

At last, McClellan took to the field that spring, moving his army up the Virginia Peninsula between the York and James rivers. He moved up the James so slowly his critics called him "the Virginia Creeper." His stalling and apprehension produced only an inconclusive victory at the Battle of Fair Oaks on May 31, and strategic losses in the clashes with Robert E. Lee during the Seven Days' Battles in late June. Lee drove McClellan far from Richmond. After the Battle of Fair Oaks, McClellan had written to his wife, "Every poor fellow that is killed or wounded almost haunts me," a sentiment befitting a nurse, or even a chaplain, but not a field commander. "Victory has no charms for me when purchased at such cost." It is difficult to imagine General Lee or General Grant expressing such feelings.

What McClellan lacked, mysteriously, was the aggressive, martial instinct—brutal, single-minded, and inexorable—that is essential for success in warfare. Nobody knew for certain whether this was a personality trait (he never went near the fighting) or a political persuasion. As Lincoln suggested on the day he called him into his office, perhaps McClellan was ambivalent about waging war against the rebels, either to preserve the Union or to put an end to slavery. At Harrison's Landing, Virginia, on July 8, McClellan presumed to advise Lincoln that the war ought to be fought against the Confederate army, rather than against the southern people or the institution of slavery. Hay and Nicolay later said that was the beginning of his career as a politician.

The president recalled that "when the Peninsular Campaign terminated suddenly at Harrison's Landing, I was as nearly inconsolable as I could be and live." If McClellan had pressed his advantage at the Battle of Malvern Hill—instead of retreating to the James River on July 1—he could have overwhelmed the battered Confederate troops and taken Richmond.

Lincoln was eager to see the condition of the army for himself. "The President made a flying visit to McClellan's army on the Peninsula this week [July 7–10]," Nicolay wrote. Satisfied that the army was "in better condition and more of it than he expected, after having passed through its long and trying ordeal of battle," Lincoln was in better spirits when he returned from Virginia, despite the heavy losses and his general's condescension. In the Seven Days' Battles there were more than twenty-five thousand casualties on both sides, and the military hospitals of the capital were rapidly filling.

"The average public mind is becoming alarmingly sensational," Nicolay observed on July 13. One of the reasons for this alarm was that the general public had more faith in McClellan than did the president, the cabinet members, or the high-ranking generals. They knew that a better general would get better results. In person, Little Mac was imperious, persuasive, and highly political—a Democrat susceptible to arguments for compromise or appeasement. His soldiers loved him, and everyone agreed that he had organized and trained the Union army superbly. In a city full of Democrats, he had—for a brief time— credibility and influence second only to Lincoln's, and the president needed him for the sake of stability.

In Mr. Lincoln's absence, Nicolay found that minding the White House included some unofficial matters. While the president was in Virginia, he wired the secretary, asking him to borrow $280 and send it to his son, Robert Lincoln. Robert was like a younger sibling to the secretaries, and particularly close to John Hay. But as long as Nicolay was in town, he handled the flow of cash through a safe in his office, so he would get Robert his money.

Upon returning, Lincoln thanked Nicolay for the personal favor.

MCCLELLAN COMPLAINED THAT THE government fell far short of giving him the support he needed to protect his men and destroy the enemy. For a year, he waged a public relations war with the White House and the cabinet over the issue, and Lincoln's secretaries had a rare view of his ingenious handling of this conflict. The general relied on his detective, Allan Pinkerton, whose reports regularly exaggerated the size of the Confederate troops arrayed against him. Battle after battle proved to Lincoln and Stanton that the Federal troops not only outnumbered but were far better equipped and provisioned than the rebels.

Yet the general never gave up criticizing Lincoln and the "hounds" in Washington he insisted were opposed to his success, and who hobbled him by retaining thirty thousand soldiers in the capital. Little Mac informed Lincoln and Stanton that if he suffered defeat, it would be *their* fault; but if the Union troops achieved victory, it would be *his* achievement. After the Seven Days' Battles in June, he had wired Stanton, "You have done your best to sacrifice this army." His audience for such insults were his own adoring soldiers, the generals who remained in thrall to him, antiadministration Democrats, and the journalists North and South who wrote to please them.

For half a year, Lincoln cultivated McClellan. He praised, indulged and forgave him, while closely observing, weighing costs against the benefits of the general's leadership—giving him enough rope to hang himself. The secretaries marveled over the president's patience. To diffuse his anger and frustration, he summoned up his great sense of humor. "If General McClellan does not want to use the army," Lincoln famously quipped, "I would like to borrow it."

The president was a fountainhead of anecdotes, puns, and ribald stories, and he welcomed them from his aides. Stoddard recalled one hot Sunday morning that summer, when the three secretaries, in their shirtsleeves, were gathered in the president's office. Stoddard had just finished sorting Mr. Lincoln's mail when Hay came in from his bedroom across the hall. He was bursting with a story, "all one bubble," Stoddard recalled. "He is sober enough most of the time, but he had heard something funny, and he was good-natured about dividing it."

The story was droll but unprintable, so we must accept that it has not come down entire—the sort of joke one would tell about a man homeward bound from the tavern who blunders into the wrong house. Hay told a story better than most men his age, but on this Sunday he kept breaking up before he could get well into it. The door was open, and soon Nicolay came in, hearing Hay's peals of laughter as he struggled to get control of the narrative. Nicolay, always busy, had a pen in one hand and a long scroll of paper in the other, but he took a chair to listen. Hay began again for his friends' benefit, and performed tolerably well until he reached the first point—perhaps where the drunkard realizes his furniture has been rearranged . . . Hay got the giggles. It was not so much the story itself, but the men's need to laugh on a quiet morning during a war, "a first-class excuse for a laugh," Stoddard recalled, "and all three of us exploded as one."

The entire second floor of the White House had been as still as a graveyard until this raucous laughter broke up the silence. The secretaries had forgotten that anybody else was within earshot until they heard the soft, pleading voice:

"Now John, just tell that thing again."

There stood President Lincoln. He had entered from the hall silently—or at least without being heard beneath their racket. He sank into Andrew Jackson's chair, facing the table where Nicolay sat across from him, and Hay stood by the mantel, where he had been holding forth. Now the story was even better told the third time, "up to its first explosive place, but right there a quartette explosion went off. Down came the President's foot from across his knee, with a heavy stamp on the floor, and out through the hall went an uproarious peal of fun." The laughter rose to its climax, and was subsiding; Hay was about to forge ahead, when:

"Mr. President, if you please sir, Mr. Stanton is in your room."

It was the doorkeeper, old Edward McManus, looking penitent, calling attention to the arrival of the formidable secretary of war. Senator Trumbull had also entered the building, on some special errand.

Stoddard recalled, years later, that "there was something all but ghastly in the manner of the death of that story. Through all the sunny, laughter-filled chambers of the Executive Office poured thick and fast the gloom and glamour of death in life that belonged to them."

THAT AUGUST, NICOLAY TRAVELED north to visit his fiancée, and to negotiate treaties with the Sioux in Minnesota. Hay wrote to him on August 27: "Where is your scalp? If anybody believes you don't wish you were here at home, he can get a pretty lively bet out of me. . . . If in God's good providence your long locks adorn the lodge of an aboriginal warrior and the festive tomtom is made of your stretched hide, I shall not grudge the time thus spent." Washington, he adds, is not an alluring village at present, except for a Miss Kennedy, a lady Stoddard is "spoony" about.

With Nicolay away, Hay alone served as Lincoln's confidant. As of midsummer, Lincoln still needed McClellan, and so he endured him—his military blunders as well as his insubordination—until McClellan's behavior began to show signs of irrationality, panic, and paranoia. Hay recalled that on a Saturday morning, August 30, 1862, he rode out to the president's summer residence, the Soldiers' Home, a gabled cottage on a tree-shaded hill three miles north of the city. He found Lincoln's horse by the door, saddled up and ready, and so the two men rode the turnpike into town together, conversing all the while.

This was the last season that Lincoln would be permitted to commute without a cavalry guard. He rode well, the veteran of some twenty years of pounding the dirt roads of the Eighth Judicial Circuit of Illinois. Now he stole sidelong glances at his companion, watching Hay cling to the horse's neck now and then for purchase, bobbing awkwardly when his mount broke into a trot, fearful of falling off.

The Second Battle of Bull Run was under way in northern Virginia, and the president was trying to comprehend the intrigues among his commanding generals. In July, he had appointed the brusque and beetle-browed Henry Halleck general in chief, effectively replacing McClellan as commander of the Federal armies. As commander of the

Army of the Potomac, McClellan now reported to Halleck, and this irked him. His army had stood within twenty-five miles of Richmond when Halleck ordered him to withdraw and march to support General John Pope's Army of Virginia near Manassas, where Pope fell afoul of Stonewall Jackson's legendary troops. McClellan resented Pope's recent promotion in Virginia, and thought him a fool, which Pope soon proved himself to be in this disastrous field command. Pope, for his part, considered McClellan ineffectual, and began by questioning the courage of his former soldiers.

"It really seems to me," said Lincoln, giving the horse his head on the straight, dusty road, "that McClellan wants Pope defeated."

Hay listened closely as the road curved and they made their way along Rock Creek Church Road through a landscape despoiled of trees. The army had used them for firewood and battlements.

"There was a dispatch from McClellan in which the General proposed, as one plan of action, to leave Pope to get out of his own scrape, and devote ourselves to securing Washington," Lincoln continued. McClellan characteristically dawdled while Robert E. Lee and James Longstreet joined Jackson to trap Pope's troops and kill or wound ten thousand Federal soldiers before they fell back to the heights of Centreville on the Washington side of Bull Run.

Lincoln told Hay that McClellan had been so panicked the night before that he had ordered that "Chain Bridge" (over the Potomac, joining Washington and Georgetown) be blown up to protect the capital from invaders. Halleck had revoked the order. McClellan had also recalled the Sixth Corps of his Army of the Potomac after it had marched seven miles toward Manassas. The men could hear the cannon fire in the distance as Pope's troops fought for their lives. Halleck was livid. When the Sixth Corps "had been sent ahead by Halleck's order, [McClellan] begged permission to recall them again," Lincoln told Hay, "& only desisted after Halleck's sharp injunction to push them ahead till they whipped something or got whipped themselves."

"I think he's a little crazy," Lincoln confided to Hay, turning in the saddle. "Envy jealousy and spite," Hay reflected, "are probably a better explanation of his present conduct. He is constantly sending dispatches to the President and Halleck asking what is his real position and command. He acts as chief alarmist and grand marplot [spoiler] of the Army."

From the toll gate on the Seventh Street turnpike, the horsemen could see above the steeples and chimneys the white columns bearing the skeleton of the unfinished Capitol dome. They turned west on Rhode Island Avenue, passing the camps of freed blacks near Iowa Circle. As they entered the city on Vermont Avenue, the traffic thickened—carriages and wagons, drays bound for market, men in linen dusters and straw hats going to work in the shops and departments. Word of the president on his horse ran a hundred yards ahead of Lincoln and Hay, so their conversation was curtailed as the president touched his hat and waved a cordial hand, or nodded to the citizens who greeted him.

If they had hoped for significant news from the telegraph office upon their arrival at the Executive Mansion, they were disappointed. There would be many rumors that Saturday, and much speculation among the officers in the War Department, but no reliable reports of the battle. In the evening, the president and his secretary dined with Stanton and his wife, "a pleasant little dinner and a pretty wife as white and cold and motionless as marble," Hay recalled, "whose rare smiles seemed to pain her." Ellen Stanton's cool demeanor during this trying time stood in contrast, and as a domestic counterweight, to the candid fury of the secretary of war. Stanton railed against his former friend, McClellan. The man did nothing but send him whining dispatches, complaints, and excuses while flatly disobeying General Halleck's orders to advance. "After these battles," Stanton growled, "there should be one Court Martial, if never any more." When agitated, Stanton would twirl a lock of his silver beard with his forefinger. His gray eyes smoldered. "Nothing but foul play could lose us this battle, and it rests with McClellan and his friends." At that point, Hay observed, both Stanton and Lincoln put their faith in General Pope.

Optimism prevailed in the White House at the end of the day, "and we went to bed expecting glad tidings at sunrise." But the next morning at eight o'clock, while Hay was dressing, a hollow-eyed, despondent

Mr. Lincoln knocked at his bedroom door. "John!" he called, and Hay let him in. "Well John, we are whipped again, I am afraid. The enemy reinforced on Pope and drove back his left wing and he has retired to Centreville where he says he will be able to hold his men." The president frowned. "I don't like that expression. I don't like to hear him admit that his men need holding."

As the day wore on, bringing more details of the defeat, Hay observed that Lincoln was just as defiant as he was disappointed. He kept repeating the phrase "We must hurt this enemy before it gets away." Church bells tolled over the city—a death knell. The next morning, it was pouring rain. Ambulances slogged through the mud with their burden of wounded and dying men on their way to Armory Square, Judiciary Square, Campbell Hospital, and thirty other military clinics recently set up around the city. But when Hay acknowledged "the bad look of things," Lincoln would hear no more of such talk.

"Mr. Hay, we must whip these people now. Pope must fight them, if they are too strong for him he can gradually retire to these fortifications. . . . if we are really whipped and to be whipped we may as well stop fighting." Hay credited Lincoln's "indomitable will, that army movements have been characterized by such energy and clarity for the last few days." The president would not give in to despair.

As for McClellan, Pope, and Halleck, the discordant trio that had produced the military calamity, there was no way that Hay could have predicted the denouement of their drama. On Tuesday, Lincoln summoned McClellan to the White House. Having heard that General Pope had questioned the bravery of nearly every Union soldier in Virginia, Lincoln asked McClellan to ameliorate any negative sentiments on the part of the Army of the Potomac toward Pope. On Wednesday, Lincoln and Halleck called upon McClellan at seven o'clock in the morning. They requested that he take command of all troops falling back to defend the capital. No one could have been more surprised than McClellan, who had been roundly censured for his antics during the recent battle. At noon, the president announced this decision to the cabinet. Stanton was astounded, outraged; so was Salmon Chase.

Seward was in New York. For four hours, the cabinet members took turns railing against McClellan, and disputing the new command, until the president sent them grumbling away.

What was Mr. Lincoln thinking? First, he had learned quickly that Pope had blundered at Manassas, leading his men into a trap laid by Stonewall Jackson and James Longstreet. Moreover, Pope had added insult to injury by blaming everyone around him—accusing Major General Fitz John Porter of disobeying orders and calling into question the bravery and manhood of both Federal armies of Virginia. The cabinet and the public may have sided with Pope against McClellan at this point, but the fighting men still loved Little Mac, and hated the high-handed, patronizing interloper Pope, who had gotten so many of them killed.

On Friday morning, Hay walked with Lincoln to the War Department, hoping for news of Confederate troop movements. There was continuing anxiety that the city would be attacked, and rumors that Stonewall Jackson had crossed the Potomac. Lincoln talked of McClellan and how hard he had been working to repair his image after the recent battle. "I am of the opinion that this public feeling against him will make it expedient to take important command from him." He told Hay that the cabinet was unanimous in their opposition to McClellan's command and threatened to denounce the president publicly for ordering it.

Nonetheless, said Lincoln, approaching the door of the small brick building that housed the War Department, "We must use what tools we have." Hay observed that the little man had become, in Mr. Lincoln's precise parlance, a tool. "There is no man in the army who can man these fortifications and lick these troops of ours into shape half as well as he." Hay had spent much of the week at his desk wielding a paper knife, reading the president's mail. He reported that the feeling against McClellan extended from the cabinet to the greater public, to which Lincoln replied, "Unquestionably he has acted badly toward Pope! He wanted him to fail. That is unpardonable. But he is too useful just now to sacrifice. . . . If he can't fight himself, he excels in making others ready to fight."

SECRETARY OF STATE WILLIAM Seward had been in New York City during the Second Battle of Bull Run. The things he heard from the president and the War Department about the generals' conduct he found profoundly disturbing.

Hay was entering the White House as Seward was coming out. Seeing Mr. Seward at the brink of tears, his friend turned back and fell in step with him, hoping his presence might afford some comfort. They walked across the park in the heat of late summer. Seward muttered something about the confusion of foreign affairs, but Hay knew that this was not the thing that was really troubling him.

"Mr. Hay," he said, turning to the young man with the deep, comprehending eyes. "What is the use of growing old? You learn something of men and things but never until too late to use it." Hay made a mental note to preserve those words in his diary. "I have only just now found out," Seward continued, wiping his face with a handkerchief, "what military jealousy is." The sorrow in his voice was tinged with anger. For months, he had hoped to take a few days to visit relatives in New York, and he could not, so long as he thought the scattered troops were in danger. But he had reviewed General McClellan's men just the week before and was convinced that the Federal armies were virtually united, and thus invincible.

"I went home," he said, "and the first news I received was that each had been attacked and each, in effect, beaten. It never had occurred to me that any jealousy could prevent these generals from acting for their common fame and the welfare of the country."

Hay replied that it seemed impossible to him that a general could write to the president proposing that "Pope be allowed to get out of his own scrape his own way." A total of 1,724 Federal soldiers had died at the Second Battle of Bull Run, and 8,372 had lost arms, legs, eyes, or had been otherwise mutilated by bullets or bayonets so as to be of no use to the army or anyone else for some time, if ever.

Sighing, Seward replied, "I don't see why you should have expected it. You are not old. I should have known it." Hay accompanied his friend to the door of his home across the square.

And that autumn Hay watched, in wonder and admiration, as the president used McClellan to restore morale in the ranks that the mean-spirited Pope had broken. General Pope had been summarily removed from command and sent to Minnesota to keep the peace among the settlers and the Sioux. When Robert E. Lee invaded Maryland in early September of 1862, McClellan was again in command. A corporal of the Union Twelfth Corps spied an envelope lying on a campground recently vacated by the rebels in Frederick County, Maryland. Inside the envelope was a paper wrapped around two cigars. On the paper was written General Lee's Special Order No. 191, which described in detail Lee's plans for uniting his scattered forces in western Maryland. It is the sort of fluke that proves war to be a crazy game of chance. Some say that God takes care of fools and children, and George McClellan was always a little of both.

His possession of Lee's tactical order leveled the playing field. McClellan's narrow defeat of Lee's forces at the Battle of Antietam near Sharpsburg, Maryland, in mid-September, gave Lincoln the military success he needed to issue the Emancipation Proclamation, freeing the slaves in the insurgent states. Without a show of military strength, the act of emancipation might appear to the world a measure of desperation rather than of conscience.

But McClellan's victory raised questions. His army had stopped the invasion of Maryland. But why had he not pursued Lee's stricken troops as they retreated over the Potomac River, attacked them as they fled, and destroyed them? He had thirty-six thousand fresh troops to finish the business, and outnumbered the enemy by more than two to one.

A week later, on a Thursday evening, September 25, Hay and Lincoln mounted their horses and set out on Vermont Avenue and the turnpike headed toward the Soldiers' Home. The heat and humidity downtown was withering, and the riders welcomed the cool drifting in from the high ground north of the city. The president was pensive, concerned about a rumor he had just heard "of an officer who had said they did not mean to gain any decisive victory but to keep things running on so that they the army might manage things to suit themselves." This would explain—as Lincoln phrased it—why McClellan "did not bag them after Sharpsburg [Antietam]." Lincoln told his secretary that he would have someone investigate the matter, "and if any such language had been used, his head should go off." It was a capital offense.

Hay was worried—not to say alarmed—and did not scruple to call it a treasonable conspiracy: the McClellan conspiracy, in fact. Hay recalled and recounted the general's behavior from the night he left Lincoln and Seward in his parlor and went to bed, to his sabotaging of Second Bull Run, to his failure to pursue Lee after Antietam. Again and again, he asked the president if it was not so, that McClellan did not want victory but rather a war of attrition that would lead to a truce, with slavery preserved. As they rode on in the twilight, the president remained silent, while Hay went on in this vein for miles. At length, Lincoln turned in the saddle toward his young companion and replied that "McClellan was doing nothing to make himself either respected or feared."

On October 1, 1862, Lincoln and a party of a dozen officers and politicians took a special train to Harper's Ferry, to visit the headquarters of the Army of the Potomac, review the troops, and consult with General McClellan concerning military strategy. At sunrise on October 3, standing with an old friend on a hilltop, surveying the acres of tents, pennants, horses, and artillery, Lincoln muttered: "This is General McClellan's bodyguard." For two days, he had been conferring with McClellan, encouraging him to take the initiative, to *move,* to cross the water and advance upon Lee's army in Virginia. The general, relaxed at his field desk in the shade of the white tent, temporized. The center post of the high tent stood between them like the dividing wall on a stage set. McClellan, sullen, patronizing, suggested that his men needed fresh horses.

"Will you pardon me," said the president, sitting stiffly across the desk from McClellan, "for asking what the horses of your army have done since the Battle of Antietam that fatigues anything?"

Nicolay returned from Minnesota in time to greet the president as he arrived from Harper's Ferry. "I have of course had my hands full of the deferred and delayed business," he wrote to Therena. Because the president had been absent for several days, he was overwhelmed with visitors upon his return. Lincoln was not too busy to instruct General Halleck on October 6 to order McClellan to "cross the Potomac and give battle to the enemy or drive him south. Your army must move now while the roads are good."

McClellan wanted reassurance, and so he turned to the intelligence agent in his service, Allan Pinkerton. On October 12, Pinkerton met with Nicolay in Washington. Drawn into the intrigue, and knowing the president's desire to express confidence in his general now if not next week, Nicolay assured the detective "that the president was much gratified at his visit to you." Pinkerton wrote to McClellan, "and had since then repeatedly expressed his confidence in you and his lack of confidence in Halleck, and from what Nicolay said I have no doubt but that after you give the Rebels one more good battle you will be called here to the command of the whole Army."

But there would be no more battles for that precocious general who was so loathe to lead a charge. On November 7, 1862, George Brinton McClellan was removed from command of the Army of the Potomac. On November 9, Lincoln replaced him with Ambrose Burnside, who led the army into the tragic Battle of Fredericksburg only a month later. Burnside, Joseph Hooker, George Gordon Meade—no Union general satisfied the president until he appointed Ulysses S. Grant commander in chief in March of 1864.

In sixteen months, Lincoln had made the best use of Little Mac as a tool that had transformed the beaten army of the First Battle of Bull Run into a magnificent fighting force of nearly a hundred thousand soldiers.

"He is an admirable engineer," Lincoln confided to a visitor, "but he seems to have a special talent for the stationary engine."

CHAPTER SEVEN

FROM HELL
TO PARADISE

B y the second week of October 1862, when Nicolay returned from the West, both Hay and Stoddard were worn out. October 12 was Hay's twenty-fourth birthday. As it was a Sunday, the three friends might celebrate at leisure, lifting a glass of whiskey at the Willard's bar, or at the new Metropolitan Club, with its dark wood paneling and marble chimneypieces, on the northwest corner of Lafayette Square.

Stoddard had made plans to take a two-week working vacation in North Carolina. The Union army, under General Burnside, had captured strategic points along the coast and the Neuse, the long estuarine river that runs through the state and empties into Ratton Bay, west of the Outer Banks. The president had given Stoddard a letter of introduction and passes to enable him to act as an agent in purchasing tar, timber, and turpentine for the navy at towns along the Neuse River.

Hay—who had little flesh to spare—had lost weight. The president's stamina was legendary, but he knew the limits of others. He granted Hay leave to go home to Pittsfield, Illinois, on October 25 for two weeks. It is proof of the enduring intimacy between Hay and Nicolay that when one of them was out of town they continued to correspond, playfully and informatively. Sometimes there is intelligence that might well be intended for the president, as in Hay's letter to Nicolay of October 28: "You cannot imagine the earnestness of denunciation which fills the West in regard to McClellan. . . . If he should be sent West to command our troops his presence would demoralize the army. His continuance in command in the East begins to shake the confidence of some of our best friends in the Government." If Lincoln had been contemplating a *transfer* for McClellan, one week before dismissing him, such a report from his secretary would have discouraged any such indulgence.

More often, the letters back and forth between the friends are full of gossip and collegiate humor about parties and women and family. Nicolay writes to Hay on the twenty-sixth, of the Washington social scene: "Two little howls came off last night—one at Mrs. Judge Merrick's (Mrs. M and Lt.Col.Webb expressed numerous regrets at your absence) where I saw a whole bevy of new secesh beauties, and the other [Seward's assistant, James O.] Clephane's reception, which didn't 'pan out' much, though he has got a reasonably good-looking wife." Hay replies that he is "having a quietly good time," sitting by the fireside conversing with his mother, "and at night I do a little unobtrusive sparking," by which he means courting the ladies.

"I am perfectly idle, and you, who always insist on being busy even when you ought to be pleasuring, can have no adequate conception of the enjoyment of the genuine dolce far niente [sweet idleness]. Just keep the army still for a week or so and I will bless you with my latest breath."

JEAN MARGARET DAVENPORT LANDER, whose beauty and wit had so impressed John Hay a year and a half earlier, had been a widow for nine months. Observing a respectable period of mourning, she had lived mostly in seclusion—with her mother who had come from England to console her— dividing her time between her summer home in Lynn, Massachusetts, and her wood-frame "cottage" on Capitol Square, Southeast, Washington, D.C.

Agents and theater managers begged the great actress to return to the stage where she belonged, but she resisted for reasons known only to her. Mrs. Lander, the famous widow of a martyred patriot, was in a patriotic frame of mind. A native of England who had spent nearly her entire life in the public eye, she knew the impact her least action would have upon public opinion—the war effort as well as her own reputation. She must make a gesture, strike a pose so altruistic and grand that it would be remembered as long as her rendition of Camille. She was well connected in political circles: General Lander's funeral, held in Salmon Chase's mansion, was attended by President Lincoln and most of the cabinet. Among her friends she numbered Chase's daughter, the statuesque beauty Kate, and Kate's friend John Hay, with whom Jean passed more and more time in the late autumn of 1862 and the winter of 1862–63. It is possible that Hay put Mrs. Lander in touch with Dorothea Dix, the dour and strict superintendent of nurses. Or it might have been Hay's friend General David Hunter.

As 1862 drew to a close, there were more than twenty-five thousand sick and wounded soldiers in Washington hospitals, and hardly enough nurses to care for them. If Mrs. Lander could not take up a sword, like Joan of Arc, and lead men into battle, was it possible she might serve her adopted country as a humble nurse?

The idea of the glamorous Jean Margaret Lander serving the Union army as a field nurse flew in the face of Miss Dix's carefully considered principles and inflexible requirements for nurses. An applicant had to be within the ages of thirty and forty-five and in good health, qualifications that presented no problem for Mrs. Lander, who had reached the age of thirty-three on May 3, and enjoyed robust good health. But then, the would-be nurse had to be homely, like Miss Dix herself, and preferably a maiden lady of impeccable character who would not inspire or be distracted by thoughts of romance as she passed among the bedridden men, dispensing mercy. Jean Margaret was dazzlingly beautiful. And for all her character references during her brief marriage to the brawling general, she was known chiefly as a stage actress (the incarnation of Camille, no less!), one of a profession whose members were generally banned from most hotels in Boston and Philadelphia, a sorority only lately differentiated from the painted women of the demimonde. No, Mrs. Lander was not plain, nor was she a virgin, nor was she a woman of "good character"—unless good character solely consisted of letters of reference from powerful gentlemen.

Nonetheless Mrs. Lander desired to serve the Union army as a nurse, and she was accustomed to getting what she wanted. She was also—as we have noted—very well connected, with at least one personal friend in the cabinet and another in the president's office, men who were in a position to support Dorothea Dix's program as she wrangled and bargained with hospital administrators, the army medical bureau, and the U.S. Sanitary Commission to do right by the wounded soldiers. One man in particular, Hay's friend General David Hunter, had been put in command of the Department of the South in March 1862. In the Port Royal area of South Carolina, there were dozens of hospitals under construction, and Clara Barton herself served Miss Dix there.

And so, sometime that winter, Miss Dix made her peace with Mrs. Lander, and under terms of strict secrecy, the former actress accepted her appointment as a supervisor of hospitals in the area of Port Royal, South Carolina. No one other than the doctors and military officers with whom she worked was to know her true identity, and journalists covering events there usually would refer to the nurse by affectionate, revealing descriptions; when they printed her name, they were careful not to mention her official role.

She would not leave Washington to go to Port Royal until the New Year. When Hay returned from Illinois in mid-November, they would have time together. And certain verses from the poet's pen at that time resonate with the theme of longing for a soul mate and an unattainable ideal—unattainable because of a disparity of ages.

TOO LATE

Had we but met in other days,
Had we but loved in other ways,
Another light and hope had shone
On your life and my own.

In sweet but hopeless reveries
I fancy how your wistful eyes
Had saved me, had I known their power
    In fate's imperious hour;
. . . .
God knows why this was not to be.
You bloomed from childhood far from me,
The sunshine of the favored place
    That knew your youth and grace.

And when your eyes, so fair and free,
In fearless beauty beamed on me,
I knew the fatal die was thrown
    My choice in life was gone.

The clever poem speaks of the older lover's temptation and ulti-mate renunciation of the younger beloved, and how each must go his way with the other's blessing.

A vague regret, a troubled prayer,
And then the future vast and fair
Will tempt your young and eager eyes
    With all its glad surprise.

And I shall watch you, safe and far,
As some late traveller eyes a star
Wheeling beyond his desert sands
    To gladden happier lands.

It is a common poetic artifice, the dramatic lyric. The speaker is the older lover—who could not have been John Hay in those years, but who certainly could have been Jean Lander. Hay was writing his poems for publication. He would not have embarrassed the lady by writing, transparently, as the young man in love with a woman nine years older than he. By the late summer of 1862, the intimacy between the widow and Lincoln's secretary would have been difficult to keep secret in the gossip-hungry drawing rooms of the capital.

The weather was beautiful, a perfect Indian summer that Hay would commemorate in romantic poems a year later.

Thanksgiving Day, November 27, 1862, Nicolay, who was usually with Hay on holidays, wrote mournfully to Therena Bates that he had dined "solitary and alone" at Willard's, "making it a mere business proceeding to mend up the wear and tear of tissue."

His best friend, the poet, had chosen other company.

THE FIRST WEEK OF December brought the cold wind and the snow that covered the dreary dun streets and sooty roofs of the federal city. "I pity the poor soldiers who had to do guard duty last night," Nicolay wrote to Therena on Sunday, December 7. He was bringing his fiancée up to date on the winter social scene when he was interrupted by one of the porters, who brought a message from Mrs. Lincoln. He opened it with anxious curiosity. It was an invitation for Nicolay, Hay, and Stoddard to join her for dinner at five o'clock that evening. What could she mean by it? "This is a startling 'change of base' on the part of the lady, and I am at a loss at the moment to explain it. However as etiquette does not permit any one on any excuse to decline an invitation to dine with the President, I shall have to make the reconnaissance, and thereby more fully learn the tactics of the enemy."

Nearly ten months had passed since Willie's death from typhoid. With much rest and reflection, and the intervention of spirit mediums who brought occasional tidings from Willie's ghost, Mrs. Lincoln was recovering from her trauma. She had grown strong enough to travel, and was gone for much of the autumn—from October 20 to November 27—staying in New York and Boston. Now she wished to resume her responsibilities as mistress of the White House. It would be wise to begin with small parties before confronting the public at the crowded, chaotic levees and holiday receptions. Also, she had begun to measure the depth and vehemence of public sentiment against her and yearned for harmony within the four walls of her own house. Stoddard she could depend upon. The other secretaries seemed to be aligned against her, so it was time to try to win them over.

So that evening of December 7, the three secretaries dined in the private dining room with Mr. and Mrs. Lincoln, looking out the north window on the snow-covered park. The other guests were old friends from Illinois: Senator Orville Browning, Judge David Davis—Lincolns' campaign manager—and Isaac N. Arnold, a congressman and lawyer from Chicago. "In a company thus composed there could be no conversation except of the most general character," Browning wrote in his diary. They discussed the news of the day, and how General Burnside's shivering troops, approaching Fredericksburg, suffered for a lack of blankets. "The northwest wind howls drearily through the half-deserted streets of the city . . . ," Stoddard observed, and "the suffering in the army must have been great for the past ten days. . . ." Ice two inches thick formed over the Potomac.

The moon was full and shone on the snow-covered square, and on the statue of Andrew Jackson. The pavements were slippery despite the ordinance that they must be cleared five hours after the snow had fallen. "If people will not clear their pavements of snow and ice, if they deem it cleanly or ornamental," a journalist scolded, "let them sprinkle a little coal or wood ashes, or a little salt . . ." There was a long list of "Deaths of Soldiers" in the paper, as usual, and an article about the new Campbell Hospital under construction at the north end of Seventh Street, eleven wards each 212 feet by 20 feet with a kitchen, guardhouse, and dwellings for the Sisters of Charity who would be employed as nurses. Mrs. Lander, Hay knew, would not be among these. But the president, Mrs. Lincoln, and her lady friends would visit Campbell Hospital, as they had frequented so many others, bringing gifts and words of encouragement to the soldiers.

The night before, at the nearby corner of Eighteenth and K streets, a house and a barn burned to the ground, but fortunately the firemen contained the blaze. Fires in winter were terrifying in northern cities because the pumps and hoses froze and the flames thrived on dry air.

Stoddard had noted, as he did every day, the price of gold, selling at $132 per ounce, and knew it would go even higher if Burnside failed in Virginia. Some rascal had smashed the streetlamp at the corner of Tenth Street and Louisiana Avenue, which was a nuisance to Stoddard, who would have to walk that way to get home. Tonight, the moon was so bright no artificial light would be needed.

"Cold, Cold, Cold," read the headline in the newspaper. "Cloaks and overcoats, furs and mittens were in good demand . . ." But for these friends from Illinois, familiar with the arctic gusts on the prairie, it was a minor discomfort. The wind blew the snow in swirls, "the ladies' cheeks and noses looked fresh as full-blown roses, the North wind whistled, and old Jack Frost reigned supreme," wrote one newsman.

Within the Executive Mansion, after a peaceful dinner, the Lincolns and their friends enjoyed a jolly evening in the Red Room around the glowing hearth, listening to Mr. Lincoln tell stories.

HAY WAS EAGER TO see as much of Jean Margaret as he could that December. On the twelfth of the month, he sent her his photograph, so she could see something of him even when they were apart.

> My Dear Mrs. Lander,
> I send you with this the picture I promised.
>   Whenever you see it, pray do not fail to remember that it is the counterfeit presentment of your most obedient servant.
>
> > John Hay

Exactly when he had promised her his picture we do not know, but it certainly would have been in response to her desire to have it, and he would not have delayed in obliging her. An intriguing quality of this note is the richness of sentiment the poet has encoded beneath his formal tone. "Presentment" is a rare, lawyerly word with a specific connotation. Presentment is the act of offering, at the proper time, a document, such as a bill of exchange, that calls for repayment. He is sending her an image of himself, a "counterfeit" meant to represent the real man, and begging her to remember—each time she looks at it—how much it would gratify him if the real woman would repay him in kind.

December 12, 1862, was a day of intense activity in Washington and on the battlefield in Virginia. That day, the president sent John Nicolay to Fredericksburg with a letter to General Ambrose Burnside, saying, lightly, "Please treat him kindly, while I am sure he will avoid giving you trouble." Lincoln wanted him on the scene, "on the eve of great events," as Nicolay wrote to Therena, to be the president's scout. He did not return until the seventeenth, after the tragic defeat of the Federal forces on the terraces of Fredericksburg. Burnside foolishly ordered his army to charge the middle of Lee's well-designed defenses along Marye's Heights behind the town. Back in Washington, Stoddard wrote in his column: "The cloud of uncertainty did at last lift from over the banks of the Rappahannock, but we would almost prefer the suspense to the grizzly horror of this reality." Eighteen thousand Federal soldiers were killed or wounded there. After the battle, the president remarked, "If there is a worse place than Hell, I am in it."

With Nicolay on assignment in Virginia, Hay struggled to keep order in the president's office. Politicians, military officers, and outraged citizens thronged the corridors and waiting rooms, demanding some explanation for the military fiasco, complaining that Lincoln should resign or be impeached, whispering that General McClellan ought to stage a military coup—an idea that Little Mac did nothing to discourage.

Before the year was out, the reversal of military fortune had put such partisan pressure on the government that first Seward, and then Chase, submitted resignations. Lincoln refused to accept these, replying "that the public interest does not admit of it." Appealing to the better angels of their nature, he persuaded the fractious cabinet to stay together. John Hay would not have a good night's sleep until Nicolay's return. Late-night ramblers and insomniacs knew that no matter what darkness covered the rest of the city, the second floor of the White House would be lighted, nearly every night, from dusk until dawn.

The senior secretary returned in time to do some holiday shopping and send a box of presents to his sweetheart in Illinois. "I send the accompanying little box of trinkets with 'A Merry Christmas' but also with a heartier wish that I might be with you to enjoy it. I fear that, separate, neither of us will have enjoyment adequate to the occasion; if we could put our happiness together, we might present a more suitable offering to the gods of gifts and glee who rule the day." It would be a cold Christmas for all, at the end of a disastrous year.

In the Yuletide season, with deep snow on Pennsylvania Avenue, and horse-drawn sleighs jingling past him, John Hay walked the two miles up the hill to the house with the view of the lighted Capitol, where Jean Margaret awaited him. We have a single note from her to Hay that year—Colonel Hay, she calls him, although he was only a bre-vetted major—inviting him to join her and friends of the Washington literary society on Saturday evening, December 27, at her "cottage" at 8:30; but we know that this was not the first or the last time he visited her there. If Jean Lander wrote him other letters, they have not sur-vived the censors of Hay's papers.

On December 28, Stoddard, anticipating his editor's demand for a New Year's column, took up his pen to describe the current state of affairs in the capital. He notes that after much turmoil the cabinet has resumed its routine, for better or worse. The army is camped on the Rappahannock, anxiously awaiting an opportunity to strike.

"We still feel the effects of our severe check at Fredericksburg, but they are steadily wearing off, and are now manifest in the great cities of the North, rather than in the army." Stoddard refers to the crisis of faith in the administration—in New York, Boston, and Washington itself, among businessmen and bankers as well as the public. He had his eye on the stock exchange, especially the gold and currency markets, where he hoped to make his fortune. "At all events, New Year's Day is here, and we are apparently but little nearer the end of the war than when we bade good-bye in 1861."

THE SOCIAL SEASON IN the capital commenced with New Year's Day and ceased with Lent (February 24, 1863). During those weeks, the secretaries attended a whirl of parties. The Lincolns, still in mourning, did little entertaining in the White House, but Hay and Nicolay were out on the town almost every night that winter. Nicolay's letters to Therena glitter with details about the social calendar. Either she has insisted on complete reports, or he prefers that she hear of his escapades from him rather than from her relatives in the city. On Sunday, January 11, he mentions one party, two receptions, and a wedding during the week previous; on Thursday the fifteenth, he writes: "This has been a sort of 'gayety week' thus far. On Monday evening I went to a little musical soirie, on Tuesday evening to a little dancing party at the Carroll's [William T. Carroll, clerk of the Supreme Court], last night to a regular Hop at Willards (a very nice party indeed), tonight I go to a stand-up party at Senator [Lyman] Trumbulls, with still another prospect for tomorrow evening." He admits that at this pace he and John Hay will not survive the season, but believes that soon, when the "transient guests" have departed, the city will sink again into "its original Rip Van Winkle somnolence."

Nevertheless, on Sunday the eighteenth, he reports that he finished out his "fifth night of party-going . . . by dancing until 2 a.m. at the Marine Barracks. . . ." There was "good music but too large a crowd. Ball dresses suffered terribly, I can assure you, and it required a quick eye and skillful pilotage to whirl an extensively be-crinolined beauty unscarred through the dense crowd in a gallopade." He flatters himself with a pun about having "dexterous feets," and deserving "a diploma of chief engineer in the whirligig business." One wonders if Therena is amused, or curious about where her lover whirls away to *after* the dance with the "becrinolined beauty." He does not mention Netty Sheppard's bawdy house, the notorious establishment of Sally Austin on Sixth Street, or a dozen other fancy houses the men must pass on the way home to bed.

These were young men of good character whose indulgences, we may assume, did not exceed a glass or two of whiskey before dark, an occasional turn at the roulette wheel, or a stolen hour or evening with a lonely stage actress. "Every house was a barroom and so were most of the public offices," Stoddard wrote. "All over the city, drinking went on almost without cessation." Hay's diary confirms this—he was never without a bottle in the desk drawer to take the edge off of bad news from the front, or the chill off a January night, or to ease inhibitions in his visitors. When Robert Lincoln came home from Harvard to find his father depressed and his mother ailing, Hay would comfort him with cheese and whiskey.

The pace of social events accelerated as Lent approached, so that on Sunday, February 15, Nicolay admitted to his fiancée there was no news other than "a recital of how gay and dissipated we have been here this week." Of course, parties were an opportunity for the secretaries to gather intelligence on the subtle currents of political sentiment. Tuesday they went to a reception given by the officers and convalescents at Campbell Hospital. Wednesday Hay and Nicolay attended a ball at the National Hotel, and two more parties afterward. On Thursday evening, the men went to a hop at Willard's, then to a gathering at Marshal Ward Hill Lamon's home before rushing off to a dancing party at the home of Rhode Island senator Samuel Green Arnold. After they had turned the lights off at Arnold's, they "returned to Willards and finished out the evening." Mr. Lincoln would be amused, and enlightened, to hear their lively reports.

Very little was accomplished in the White House the next day apart from a reception Mrs. Lincoln held for the midgets Tom Thumb and his new bride, Lavinia Warren, which the secretaries attended. Afterward, they hurried off to a gathering at the home of Galusha Grow, Speaker of the House, and his wife, before attending a small party at a Mrs. Bacon's and a large party at the Russian embassy. Nicolay does not mention the public reception at the White House on Saturday—which was thronged—and at which he, Hay, and Stoddard were obliged to assist. A reporter for the *New York Herald* noted that "the President was cordial in his greetings, and Mrs. Lincoln manifested toward all visitors the affability for which she is distinguished," while another noted that the president looked "haggard and careworn . . . yet he preserves his good nature." Nicolay does record that before this, they attended a morning reception hosted by Marshal Lamon's wife; at 2:00 p.m., they rushed off to a dancing matinee in the enormous arsenal at the southernmost tip of the city, Greenleaf Point on the Potomac. They danced from two until six, "and at night [went] to a little party at Mrs. [Stephen] Douglas's.

"There," he writes Therena, "isn't that doing pretty well for one week. . . . For next week we have a party at the French minister's on Monday night, and a hop at the National on Tuesday night."

The president's secretaries must have spent a good portion of their salaries on shoe leather.

THE WORST SNOWSTORM OF the winter came at the end of February, but in early March, Nicolay noticed the spring buds swelling on the trees and bushes. Congress adjourned, and the hotel parlors that had been "filled to overflowing with ladies, are now almost entirely deserted," he recorded, wistfully.

In the last bone-chilling weeks of winter, John Hay wanted a change of scene. The president, knowing how hard his aides worked and partied, was always open to their requests for leaves of absence—particularly when a journey might intersect with some military or political event. "When the President had any rather delicate matter to manage at a distance from Washington, he rarely wrote, but sent Nicolay or me," Hay noted. Where did he want to go, in March of 1863, that would be agreeable? Where should he go where he might serve the president and his country?

It was probably Hay's idea to sail to Hilton Head, South Carolina, on April 2, and remain there until June, leaving Stoddard and Nicolay to manage the Executive Office as the war heated up again. Federal forces had established beachheads that extended to the southern tip of South Carolina. Hay certainly had his eye on the map and the weather. The islands south of Charleston are beautiful in early spring, and in fact his original plan was to sail from New York to the islands on March 13. But arriving in Manhattan on the twelfth, he felt so sick and weak he decided to return to Washington and "make repairs before setting out." While his eye was on the map, Hay's ear was attuned to military developments. The president was preoccupied with the movements of the Union fleet of ironclads and the South Atlantic Blockading Squadron steaming toward Charleston Harbor under the command of Admiral Samuel Francis Du Pont. The navy planned to attack Fort Sumter, hoping that the city of Charleston might yield to Du Pont's fleet.

Another snowstorm had blanketed Washington in mid-March. Longing for blue skies and knowing the navy's plans to invade Charleston Harbor, Hay offered his services as an envoy in case Secretary of the Navy Gideon Welles or Mr. Lincoln had any dispatches they wished to convey to Admiral Du Pont. Hay wanted to see Hilton Head, and had a brother, Lieutenant Charles E. Hay, who was aide-de-camp to General David Hunter. The secretary could deliver dispatches, visit his brother, and report to the president on military developments in the Department of the South.

There was no need for him to tell Mr. Lincoln or anyone else that one reason he had chosen Hilton Head—when he might have made himself as useful below Vicksburg with General Grant, or with the Army of the Potomac upstream from Fredericksburg—was that Jean Margaret Lander had been stationed in Port Royal, not fifteen miles north of Hilton Head, for two months. On April 4, Dr. Seth Rogers, a surgeon in the Federal army, wrote to a friend: "Mrs. General Lander drew up on her splendid steed before my tent door this afternoon and assured me she would do all in her power for our General Hospital for colored soldiers, now being established in Beaufort."

Hay might have gone anywhere in America, but he chose to travel five hundred miles to the one field of operations where Jean Lander was stationed as a supervisor of nurses. If this was a coincidence, it was a happy one for these two friends, who had not satisfied their desire to see each other in the fishbowl of the nation's capital. They would find plenty of opportunities in the months of April and May to be together on the beaches of Port Royal Sound, and in the tropical gardens of Beaufort, where Mrs. Lander lived.

NICOLAY WROTE TO THERENA on Sunday, April 5, 1863, to say that he was literally alone in the White House. The president and his family had gone to review the Army of the Potomac at General Joseph Hooker's headquarters, in Falmouth, Virginia. And "John Hay left last Thursday (April 2) morning for New York, and sailed on the 'Arago' yesterday morning for Hilton Head. He expects to help Gen. [David] Hunter capture Charleston," Nicolay continues, with subtle irony. "I hope he may—but I am afraid that Charleston problem is a harder one than we imagine."

The "Charleston problem" that Hay was sailing toward on the USS *Arago* represents a fascinating chapter of Civil War and naval history, and the sad end to the heroic career of Rear Admiral Samuel Du Pont. A rugged old campaigner of nearly sixty, Du Pont had cleared Mexican warships from the Gulf in the war with Mexico in 1848, had helped found the U.S. Naval Academy at Annapolis, and was the mastermind of naval strategy against the Confederacy at the start of the war. Appointed flag officer in September 1861, he was placed in charge of the South Atlantic Blockading Squadron, with seventy-five ships, the largest fleet any American officer had ever commanded. Du Pont swiftly did a remarkable thing: he attacked the rebel fortifications at Port Royal harbor in South Carolina (fifty miles south of Fort Sumter—where the war began). By November, the Union navy controlled the southern waters of the entire eastern coast from Georgia to Florida, enforced an effective blockade, and established a formidable southern base for Federal ground troops below Charleston. This tactical success won Du Pont a formal commendation from Congress and a promotion to rear admiral.

Du Pont was the first U.S. officer to command a fleet of ironclads, and probably knew more about their strengths and flaws than anyone. While rumors and sensational journalism led the public and politicians to believe the "ironsides" were invincible, Du Pont knew better. In an attack on Fort McAllister, in Georgia, he had seen them falter because they shipped fewer guns, and those guns fired slowly.

So when the Navy Department, Secretary Welles, and Assistant Secretary Gustavus Fox ordered Du Pont to invade Charleston Harbor and retake Fort Sumter with his "insuperable" ironclads, the rear admiral brooded. He maintained a lively skepticism about this project that those ambitious landlubbers did not comprehend—with the exception of Mr. Lincoln, who had an uneasy feeling about it. On March 29 and April 2, just before Hay's departure, Lincoln complained to Welles and Fox about the planned invasion. Although we do not have the secret dispatch that Hay carried on his person as he sailed on the *Arago,* it was issued too late to have been the actual order to launch the attack. Judging from Hay's account of his meeting with Du Pont after the offensive, and Hay's letters to Nicolay on April 9 and to Lincoln on the tenth, the dispatch contained advice from the president that the fleet must be preserved—beyond Charleston—for even more important business in New Orleans.

Hay arrived at General David Hunter's headquarters at Stono River, South Carolina, on the evening of April 8, 1863, having landed at Hilton Head the day before. He wrote to Nicolay at once, a long and effusive letter praising the army, the navy, and the tropical scenery. "I hear nothing but encouraging accounts of the fight yesterday in Charleston Harbor. Gen. [Truman] Seymour, Chief of Staff says we are sure to whip them. . . . The monitors behaved splendidly. The Keokuk was sunk and the Patapsco somewhat damaged . . ." but as a whole the fleet's performance, Hay believed, exceeded all expectations. Now an army expedition was afoot to attack Charleston by land. Although greatly outnumbered, the Federal troops, Hay reasoned, were more advantageously positioned and had the element of surprise.

He conveys the "kindest remembrances" from General Hunter to Nicolay. They had all been aboard the presidential train from Springfield to Washington two years earlier. Hunter must have been consulted when Mrs. Lander was assigned to his military department. He now saw her often, since she became supervisor of the nurses in the several Port Royal hospitals. Hay would be seeing her soon as well.

"I wish you could be down here," he writes to his office mate. "You would enjoy it beyond measure. The air is like June at noon & like May at morning and evening. . . . The sunsets unlike anything I ever saw before. . . . not gorgeous like ours but singularly quiet and solemn. The sun goes down over the pines through a sky like ashes-of-roses and hangs for an instant on the horizon like a bubble of blood. Then there is twilight, such as you dream about."

While the scenery continued to enchant him, Hay was soon disillusioned with the navy's performance. The next morning, he wrote again to Nicolay: "Alas for the pleasant prognostications of the military men! . . . the attack has been a failure! . . . Charleston is not to be ours as yet, and another instance is added to the many, of the President having clearer perceptions of military possibilities than any man in the Cabinet or the field. He thought it would fail." He had watched Lincoln argue with Welles, Fox, and Stanton over the plans to invade Charleston, and again he marveled at the superior military instincts and common sense of the prairie lawyer.

That morning, the secretary's business was to deliver his dispatches from the Navy Department and the president to Admiral Du Pont. He found Du Pont on board *Ironsides,* lying inside the "Bar" in Charleston Harbor with the rest of the monitor fleet, in the place where they had anchored after the engagement of April 8. While Du Pont was reading the messages, Hay conversed with Captain Christopher R. P. Rodgers, fleet captain of the South Atlantic Blockading Squadron. Even with the finest officers and perfect management, the experiment of taking the fortified harbor without powerful land forces was doomed. They had fought for forty minutes. Had they kept it up for twenty minutes more, the whole fleet would have been sunk. Rodgers allowed that "the failure would of course produce a most unhappy effect upon the country, which had so far trusted implicitly in the invincibility of the Monitors." Then he testified that every one of his officers believed that what they had attempted was impossible, and that they ought to be congratulated that "what is merely a failure had not been converted into a terrible disaster.

"This would have lost us the command of the coast, an irremediable disaster," Rodgers continued. "So the Admiral took the responsibility of avoiding the greater evil, by saving the fleet . . ."

Du Pont looked up from his reading, nodding in assent to Captain Rodgers's explanation. He added, touching the papers, "And as if we were to have a visible sign that an Almighty hand was over us for our good, the orders you have given me show how vast was the importance of my preserving this fleet . . . for the work which I agree with the President in thinking most momentous, the opening & the control of the Mississippi River."

There were tears in Du Pont's eyes, Hay informed the president—in a letter of April 10 detailing the entire scene—and "their whole conversation was as solemn as a scene of death." It consoled the admiral that the dispatches expressed Mr. Lincoln's opinion that the fleet of ironclads had more important work to do than the ill-advised invasion of Charleston Harbor. Du Pont had been opposed to it; his officers had denounced it; the commander in chief himself had thought ill of it; and the invasion was a significant military failure. Hay was witnessing one of the more pathetic personal tragedies of the Civil War.

In closing his letter to Lincoln, Hay writes: "I was several times struck by the identity of opinion and sentiment between Admiral Dupont and yourself. You had repeatedly uttered, during my last week in Washington, predictions which have become history." He wanted the president to know of the admiral's sadness and profound regret. Hay expresses his hope that "however the news may be received, that due honor may be given those who fought with such bravery and discretion, the losing fight."

During the next two weeks, Hay was stunned to hear of the bitter feelings toward Du Pont in the Navy and War departments in Washington. On April 16, General Hunter and Admiral Du Pont received orders to continue operations against Charleston, and Hay reported that the general was willing but the admiral was not. On the twenty-third, Hay expressed dismay that there was "much wrath at the report that Dupont intended to withdraw his fleet and abandon his [position] . . . He would have obeyed orders," wrote Hay—knowing Lincoln's wishes—"had he done so." It was just those orders to withdraw that he had delivered in his dispatch.

To his horror, Hay was observing the mad dissonance between the political leadership in the Navy Department under Gideon Welles and the commanders at the front, Hunter and Du Pont. Soon it would so demoralize the admiral that he would not act at all. "It is not for me to say," Hay wrote Nicolay, "what is or is not possible. My old ideas have been horribly shattered when I have seen two men [Welles and Du Pont] each of whom I had formerly considered an oracle on every subject connected with ships, accusing each other of ignorance and charlatanerie."

He adds that Du Pont is neither a fool nor a coward, and that he, Hay, is convinced that while the monitors have excellent defensive capabilities, Charleston Harbor proved they were not fit for aggressive operations. Hay's letters to Lincoln and Nicolay were helpful in easing relations among the White House, the Navy Department, and the command at Hilton Head. The attack on Charleston was indefinitely postponed, and the congressional commission appointed to investigate Du Pont's conduct proved inconclusive.

Secretary of the Navy Gideon Welles blamed Du Pont, and as commanding officer he was responsible. The admiral asked to be relieved of his command, and he would spend the rest of the war pushing papers in Washington, dying in 1865 at the age of sixty-one, a bitterly disappointed man.

HAY'S OFFICIAL RESPONSIBILITIES BEGAN with the delivery of the dispatches to Du Pont on April 9 and ended with his report of April 23, paraphrased above, but he found reasons and excuses to remain in that tropical paradise until June.

One of the reasons Hay went to South Carolina was to see his brother Charles. In his diary, he mentions briefly that Charlie was sick on April 12, and three days later noted, "Took Dr. Craven to visit Charlie. Pneumonia." His letters to his mother, his grandfather, and

Nicolay during the months of April and May tell the terrifying tale of Charlie's illness, how John saved his brother's life when the physicians couldn't, and how he could not possibly return to Washington until he was sure of Charlie's safety. On April 23, he told his mother that it was "absolutely providential that I came down here as I did." He writes that Charlie was misdiagnosed by the doctors as having bilious fever, and only when John insisted on a second opinion was the pneumonia discovered and treated. "It would have been an even chance, that in another week he would have had his lungs damaged for life, by ignorance and incompetence."

Hay was a devoted brother, and a fine writer, but a clumsy liar. Medical care in the area was excellent, and pneumonia cannot be mistaken for bilious fever. There was no treatment for pneumonia in those days other than bed rest; but on April 23, the brothers went on a weeklong cruise to Florida, where they took long walks and went horseback riding on the beaches. There is no more mention in Hay's diary of Charlie's illness—he appears there in glowing health. Yet on May 12, Hay writes to Nicolay, "I had intended to leave for the North today, but the uncertain state of Charlie's health prevents me," and on May 24, he apologizes: "I am very sorry that I have to leave. . . . But I have been away as long as my conscience will permit to tax yr. forbearance. Poor Charlie is in bad health. His lungs are affected. His physician thinks he must go North, which he flatly refuses to do as he thinks nothing ails him . . ." The next day, the brothers went horseback riding on the beach not once but twice. Hay does not report this to his mother or Nicolay.

So what was keeping John Hay in the neighborhood of Hilton Head Island and Beaufort, South Carolina, for two months in the spring, apart from five letters of military advice to John Nicolay? The fact is that he was having the time of his life sailing around the Sea Islands in the company of General David Hunter, a witty Irish journalist named Charles G. Halpine, who was serving as an adjutant to Hunter while writing for the *New York Herald,* and Jean Margaret Lander. Mrs. Lander lived in a magnificent rented house in Beaufort. Being an excellent equestrienne, she cantered all over the Port Royal area in her capacity as supervisor of nurses, to hospitals as far south as Parris Island and as far north as Edisto Beach.

Hay first visited Beaufort on Sunday, April 12. His diary that spring was constant but fragmented, poetically elliptical, with lists of names and impressions: "The forests. the Shell Road. Moss. the flowers Dogwood, Cherokee Rose, Honeysuckle, Jasmine . . ." Mrs. Lander's name appears several times in Hay's diary that spring, above and below ellipses and cross-hatchings.

He first mentions her on a Sunday, April 19, the day they dined with U.S. Army chaplain Mansfield French, an agent of the Freedmen's Bureau who lived in Beaufort. French, dubbed "the White Jesus" for his work on behalf of slaves and freed blacks, was one of the leaders of an extraordinary community of reformers in the Port Royal area that included General Hunter. He had formed one of the first regiments of black soldiers, and in May 1862, he had issued a proclamation freeing all slaves in his department—an unauthorized edict that Lincoln had to rescind. Many of the hospitals Mrs. Lander supervised treated black soldiers, and black nurses served on her staff. When Hunter formally appointed John Hay as a military aide, he told Nicolay, "I want my abolition record clearly defined and that will do it better than anything else . . ."

Hay visited Jean Margaret's beautiful home on May 19. On Thursday the twenty-first, he wrote that Mrs. Lander sang "Wha'll Be King but Charlie," a rousing Scots ballad in march rhythm and a minor key, a Jacobite lyric of the 1820s.

The news from Moidart came yestereen,
Will soon gar many fairly,
For ships o'war have just come in,
And landed Royal Charlie.

Come through the heather, around him gather,
You're all the welcomer early.
Around him cling, with all your kin,
For wha'll be King, but Charlie?

She had a rich alto voice, precise of pitch and accent, and Hay enjoyed her singing and reciting as much as she enjoyed performing for him.

Friday, May 22, was a perfect day—not a cloud in the sky—and the Broad River flowed toward the Confederate mainland like a wide ribbon of silver. The warblers and vireos were in tune. "Went this afternoon out to Barnwell's place on the Broad River & had a blackberry picnic under charge of Mrs. Lander. . . . the life and soul of the affair." They dined within sight of the rebel army, in a grove near the old Robert Barnwell mansion, the ancestral home of a family of secessionist U.S. legislators. It was a dilapidated Romanesque house with a large piazza. An avenue of palmettos and oaks meeting at the tops made a colonnade that ran far into the distance, where they could see the colored troops of the First South Carolina camped in their palmetto huts, and the Stars and Stripes rippling in the breeze. Near the riverbank, the brigade band began to play. John Hay and his petite companion Jean Margaret joined General Rufus Saxton and his wife in a dance as the waxing moon rose over the water.

She arranged the picnic in his honor. Then, with the help of Mrs. Saxton, Jean Lander would produce a more formal "farewell" reception at the plantation of the author and reformer Frances Dana Gage. Her mansion commanded a spectacular view of Port Royal harbor and the ocean beyond. They could see the fleet of warships near Hilton Head. On this occasion, Hay would be called upon, as a spokesman for President Lincoln, to address the freed blacks on Mrs. Gage's plantation. A journalist from the *New York Tribune* paraphrased the secretary's remarks.

> Mr. Hay, in eloquent yet to the blacks comprehensible language, as one who in official position stood near the person of their good friend, told them that the President took the greatest interest in their welfare; that he considered this military department one of the most important in the country, not simply on account of its military character, but that here great social and educational projects were being worked out, upon the success of

which would probably depend the welfare of the race. It gratified the President, he said, to hear that they were learning to read and write, to work for themselves, to accumulate property, and manifest a disposition to fight, if necessary, for its defense . . .

When Hay had concluded his speech, the blacks came forth to shake hands with him, and three cheers went up for General Saxton, three cheers for Mr. Lincoln, and then an old man standing on an old broken plow called for three cheers for the president's general—pointing to John Hay. At last, there were rounds of cheers for Mrs. Saxton, and Mrs. Lander, "given with a will which fairly made the old oak overhead thrill with joy."

The anonymous newsman from the *Tribune* attended these events and cryptically mentioned "an eye for the picturesque, and not a little true artistic genius were required to arrange and group the details so as to satisfy the most fastidious; and who more competent than the accomplished Col. [Thomas] Higginson . . . and one whose name in this connection I am not permitted to mention but who is an artist, original and pure, a Christian, sincere and active; a woman, noble and full of the best impulses." The woman whose name he must not mention in that connection, he mentions in the next column: Jean Davenport Lander.

Colonel Higginson, writing to his mother, described how Mrs. Lander had "got up" the party "for a young Mr. Hay, President Lincoln's private secretary, a nice young fellow, who unfortunately looks about seventeen and is oppressed with the necessity of behaving like seventy."

This was an oppression of circumstances that the former "Infant Phenomenon," the actress Jean Margaret Davenport, could understand all too well, and sympathize with—more than any other woman Hay would ever know.

CHAPTER EIGHT

BLOOD AND GOLD

The May week that John Hay spent in Beaufort with Mrs. Lander, William Stoddard was stricken with typhoid. Any hopes that the poet may have had of prolonging his tropical romance were in vain, as Nicolay and the president needed his help in Washington.

That month was one of the most discouraging in all of Mr. Lincoln's term of office. The failure of Admiral Du Pont's fleet in Charleston Harbor was the prelude to a series of military disappointments. General Joseph Hooker, with an army of 130,000, was beaten by Robert E. Lee's force of 60,000 at Chancellorsville, a battle that every northerner expected to win. A friend of Lincoln's who was with him on May 6, 1863, when news of the defeat arrived, said that never "did he seem to be so broken, so dispirited, and so ghostlike." He walked up and down the room, his hands clasped behind his back crying, "My God! My God! What will the country say!"

Stoddard was working late that night, and he recalled "the slow, heavy, regular tread of the President's feet, pacing up and down in his room . . ." He had letters that required Mr. Lincoln's attention but couldn't bring himself to add to the burden that resonated in the sound of those footsteps. The secretary worked until three o'clock in the morning and left stealthily; turning at the head of the stairs, he could still hear the president's footfall. Returning at eight o'clock in the morning, he looked into Lincoln's office. "He is there still, and there is nothing to indicate that he has been out of it."

General William Starke Rosecrans was stalled in eastern Tennessee. At Port Hudson, Louisiana, on May 27, General Nathaniel Banks's Federal army of 13,000 attacked 4,500 Confederates under Major General Franklin Gardner and lost 1,995 men to the rebels' 235. Lincoln would not blame any of his generals, so the newspapers, many politicians, and much of the public censured the commander in chief for all the carnage.

A letter from Nicolay to an editor of the *Chicago Tribune* on June 19 provides a view of the pressure upon Lincoln, and the new role of the White House secretary as a public relations agent. On the sixteenth, the *Tribune* editor had written to report that they had recently heard that the president had said to Senator Sumner "that he had not seen a copy of the *Chicago Tribune* for four months. Now as it is mailed regularly we wish to know whether it is received at the White House. If it miscarries we will have that corrected. If he does not want it—declines to read it—we will discontinue sending it. Please answer . . ."

The answer is quintessential Nicolay, candid and dignified, but fierce in its defense of his office, eloquent in extolling the president, and blistering in its denunciation of the editor's pretensions. He begins by assuring the gentleman that the *Tribune* is regularly received and kept with other newspapers on a table in his office. He sees it, and so do others, especially "Western men who happen here." Now then: the president requests his secretary to say, simply, that he has no desire to ban the *Tribune,* but rather would be glad to receive it "so long as in your kindness you may please to send it." That is all.

Nicolay, however, desires "to add a word on my own responsibility."

Excepting the Washington Dailies, in which he carefully reads the telegraphic dispatches, the President rarely ever looks at any papers,

simply for want of leisure to do so. In this the Tribune fares as well
as . . . all others. Still I think . . . he would have been attracted to your
journal more frequently as to an old and familiar friend, if it had
not in that time contained so much which he had a right to expect
it would at least have left unsaid.

I can assure you . . . the president's task here is no child's play.
If you imagine that *any man* could attempt its performance, and
escape adverse criticism, you have read history in vain, and studied
human nature without profit. But was it not to be expected that those
of the President's friends, who knew him long and intimately—who
understood his integrity and his devotion . . . would at least abstain
from judging him in the blindness of haste, and condemning him
in the bitterness of ill-temper? It does seem to me that this much
was due to generosity and charity for the fiery trial which he is
called upon to pass through here . . .

Let me repeat that these are exclusively my own thoughts
and not the President's . . .

Let me add that I desire to continue reading the Tribune—
reserving only the privilege of finding as much fault with it as it
finds with the Administration, which I know is unselfishly endeav-
oring to do its whole duty in the crisis.

William Stoddard also continued to do his part as the president's
advocate, in the pages of the *New York Examiner*. Stoddard's column
of June 18, 1863, praises Lincoln's letter "To Erastus Corning and
Others," a disquisition of several thousand words published in the *New
York Tribune* on June 12. Corning and other New York Democrats had
denounced the president for suspending the writ of habeas corpus for
the expedience of making military arrests. Lincoln—in his thorough
legalistic response—politely explained that the Constitution secured
"the right to a speedy and public trial by an impartial jury" before
and after a civil war, but not during times of rebellion. Now, with spies
and traitors in his vicinity, the president had no choice but to detain
them at once in order to secure public safety. "Perhaps the event of

the week," Stoddard writes, "is the reply of the President to the Albany Democrats. It is a grand document, strong, plain, simple . . . yet dignified as it becomes the ruler of a great people when the nation is listening to what he says. It should be printed in every Northern paper, and read by every citizen."

Lincoln needed public support. After the Confederate victory at Chancellorsville, Lee planned a second invasion of the North. He began moving the Army of Northern Virginia, seventy-five thousand strong, away from Fredericksburg and west toward the Potomac. On June 15, the rebels overran the Federal garrison at Winchester. General Hooker informed the president that "it is not in my power to prevent" an invasion. Lincoln called up a hundred thousand militia from the states of Maryland, West Virginia, Pennsylvania, and Ohio.

Rumors of Lee's rapid advance spread panic in the mid-Atlantic cities from Baltimore to Harrisburg, Pennsylvania. The price of gold had been rising as the result of Union defeats; now the fear of a Confederate invasion spread to the financial markets as well. The price of gold was soaring, and Stoddard—the shrewd gambler—was "shorting" the metal and piling up greenbacks. He wrote from his sick bed that "we almost pray that Lee *may* move forward, and learn at some new Antietam [where Lee had once failed] that the gates of the North are securely closed against the armies of the Rebellion."

These words were prophetic. At the end of June, General Lee was in Pennsylvania, and the Federal army—under its new commander, George Gordon Meade—was moving north to meet the Confederate invasion at Gettysburg.

"THE FOG OF WAR," a phrase coined by the Prussian military theorist Carl Philipp von Clausewitz nearly two centuries ago, has become a cliché because of its poetic precision in expressing the uncertainty of data, not only in the heat of battle but in its immediate aftermath.

Technically the three-day Battle of Gettysburg was over on July 3, 1863. But for all the hours Lincoln spent in the telegraph office reading dispatches from General Meade, it would be weeks before the men in Washington understood the epic scope of the battle or the process of maneuvers and mistakes that produced the Union victory. All that was exactly understood on July 4 is that Lee's army was retreating from Gettysburg and that there had been unprecedented carnage on both sides. The actual numbers of dead and wounded—out of 88,000 Federals engaged, 3,155 killed, 14,529 were wounded; out of 75,000 Confederate troops, 3,903 were killed, 18,735 wounded—would not be known, much less comprehended, until November, when the president and his secretaries would attend the dedication of a new cemetery on the battlefield.

Meanwhile, the Executive Mansion was in turmoil, lashed by the contrary winds of hope and dread. On July 2, Mrs. Lincoln was thrown from her carriage on the road from the Soldiers' Home, and sustained a serious wound in the back of her skull. It was suspected that a saboteur had loosened the bolts on the carriage seats. When she arrived at the White House, limping, with a bandage wound around her head, Lincoln was at the War Department reviewing dispatches from the front. Receiving word of her injury, he hurried to her side. She appeared like some twisted reflection from the tide of the distant battle.

Despite her head wound, and over the objections of many frightened politicians, Mrs. Lincoln worked with William Stoddard in making the arrangements for an Independence Day celebration. "There will be a Fourth of July celebration in Washington this year, if we can hear Lee's cannon all the while, and if we adjourn from the speaker's stand to the trenches," he wrote. The commissioner of public buildings gave him the lawn south of the White House for the speaker's stand. He engaged the Marine Band. Stoddard endeavored to reassure the president's wife that the capital was in no danger from General Lee. "No, Mrs. Lincoln, all that's left of him after beating Meade will be too lame to march as far as Baltimore."

"There was never before such a Fourth of July in Washington!" Stoddard declared. "What a procession! The Marine Band and the Marines. Regiment after regiment sweeps down the avenue, between the long files of the division which has been halted at parade rest along the curbstones on either side. How well the cavalry look, and the artillery!"

Benjamin French, the commissioner of public buildings, agreed. "It was a glorious day in Washington. Everybody seemed determined to make it known publicly that secession was at a low ebb in the Federal City." Stoddard had made it happen by sheer force of his own enthusiasm, which he suspected was shared by others. From the early morning on, one could hear the racket of firecrackers, the blasts of pistols and muskets; and the noise of bells and explosions went on until nearly midnight.

"It was really a glorious Independence, and its effect was very much heightened by the exhilarating news from our army which was received about 10 o'clock a.m. and was soon spread all over the city." The president had issued his press release, "news from the Army of the Potomac, up to 10 p.m. of the 3rd is such as to cover that Army with the highest honor." Stoddard had more than one reason to be ecstatic. "The best of it all was that good news from Gettysburg and Vicksburg came tumbling in on that celebration, to make it cheerful, and that the price of gold was tumbling at a rate that made my dinner bill of small account." He had hosted a party of event organizers at a restaurant that night, running up a high tab.

On the morning of July 7, General Grant wired the War Department that he had at last captured Vicksburg, Mississippi. Strategically, this control of the river was as significant as Meade's success, thus far, in Pennsylvania. The tide of the war had turned. And now if General Meade would prevent Lee's army from crossing the Potomac—pursue and destroy it—there would be nothing standing between the Union army and Richmond.

John Hay noticed that President Lincoln was in high spirits on July 11, "as he had pretty good evidence that the enemy were still on the North side of the Potomac and Meade had announced his intention of attacking them in the morning." Lincoln envisioned a brilliant success. Although he had been frustrated by Meade's delay since July 4, he now believed the general would "show sufficient activity to inflict the Coup de grace upon the flying rebels." As the rain pattered against the windows all the next afternoon, the men in the White House saw that even the weather moved in their favor, as it would be even more difficult for Lee's army to ford a river swollen with rain. Nicolay wrote to his fiancée "that Meade's army is perhaps today attacking the rebel force under Lee somewhere between Williamsport and Hagerstown." The armies had been so close, "a battle must almost necessarily result. . . . If Meade can gain another decisive victory the rebel cause will hardly be able to recover from the disaster."

But on Monday the thirteenth, when Meade still had not attacked Lee's stranded army, Hay saw that "the President begins to grow anxious and impatient about Meade's silence." Hay told him that indeed the enemy might escape by way of Falling Waters, just below Williamsport, Maryland, if Meade did not strike quickly. And the next morning, Hay found the president crestfallen. Meade's dispatches of the night before had been so cautious and timid that Lincoln "feared he would do nothing," and by midday came the telegram "stating that our worst fears were true. The enemy had gotten away unhurt. The Pres[ident] was deeply grieved."

"We had them within our grasp," he told his secretary. "We had only to stretch forth our hands & they were ours. And nothing I could say or do could make the Army move." The president had been in an agony of frustration with Meade for days, ever since he had heard the general's order to "drive the invader from our soil." It reminded Lincoln darkly of McClellan. "The same spirit that moved McClellan to claim a great victory because Pennsylvania and Maryland were safe. The hearts of 10 million people sank within them when McClellan raised that shout last fall. Will our Generals never get that idea out of their heads? The whole country is *our* soil."

So Lee's battered Army of Northern Virginia survived to fight for another twenty months, prolonging a war that might have been over in the summer of 1863 if the Union generals had followed the president's orders.

STODDARD HAD MADE A killing in the gold market. He was grateful for that, and the greater sense of independence that money brings. But he was unwell. "What with excitement and overwork and Potomac River malaria, I found myself out of order." His physician told him that no medicine would do him nearly as much good as a trip north to the seashore. So he applied to Mr. Lincoln for a furlough and obtained it.

Bound for Syracuse and New London with his younger brother Henry, Stoddard reached Manhattan on July 11, in the midst of the terrible Draft Riot of 1863. He was evidently able-bodied enough to be called into action by Union general Ward B. Burnett, and with holstered pistol and knife was sent down to Wall Street to guard the Treasury Building—whose greenbacks had been so kind to him. The general swore the brothers in, "and we were posted," Stoddard wrote, "that is, we were put temporarily in charge of the Treasury, under the impression that there was to be an immediate attack on it."

Gettysburg had stripped the city of militia, and the police were hardly able to control the mob. "The air was hot, sultry, full of smoke from many fires. The crowds of rushing men. The frantic women. The contradictory rumors. The swift marchings here and there." It seemed to Stoddard, in his weary state, like a nightmare that had nothing to do with the real world. He was transferred to the customhouse, and another post and another, until he passed out in a hallway of the Metropolitan Hotel. "Stronger men than I, seasoned policemen, were utterly prostrated with the heat." Sometime the next night he was "invalided" and caught the next train to Syracuse.

He would be gone for two months. The excitement and constant pressure in the Executive Mansion had also worn Nicolay down. The president granted him leave to visit Springfield and Pittsfield, then to journey to Colorado to meet William P. Dole, commissioner of the Bureau of Indian Affairs. There, Nicolay was to assist in concluding a treaty with the Ute Indians in the San Juan Valley. Nicolay left Washington on July 16, five days after Stoddard; delays and postponements of the meeting with the Indians gave Nicolay time to go buffalo hunting in the Nebraska country, and fishing in the Colorado territory and the Rocky Mountains. The senior secretary would not return to Washington until early November.

It has often been said that the relationship between Abraham Lincoln and John Hay resembled the intimate friendship between

George Washington and his young aide-de-camp Alexander Hamilton. In both cases, the friendship transcended the imbalance of power that usually characterizes the dynamic between mentor and pupil, master and apprentice. Lincoln and Hay were bonded by a similar sense of humor, a fondness for wordplay, puns, and droll stories. After Lincoln, Hay was considered the best storyteller in Washington. Hay may have been more widely read than Lincoln, but they shared a passion for Shakespeare, Poe, and poets of the vernacular like Burns and Lowell.

During the slow summer months of 1863, after Gettysburg, Hay and Lincoln consolidated their friendship. The great armies were stalled. Mrs. Lincoln had gone to the White Mountains of New Hampshire to recuperate, taking Robert and Tad with her. Stoddard and Nicolay were both on furlough. "This town is as dismal now as a defaced tombstone. Everybody has gone," he wrote to Nicolay. So, for much of the time, Hay had Mr. Lincoln all to himself, in the White House office and at the summer cottage four miles north where they spent many nights, riding off from the White House on horseback at twilight.

Hay's diary from this period includes vivid vignettes of the president in relaxed and unguarded moments. Lincoln was totally at ease in the younger man's company, and took delight in it. On July 18, Hay worked with the president and Judge Joseph Holt for six hours reviewing court-martials, a grim duty that Lincoln hated and tried to avoid. Hay "was amused at the eagerness with which the President caught at any fact which would justify him in saving the life of a condemned soldier." He was merciless only in cases where cruelty was undeniable. Lincoln was particularly averse to executing soldiers accused of cowardice, saying "it would frighten the poor devils too terribly, to shoot them." He peppered the sessions with gallows humor. He told the story of an Illinois lawyer (probably himself) who counseled a man who had stolen a hog and been arrested, and released on bail, "to go & get a drink & suggesting that the water was better in Tennessee," and how the thief was never seen again; and they all had a good laugh before returning to the awful questions of firing squads and pardons.

"It would do you good," Hay wrote to Nicolay, "to see how I daily hold the Tycoon's nose to the Court Martial grindstone."

The next morning, a Sunday, Lincoln was in high spirits, and gave Hay some lines of doggerel he had written.

GEN LEE'S INVASION OF
THE NORTH WRITTEN BY HIMSELF

In Eighteen Sixty three, with pomp and mighty swell
Me and Jeff's Confederacy went forth to sack Phil-del,
The Yankees they got arter us and giv us particular hell,
And we skedadled back again, and didn't sack Phil-del.

It had been a terrible season of droughts and heavy rains, but now the air was light and clear and the gardens blooming. On a whim, Hay went to church, where he heard "a dry priest declaim against science and human reason" and then "glorify the dogma of the Immaculate Conception." The new Jesuit sanctuary of red brick, up on North Capitol Street, had a superb painting above the altar of St. Aloysius Gonzaga receiving his first communion. Constantino Brumidi, the noted painter of the Capitol frescoes, had created the image using pastor Bernadine Wiget in the frame; and the model for Aloysius's mother was none other than Adele Cutts Douglas, the widow of Stephen Douglas.

In the afternoon, Hay rejoined Lincoln, and the men discussed "the position at Williamsport the other day." This was the town in western Maryland, on the Potomac, where Meade's army might have overtaken General Lee's. The president was still fuming over the unfinished business after Gettysburg. "Our Army held the war in the hollow of their hand & they would not close it," he told Hay. "We had gone through all the labor of tilling and planting an enormous crop & when it was ripe we did not harvest it. Still, I am very grateful to Meade for the great service he did at Gettysburg."

On a hot night in late July, Hay rode out to the Soldiers' Home with Lincoln. They discussed philology, the study of literature and language, and more specifically, the study of speech as the medium of literature, and the way language sheds light on human history. It is a science, Hay wrote, "for which the Tycoon has a little indulged inclination." More than a little. Under the influence of Walt Whitman, in 1858, Lincoln had written the curious lecture "On Discoveries and Inventions," in which he argued that the ultimate divine discovery and invention is speech, "articulate sounds rattled off from the tongue," and that "*writing*—the art of communicating thoughts to the mind, through the eye—is the great invention of the world. Great in the astonishing range of analysis and combination . . . great in enabling us to converse with the dead, the absent, and the unborn, at all distances of time and of space . . ."

That is the way these friends whiled away the hours that summer—in reading and conversation. What a privilege for the young man, and how can we help but envy him? Lincoln's intellect was at the peak of its powers, and so was his command of language. All summer long, he was using Hay as a sounding board, reading aloud to him from Shakespeare, trying out ideas on him. Within four months, he would write an address of 272 words that would put the living in touch with the dead and link his own name forever with immortal orators: Pericles, Cicero, and Daniel Webster.

On July 31, they discussed the devilishly complex alternatives for freeing the slaves: for example, the "Missouri system which is faulty in *postponing* the benefits of freedom to the slave instead of giving him vested interest therein." They discussed colonization—in Africa or America—an idea that once appealed to Lincoln; now, like Hay, he was opposed to it. "I had considerable talk with the President this evening on the subject. It deeply interests him now. He considers it the greatest question ever presented to practical statesmanship. While the rest are grinding their little . . . organs for their own glorification the old man is working with the strength of a giant and the purity of an angel to do this great work."

Nicolay was hunting buffalo near Fort Kearney, Nebraska, on August 7, when Hay wrote him a long, newsy letter, mostly about the fallout from Lincoln's recent military draft. He mentions a number of friends who have been pressed into service, including the president's black valet, William Johnson, the headwaiter at Willard's, and Henry Stoddard, William's brother, who used to come from his desk at the Treasury Department on breaks to chat with the secretaries. Hay says he is growing apathetic "& write blackguardly articles for the *Chronicle. . . .*" The piece published that very day concerns the recent elections in Kentucky—which favored the Union candidates—and the reluctance of the Democrats to accept the Emancipation Proclamation and the drafting of Negro soldiers.

In the same letter, he offers this glowing report: "The Tycoon is in fine whack. I have rarely seen him more serene and busy. He is managing this war, the draft, foreign relations, and planning reconstruction of the Union, all at once. . . ." He rules the cabinet, and "there is no cavil." Hay is convinced "that the good of the country absolutely demands that he should be kept where he is until this thing is over. There is no man in the country, so wise so gentle and so firm. I believe the hand of God placed him where he is." From his youthful skepticism of 1861, Hay has come a long way to arrive at this assessment of Abraham Lincoln. And Hay's opinion—which comforted Lincoln whether or not this was spoken outright—anticipates that of most of the leading Republicans by about four months.

On a fine bright Sunday, August 9, Hay accompanied the president to Gardner's Gallery on the northeast corner of Seventh and D Street to get his picture taken. This must have been a source of amusement, if not wisecracks, from the secretary. No president, and very few people, had ever spent as much time in photographer's lofts and studios as did Lincoln; and it would be many years before any president would see as many portraits of himself. Lincoln was not a vain man, but he courted photographers as if his mission depended as much upon his image as his presence. Perhaps he hoped that some ambrotype or silver print might reveal a part of himself that he could not discover in a looking glass, a key to self-knowledge. Maybe he saw the picture frame as a window, like writing, that opened upon future generations.

The gallery, across from the colossal Patent Office, was on the third floor of the Sutler's Books and Stationary building, an old brick structure with a pitched roof and striped wraparound awnings. Shoppers could browse the stacks of books on the sidewalks in good weather. The president and his companion passed through a side door and up the stairway to the bright studio. Mr. Alexander Gardner, in shirtsleeves, was charmed, always happy to see this customer. Mr. Lincoln, in a sleek coat of black broadcloth that fell gracefully over his knees, a white shirt with a short collar and small black satin bow tie, and a black vest with a single watch chain, was invited to stand against a gray backdrop. The fingers of his left hand made a tripod upon two books placed on a round marble-topped table with an ornate Victorian pedestal of wood. His clenched right hand was placed rather awkwardly at his waist, as if it might be holding a saw or a carving knife but is aware that it ought to be doing something in this odd moment of temporal suspension. His face was void of expression, his eyes gazing over Gardner's head in the standard stereographic pose.

Next, the photographer sat him down on a cane-bottomed chair beside the marble-topped table, and moved the tripod closer to his subject. He asked Mr. Lincoln please to cross his right leg over his left, place his elbow upon the book on the table, then relax, and look directly into the lens, as if the box camera were a friend who had come calling. Mr. Lincoln obliged. In this portrait, there is life. The beautiful gray eyes are welcoming and there is humor in the features, the shadow of a smile. This was Lincoln's favorite. "The imperial[-size] photograph, in which the head leans upon the hand, I regard as the best I have yet seen," he wrote to Gardner. Clearly Lincoln was *pursuing* something, a pictorial idea of himself that Hay and Nicolay later claimed would never be captured on the glass.

Half a dozen photographs were taken during that session, as John Hay watched and chatted with Mr. Lincoln about the war and the Confederacy. "The rebel power is at last beginning to disintegrate," he told Hay between poses. "They will break to pieces if we only stand firm now." The president stood firm for Mr. Gardner, his craggy face monumental. Talking of opposing factions in Richmond, Lincoln observed that one group believed "still in foreign intervention, Northern treason & other chimeras, and the other, the Administration party [Jefferson Davis et al.] trust to nothing but the army." Lincoln believed that "Davis is right. His army is his only hope, not only against us but against his own people. If that were crushed the people would be ready to swing back to their own bearings."

Of the images Gardner captured on that summer day, John Hay kept one albumen print for himself, a head-and-shoulders portrait of Lincoln looking gravely and intensely toward the camera. It remained with Hay and his descendants for many years, and caused a sensation when it was first published a century later.

THE REST OF AUGUST was mercifully uneventful, notwithstanding the continuing uproar over the draft in New York and Ohio. On the thirteenth of the month, the *New York Times* reported that Jean Davenport Lander had returned from Beaufort, South Carolina, due to illness, having resigned her position as supervisor of nurses. Soon John Hay would see her again.

That Thursday, Hay rode with the president and Mr. Seward up to the Capitol to inspect the statuary of the east pediment. Regarding—with a knowing eye—Hiram Powers's sculpture of the woodchopper, the president frowned disapprovingly, remarking that the axman "did not make a sufficiently clean cut." There was often sparkling conversation between Seward and Lincoln, and Hay had a fine memory for it. Seward declared, "Slavery is dead: the only trouble is that the fools who support it from the outside do not recognize this, and will not till the thing is over. . . . though slavery is dead, the Democratic party insists on devoting itself to guarding the corpse." That was the afternoon that Hay recorded the now famous, bitterly ironic comment on the marriage between politics and war. Wryly referring to New York governor Horatio Seymour, who opposed the draft with an eye to appeasement and pacifism, Seward called him "silly and short-sighted. One fundamental principle of politics is to be always on the side of your country in a war. It kills any party to oppose a war . . . If you want to sicken your opponents with their own war, go in for it till they give up."

Not to be left out of this badinage, Lincoln chimed in: "Butterfield of Illinois was asked at the beginning of the Mexican War if he were not opposed to it; he said '[N]o, I opposed one War. I am now perpetually in favor of war, pestilence and famine.'"

In the evenings, the men strolled down to the Tiber Creek behind the White House for target practice. Inventor Christopher Miner Spencer, a thirty-year-old "quiet little Yankee," according to Hay, had built a repeating rifle, a seven-shot magazine gun that was a marvel of engineering.

Against a lumber pile on the north bank of the stream, they set up targets two inches wide and took turns firing the rifle from thirty paces away. Spencer was an excellent shot. The president, being farsighted, was surprisingly good. Hay, mindful of the real purpose of the invention, archly described it as "a wonderful gun loading with absolutely contemptible simplicity and ease with seven balls & firing the whole readily and deliberately in less than half a minute." His own marksmanship "was the most lamentably bad"; he feared his eyesight was failing, as he could scarcely see the target. Hay reflected that Spencer had "sold himself in relentless slavery to his idea for six weary years before it was perfect . . ." Before the war's end, some two hundred thousand of the deadly rifles were in the hands of soldiers. Many thousands were killed or maimed by them.

On another clear evening, Saturday the twenty-second, Hay and a Mrs. Young accompanied the president to the National Observatory. Just six blocks west of the White House on E Street, the site commanded a splendid view of the Potomac. The president, fascinated by mechanical and scientific things, loved the observatory, whose principal function was the preparation of wind and current charts, hydrographical studies, and the regulation of the city's clocks. Astronomy was a secondary interest of the observatory, but there were three fine telescopes. In the West Wing was a seven-foot-long transit instrument mounted upon two seven-foot-high granite piers, used for measuring the transit time of stars and planets over the meridian. Connected to it was an astronomical clock to denote sidereal time. In the South Wing was a vertical transit, a library, star charts, and a normal clock with a gridiron pendulum everyone admired—in a year's time it was accurate within eleven seconds.

The main telescope set in the dome was more than fourteen feet long with an object glass that had a range of magnifying power from eighty to six hundred, depending upon the stillness of the earth. The slightest tremor at the height—caused, say, by cannon fire—would throw a star out of the focal plane. Mr. Lincoln, John Hay, and Mrs. Young took turns peering into the eyepiece as the superintendent adjusted the equatorial in the dome. The president, stooping and squinting, had many questions, and he would chuckle as a star came into focus. On this night, they viewed the moon in its second quarter, and Arcturus, the huge orange star in the constellation of Boötes, the "bear keeper."

Later, when they had said good night to the lady, Hay rode out with the president to the Soldiers' Home. They sat in the drawing room until a late hour, for it was the last time they would have together alone that summer. Lincoln read aloud to Hay from Shakespeare: the last act of *King Henry VI, Part 3* and the opening scenes of *Richard III*. It was an interesting choice, demonstrating just how well this president knew his Shakespeare, from the obscure trilogy covering the downfall of King Henry to the popular historical tragedy that pursues the adventures of Henry's murderer Richard Plantagenet (Duke of Gloucester).

Lincoln was fascinated by the thematic continuity from the murder scene at the end of *Henry VI* to Gloucester's famous monologue at the beginning of *Richard III*, "Now is the winter of our discontent."

KING HENRY VI

And thus I prophesy, that many a thousand
Which now mistrust no parcel of my fear,
And many an old man's sight and many a widow's
And many an orphan's water-standing eye—
Men for the sons, wives for their husbands,
And orphans for their parents' timeless death
Shall rue the hour that ever thou wast born.
The owl shrieked at thy birth,—an evil sign;

The night-crow cried, aboding luckless time
. . . .
Thy mother felt more than a mother's pain
And, yet brought forth less than a mother's hope,
To wit, an indigested and deformed lump,
Not like the fruit of such a godly tree.

Mr. Lincoln read on and on, and Hay listened, rapt; the devastation that Shakespeare prophesies was all too familiar. Was it possible that the good president in any way identified with the strangely shaped Duke of Gloucester, who declares, at the end of *Henry VI:*

Then, since the heavens shaped my body so,
Let hell make crook'd my mind to answer it.

And at the opening of *Richard III:*

But I that am not shaped for sportive tricks,
Nor made to court an amorous looking glass,
I, that am rudely stamped and want love's majesty
To strut before a wanton ambling nymph;
I that am curtail'd of this fair proportion,
Cheated of feature by dissembling nature,
Deformed, unfinished, sent before my time
Into this breathing world, scarce half made up
And that so lamely and unfashionable
That dogs bark at me as I halt by them . . .

As the hands of the grandfather clock neared the summit of midnight, Hay yawned and nodded, heading for a dream far from Shakespeare's battles and villains, perhaps a tropical idyll or some other Elysium where a dreamlike woman would be waiting, Margaret—not the Margaret of King Henry and Richard III, but the astonishing Jean Margaret, who at nine years of age had sent lightning through the theater world when she played, incredibly, the role that Mr. Lincoln was now reading in his melodious voice.

Why, I, in this weak piping time of peace,
Have no delight to pass away the time,
Unless to pass my shadow in the sun
And descant on my own deformity . . .

Lincoln—Hay recalled—with tender concern for his audience of one, read "till my heavy eye-lids caught his considerable notice & he sent me to bed."

They rose early the next morning, a Sunday, ate their breakfast, and rode to the White House. Lincoln went off to the oval library to write a long, memorable letter to James Conkling, in which he defends the Emancipation Proclamation and the arming of Negroes to fight for the Union. It is a poetic letter, infused with the spirit of the Bard of Avon.

The signs look better. The Father of Waters again goes un-vexed to the sea. Thanks to the great North-West for it. Nor yet wholly to them. Three hundred miles up, they met New England, Empire, Key-Stone, and Jersey, hewing their way right and left. The Sunny South too, in more colors than one, also lent a hand. . . . Peace does not appear so distant as it did. I hope it will come soon, and come to stay; and so come as to be worth the keeping in all future time. It will then have been proved that, among free men, there can be no successful appeal from the ballot to the bullet. . . . And then, there will be some black men who can remember that, with silent tongue . . . and steady eye, and well-poised bayonet, they have helped mankind on to this great consummation . . .

Across the hall, Hay was folding shirts, packing his trunk, preparing to leave for a two-week vacation at the seashore in Long Branch, New Jersey. He told Nicolay that he had become frightened at "The brow so haggard the chin so peaked/Fronting me silent in the glass." So he had sent for Stoddard, "who had been giving the Northern watering places for the last two months a model of high breeding and unquestionable deportment." Hay had also agreed to give the commencement speech at his alma mater, Brown University, on September 2. Stoddard would manage the office while he was gone.

STODDARD HAD BEEN ILL when he left the city in early July, and he was not altogether recovered when Hay asked him to return. Yet he reported promptly in the last week of August, and Hay passed the baton to him.

With fond amusement, Stoddard recalled the afternoon of August 26, when the president called him into his office. He was finishing up the communication to James Conkling quoted above. Lincoln had composed the letter in response to an invitation to return to Springfield and attend a meeting of "Union Men" who objected to the president's policies, particularly the Emancipation Proclamation. Since Mr. Lincoln could not leave Washington, Conkling himself would read the president's letter aloud at the meeting.

"Sit down over there," said the president, gesturing to a chair across from him at the long cabinet table. Mr. Lincoln was sitting at the head of the table with his back to the light of the open windows. A pile of foolscap paper lay in front of him covered with closely written paragraphs with blots and cross-hatchings. "I can always tell more about a thing after I've heard it read aloud, and know how it sounds."

So Stoddard took his seat. He asked Mr. Lincoln if he would like him to read the letter to him.

"No, no," said the president, fixing his spectacles on his nose. "What I want is an audience. Nothing sounds the same to me, when there isn't anybody to hear it and find fault with it."

"I don't know, Mr. President," the secretary replied, with humility that the president doubted Stoddard possessed, "that I'd care to criticize anything you'd written." Mr. Lincoln knew from Stoddard's journalism that he criticized everything, including presidential speeches. And so he insisted. "Yes, you will. Everybody *else* will. It's just what I want you to do." While he was speaking, Mr. Lincoln was touching up the manuscript with his pen, drawing lines through words and scribbling notes. When he first began to read, Stoddard had the feeling that Lincoln had forgotten about him. The feeling was short-lived. "He is more an orator than a writer," Stoddard said, "and he is quickly warmed up to the place where his voice rises and his long right arm goes out, and he speaks to you somewhat as if you were a hundred thousand people . . . and as if he believes that something like fifty thousand of you do not at *all* agree with him."

Now and then Lincoln would pause, take a deep breath, and look across the table at his secretary to see how he was taking it. "I concealed my thoughts artistically," Stoddard recalled, knowing the president's powers of intuition, "but it was a long and clearly significant letter, now famous, to all mankind by way of certain eminent citizens of Illinois . . ." When Lincoln had reached the end, "Let us diligently apply the means, never doubtful that a just God, in his own good time, will give us the rightful result," he put down the page and laughed silently.

He asked his secretary if there was any criticism he wanted to make. The audience of one demurred, saying that he thought the letter "as nearly beyond criticism as it well could be," but as the president looked steadily at him, Stoddard admitted, respectfully, "there's one place . . ." Lincoln handed the pages over, and begged him to point to the spot.

So Stoddard drew Mr. Lincoln's attention to the long paragraph in which he extols the valor of the army and navy. "Some people," he said, "will find fault with this: 'Nor must Uncle Sam's Web-feet be forgotten. At all the watery margins they have been present. Not only on the deep sea, the broad bay, and the rapid river, but also up the narrow muddy bayou, and wherever the ground was a little damp, they have been, and made their tracks.'"

Now the president's silent laugh became an audible chuckle. He allowed that he believed it might be just that part that the journalist would find fault with. But then he said he thought he would leave it as it was—that people would get his meaning.

"I never saw a web-footed gunboat in all my life," Stoddard insisted.

"Some of them did get ashore though," said the president, grinning, before thanking his secretary for his attention, and then excusing him. He never did change the bizarre phrase.

"Lincoln knows just how that thing will sound in the ears of millions," Stoddard wrote, "and he doesn't care a corn-husk for the literary critics here or in Europe."

THOSE QUIET DAYS IN August and September were likely the only ones when Stoddard had the president all to himself, so several of his undated memories and impressions of Mr. Lincoln belong to that season.

"The White House is deserted, save by our faithful and untiring Chief Magistrate, who . . . is always at his post," Stoddard wrote on August 31. "He looks less careworn and emaciated than in the spring, as if, living only for his country, he found his own vigor keeping pace with the returning health of the nation." He mentions "rumors" of the public letter which he had just critiqued, "another of those homely but powerful appeals . . . almost equal to battles won." And so Stoddard has become—doubtless with the president's approval—the main source of the White House rumor, devoting his column to the arguments for the Emancipation Proclamation voiced in the Conkling epistle.

On September 7, he praised the autumnal weather, "days sunny but not too warm, and nights cool and breezy." He does not mention, in any of his writings, ever visiting the Soldiers' Home. Of the three secretaries, it appears that only John Hay was a regular visitor there. In the cool of the mornings, when there was a golden mist on the river, Stoddard went with the president to the South Lawn with some new rifles for target practice. Unlike Hay, Stoddard was a crack shot, and Mr. Lincoln relished his company as they tried out all the new breech-loaders and repeaters, firing away at targets fixed on the woodpile near the riverbank.

"General Ripley says, Mr. Lincoln, that men enough can be killed with the old smooth-bore and old cartridges, a ball and three buck-shot."

"Just so. But our folks are not getting near enough to the enemy to do any good with them now. We've got to get guns that'll carry further."

A hundred paces from the woodpile, Lincoln kneeled and fired away at a board until it splintered. A sergeant and several corporals on guard duty in the distance, hearing the gunshots, called out for them to cease fire—louder and more profanely as they approached—until the president stood up to his full height. "Perhaps the president heard him," Stoddard recalled, "perhaps not, but his tall, gaunt form shoots up, up, up, uncoiling to its full height, and his smiling face looks down upon the explosive volunteers." Their faces looked up at his, "and all their jaws seem to drop in unison." Without a word of command all turned "right about face," and ran away to the Avenue, leaving only "a suppressed breath about having cussed Old Abe himself." Stoddard noted again the peculiar manner of Mr. Lincoln's long and hearty, semisilent laugh. Stoddard said of the soldiers only that "they might have stayed to see the shooting."

Then it was back to the office and the mountain of mail and parcels that kept the lone aide occupied for the rest of the day. By late afternoon, he had a number of letters to show the president, but Mr. Lincoln had other business in mind. He was bound for William Seward's house across the square. Mr. Lincoln stood in his office in the dwindling light, a large portfolio under his arm. Stoddard entered with his stack of mail.

"Not now. Not now," said the president, "come!"

Seeing that Mr. Lincoln was "intensely absorbed in something . . . it is best to take the portfolio and follow him in silence." Reaching the front door, they noticed that it had started to rain. The old Irish doorkeeper Edward McManus was standing there, rubbing his hands together, "his perpetual half-smile of suppressed humor flickering across his face."

Lincoln asked his doorkeeper please to go and fetch his umbrella, up in his office in the corner behind his desk. In the few minutes Edward had taken to go up the stairs and come back down, Stoddard learned they were bound for Seward's to meet General John Dix. McManus reported, "Your Excellency, it's not there," rubbing his hands dryly, with a twinkle in his eye. "I think the *owner* must have come for it, sir," said the old man mischievously, descanting upon the evanescence of all umbrellas, as opposed to top hats, which must fit their owners, and how even a president might take one that did not belong to him.

"I'll get another—just a minute, sir."

While McManus was gone on his errand, the president recalled a story about this fellow. He had served under President Zachary Taylor, who died in office after a year; Vice President Millard Fillmore took his place in 1850. Fillmore needed a new carriage. Hearing that a gentleman nearby was breaking up housekeeping and had a vehicle for sale, the president asked his doorkeeper to accompany him and evaluate the carriage. It looked pretty good, but the fastidious Fillmore eyed it with suspicion. He turned to the worldly-wise servant: "How do you think it will do for the President of the United States to ride in a second-hand carriage?"

"Sure, your Excellency," replied Edward, and here Mr. Lincoln had the skill of mimicry to echo the Irish accent and the sidelong glance of the gleeful servant, and "you're only a *second-hand President* yourself, you know."

Such was the nature of Stoddard's memories and impressions—affectionate and humorous. His writings do not often account for momentous events, or provide political or military revelations (as Hay's and Nicolay's do); evidently such things were not confided to him. He had little to say about the meeting with General Dix at William Seward's house, as the rain glanced against the windowpanes, except that maps and charts emerged from the portfolio he carried, and these were spread out upon a center table in a businesslike reception room where a wood fire blazed upon the hearth. The men discussed military strategy for the border states. When it was over, Stoddard asked the president what he had thought of Dix, whom neither had ever seen before, and Lincoln replied only that he seemed "a very wise man."

There is an old adage to the effect that "Water rises only to its own level," and William Stoddard's view of Abraham Lincoln—not to be faulted—rarely shows the depth of perception evident in Nicolay's letters and journals, and never reaches the fathoms plumbed by John Hay.

It appears that the wise president, valuing his three wards as he did, gave of himself to each according to his ability to receive.

"Does the President take any interest in Wall Street gambling operations?" Stoddard asked rhetorically in his memoirs. "Of course he does, for the currency is the life of his policy." If this was true, only Stoddard remarked upon it. Over dinner one evening, they were discussing precious metals.

"What is the price of gold this morning? Is it up or down?" Lincoln asked his secretary.

"Up, Mr. Lincoln. The street is wild." In the late summer of that year, Confederate victories in the Chickamauga campaign and General William Starke Rosecrans's precarious entrenchment at Chattanooga proved that the war was far from over, despite the triumphs at Gettysburg and Vicksburg.

"Well now," the president replied, "they don't know everything. If I were a bear on Wall Street, and if I were short of gold, I'd keep short. It's a good time to sell." He gave no explanation—never did, according to Stoddard—but did add some bitter comment "about bulls that may be tossed themselves." Then the two men folded their napkins and left the table to go back to work upstairs.

In the waiting room, Stoddard saw the tall, "hawk-eyed" Thomas Clark Durant, a director of the Union Pacific Railroad. He was pacing up and down, muttering to himself: "I'll stop, right where I am! If it goes on up, it'll break me!" The secretary asked him what was the matter, and Durant told him he was short of gold. "Sold my head off!" he cried, panicked. "And now it's just booming." If Durant had not been on the patriotic side of the wager, Stoddard might have told a different story. "Time for me to take it in, I guess, and stand my losses just as they are."

"Now, Dr. Durant," said Stoddard, calmly, echoing his boss, *"they don't know everything. If I were a bear on Wall Street, and if I were short of gold, I'd keep short. It's a good time to sell."*

"Is that so?" the businessman inquired. If he had other sources of information on the gold market, you would not know it from Stoddard's account. Durant asked for a telegram blank and ordered Stoddard to wire the brokers to sell more gold.

"Telegram after telegram is dashed off rapidly by the relieved bear," Stoddard wrote, "and a messenger carries them out after him." He hoped that the price of gold would drop heavily, for this patriot was using his money to build a railroad that would "save the Pacific slope to the Union." Then he adds, defensively, that "as to the President's unintentional suggestion, no other such instance has occurred or probably ever will. Nothing done in or about the White House has anything to do with the course of things on Wall Street."

We must admire William O. Stoddard for his daring memoir. If he had cared for his reputation nearly as much as he loved a good story, he would have kept this anecdote to himself. Either it never happened, or such instances were commonplace. The truth is that by 1863, Stoddard was involved with financiers eager to reward the private secretary handsomely for inside information about events that might affect the currency markets.

A land-claim scandal that surfaced fourteen years later brought to light testimony as well as letters and telegrams that exposed the secretary's conduct. New York financier Clinton Rice testified that he made Stoddard's acquaintance in 1862, when he told Rice "he enjoyed superior facilities for obtaining in advance all information of a political, official and diplomatic character likely to affect gold, stocks, and other commodities. I entered into an arrangement with him [Stoddard] to furnish me telegraphic cipher dispatches." Rice would use the information to invest in stocks or gold, and divide profits with Stoddard "share and share alike." As soon as there was "any important action of the Cabinet, or on receipt by the President or heads of departments of any important military or naval . . . operation" or diplomatic development, the secretary would wire Rice at once in cipher and the financier would place his bets. A day or two later—to cover their tracks—Stoddard would write him "a letter of explanation and advice," and sign it with the nom de plume "Two Hundred."

On October 15, 1863, the secretary allegedly wrote to Rice: "I am anxious to see you and talk over matters. I have made a grand combination which will give me the entire control of the New York press through their Washington correspondents. This alone is an immense thing." If true, it was also immoral. "In order to keep it up, however, we must have some money, and that soon." And the next day he refers to the "hollow" Union victory at Bristoe Station three weeks earlier, and how much the press had exaggerated the importance of the event. "I think I could run a gold line here better than anywhere else. Will pay all the expenses for half the net proceeds. About ten thousand would do. Account rendered every thirty days." Multiply the dollar amount by fifteen to get an approximate equivalent in today's currency. Stoddard was playing a dangerous game for very high stakes; and his naïveté, as he describes it, is incredible.

"I am awfully busy," Hay wrote Nicolay in late September, and "Stoddard is more & more worthless. I can scarcely rely upon him for anything." On October 5, Hay left for Illinois for two weeks, to celebrate his birthday and attend his sister's wedding, leaving the office entirely in Stoddard's care during the period when he was establishing his gold line on Pennsylvania Avenue.

Soon after Hay's return on October 18, Stoddard departed for New York to confer with Rice. Later that month, he sent a letter to Hay, who noted in his diary, "Received a more than usually asinine letter from Stoddard who is in New York stock jobbing & writes to me pretending he is working for the [local] election."

"All who knew me at the time," Stoddard recalled, especially his colleagues in the Executive Mansion, "were already well aware of that fact. Stock and gold gambling was the mania of the day, and for a time I had it very badly. . . ." Stoddard's mania, or obsession, with the markets was distracting him from the daily business in the White House, which paid him not 10 percent of what he was earning in stock transactions. It must have begun to seem less like a position of high responsibility than as a mine of information.

CHAPTER NINE

THE TIDE TURNS

In late October of 1863, John Nicolay began his journey home from the Colorado territory by stagecoach and railroad. He had made a successful treaty with the Ute Indians, and now was on his way to Pittsfield to pick up his fiancée, Therena, who would accompany him to Washington. She planned to spend the next three months in the capital, staying with an old friend, Mattie McCook of Ohio, now married to a Mr. Davis.

The couple arrived in the capital on November 5; Nicolay delivered her to the Davis residence and then reported to the White House.

If Nicolay's fiancée attended the theater, or the social events John Hay records in his diary, he makes no mention of it. Her name never appears in Hay's detailed diary, or in any other known record of that time and place. As there is no correspondence between the lovers— save a note dated January 2 explaining that he is too busy at the New Year's levee to see her—we know next to nothing about their time together.

We have little information about Therena Bates. A single broken daguerreotype survives, showing a young lady with strong features, posing in a dress of vertical stripes, dark hair center-parted and brushed back over her ears, and fine wide-set brown eyes.

Her daughter Helen, writing her father's biography in 1949, adds: "Therena Bates had relations in Washington. She visited them to get a glimpse of life at the capital, which, that year, was very gay. She used her dark eyes to advantage at the White House, as is plain from the questions she asked about the furniture—details that my father had never even noticed." So Therena was welcomed, at least once, to the White House, where she admired a round marble table in the Blue Room. They took a pleasure trip to Mount Vernon.

From letters Nicolay wrote after her departure on February 9, we know that he missed her terribly after she left, which would not have been the case had he neglected her while she was there.

Did they discuss their future during those winter months? Did Therena ask when they would be married? Presumably they did raise such questions. In those days, most men and women in their late twenties and early thirties were already married with children. Because these two eventually married, we have called her—from the beginning—his fiancée. Yet Nicolay was evasive and had many excuses for postponing the date. As Helen Nicolay wrote: "The engagement had been of such long standing that their intimates had teasingly wondered whether a wedding would ever take place." Because Nicolay kept his end of the bargain they had made to destroy each other's letters, we have none of Therena's. But we know of her silences during weeks when Nicolay would complain that he had heard nothing from her, silences that betray her frustration and anger, and speak louder than words.

ON NOVEMBER 8, STODDARD noted, the weather was "magnificent—bright, sunny, cool but not cold, a trifle windy, but just the weather for marching and fighting." Federal cannons bombarded Fort Sumter in Charleston Harbor without vanquishing that stubborn stronghold.

Meade's Army of the Potomac pushed across the Rappahannock, driving Lee's force back to the Rapidan River. Fighting intensified in Tennessee as the rebels moved against Burnside's troops in the eastern part of the state.

On that brisk, quiet Sunday, Nicolay and the President strolled around the Treasury Building and across F Street to Gardner's photo gallery. John Hay and Evelina Ames, wife of Congressman Oakes Ames of Massachusetts, were waiting for them. In the clear afternoon light Gardner took many pictures of the president, including one of the most famous, that forthright, frontal head shot in which the powerful, serene glance meets the viewer's—although the left eye is ever-so-slightly rolled back, showing more white than the other. Art teachers sometimes use this image to illustrate the asymmetry of the human physiognomy: cover the bright unassuming left hemisphere of Lincoln's face, and the right side, dark, multilayered with expression, pierces you with its sly, humorous gaze.

"We had a great many pictures taken," Hay recalled. "Some of the Presdt. the best I have seen. Nico & I immortalized ourselves by having ourselves done in a group with the Presdt." This photograph of the president seated in an armchair, his hands folded, looking toward Nicolay in a cane chair to his right while Hay stands to his left, looking over their heads, is a masterful triple portrait. It captures the personalities of the three men and the dynamics among them. Lincoln in his black suit and satin tie, his hands in his lap, legs crossed at the ankles, looks positively monumental. The beardless Hay—wearing a tweed jacket fashionably loose on him, white necktie, and light-colored trousers—affectionately drapes his right arm over the back of the president's chair, left hand on his hip, clutching his black hat. He looks transient, ready to move. The only man to confront the lens is the goat-faced Nicolay, holding his portfolio in his hand, ever vigilant, protective, as if about to inform us, gruffly, that Mr. Lincoln is not, at present, available.

The next evening, Mr. and Mrs. Lincoln, along with the wife of General David Hunter, Simon Cameron, Hay, and Nicolay, all went to

Ford's Theatre to see John Wilkes Booth in the Charles Selby melo-drama *The Marble Heart.* Booth played the sculptor Phidias, who falls in love with one of his creations while abusing the real woman who loves him. Hay pronounced it "rather tame than otherwise," but the president was enthusiastic. According to one journalist, Lincoln "ap-plauded the actor rapturously. . . . Booth, when told of the President's delight, said to his informant that he would rather have the applause of a Nigger. The President sent word backstage that he would like to make the actor's acquaintance, but Booth evaded the interview."

That was the week of Kate Chase's wedding to Senator William Sprague of Rhode Island, the multimillionaire textile heir. The day after *The Marble Heart,* November 10, John Hay, a close friend of Kate's, arranged a party for her bridesmaids, her sister Janet, Miss Ida Nichols, and Miss Helen Skinner. Others on that snowy afternoon excursion to Mount Vernon were Mrs. Ames, Captain Thomas Ives, John Nicolay, and Jean Margaret Lander.

Mrs. Lander had returned to Washington, having spent seven months working in the hospitals at Hilton Head and Beaufort. There "aided by an excellent corps of nurses of her own organization, she has done a blessed work for the sick soldiers," said the *New York Times.* Her services had been "especially valuable since the bloody repulse of our forces at Fort Wagner," a bastion guarding Charleston Harbor where Federal brigades lost nearly two thousand troops, most of them black soldiers. The *Times* regretted "that Mrs. Lander's return North has been made imperative by the enfeebled state of her health, resulting from the arduous duties that she has so cheerfully performed." Mrs. Lander never returned to the field as a nurse. She spent the rest of that year and much of 1864 in Washington, D.C., and Lynn, Massachusetts.

During the month of September there is one signed letter from John Hay to the actress, dated the nineteenth, enclosing a poem by the contemporary poet George Henry Boker. "Here is that wonderful lyric of Boker's. Some of these times I want to hear you read it." Although the poem Hay enclosed in his letter has not survived, much of Boker's work can still be found. He wrote love sonnets, such as this one.

When with the courage lent me by thy smile,
I laid my hands upon thy sacred form,
Dared, passion-wild, thy scented mouth to warm
With cleaving kisses, unrepelled the while;
Was it thy patience or my venturous guile
Shook virtue's outworks with a fiery storm,
And made her guards the trembling ramparts swarm,
To meet a foe who came in friendly style?
I know not, Love; but since that trustful day
I grow more careful of myself, less stained
By worldly touch, as though that touch profaned.
I am all thine, more like thee; if thou'lt say
Those kisses brushed thy purest bloom away,
Say also this, that what thou lost, I gained.

Reading aloud was a passion the two friends shared. Jean had made a profitable sideline with public recitations of the great poets between theater appearances; now she had a most appreciative audience of one. There are other communications that have been stripped of envelopes and signatures, but are in Hay's handwriting. For example: "To An Unidentified Correspondent, Washington, 15 September 1863":

Your note is so very suggestive,
That I'll come, led by motives digestive—
    For Willards I ban
    Whenever I can—
I close for your henchman grows restive.

And another is dated the twenty-fourth of that month, rejecting a gentleman's invitation to dinner, in favor of an unnamed lady.

Mon cher I cannot dine with thee
For a beautiful dame hath invited me

With her to dine
So your talk and wine
I resist, and like the Devil, they flee

I go in beauty's smile to bask
And hang on her lips (a Ravel [sic] task)
While her sweet eyes shine
O'er the sparkling wine
And flavor it so I could drink a cask. . . .

Then there is a suggestive note to a "Mariner Brave" on October 26, begging to be excused from a rendezvous: "I have so much work to do that I cannot come. I must 'scorn delights & live a laborious day. I expect to go to the Devil for it but must toil this sabbaday. Yours, feeling the cuss of Adam in its fullness."

These notes from Hay—apart from the one Mrs. Lander kept—have a curious provenance. Somehow all three landed in the papers of James Wadsworth, a wealthy New Yorker who became military governor of Washington, D.C., and then died in the Battle of the Wilderness in 1864. An acquaintance of Hay, Lincoln, and Daniel Sickles, and a familiar figure in Washington society, he probably knew Mrs. Lander also; but how these private billets-doux ended up with Wadsworth's papers remains a mystery.

HAY'S DIARY, NOVEMBER 18, 1863, a Wednesday: "We started from Washington to go to the Consecration of the Soldiers' Cemetery at Gettysburg. On our train were the President, Seward, Usher & Blair: Nicolay and Myself ..." as well as the French and Italian ambassadors; two Italian naval officers; Charlotte Wise, daughter of Edward Everett, who would speak before Lincoln on the battlefield; and Hay's friend Wayne McVeagh, chairman of the Pennsylvania State Republican Committee and an outspoken radical. McVeagh "pitched into the President coming up and told him some truths," insisting that Mr. Lincoln needed it from time to time, Hay recalled.

Several good books have been written about Lincoln's most famous speech and the event that occasioned it, and as the secretaries played no special part in it—being no more than two fellows among thousands who witnessed the ceremony—we will not dwell long upon the little town. Arriving a day early in the late afternoon, the president parted with the company from Washington. He was the guest of David Wills, an organizer of the ceremony, whose house was the grandest on the town square. Hay and Nicolay lodged with some other men at the home of the banker Charles Fahnestock. There they met up with the publisher John W. Forney, a friend of Hay's who was somewhat the worse for the whiskey he had been drinking all day. The secretaries lost no time in catching up with Forney. On the eve of that historic occasion, under the bright moon and clear sky, the friends passed the bottle around as they followed the crowds and the music of the serenades.

"The President appeared at the door and said half a dozen words meaning nothing & went in," Hay recalled. That was true enough. When Lincoln was unprepared for a speech he knew just how to dismiss an audience without angering them. First, he thanked the people for their invitation. He said it was likely they would hear him for a little while if he started to make a speech. Then he said he had no speech, and "in my position it is somewhat important that I should not say any foolish things."

Someone in the crowd shouted: *If you can help it.*

"It very often happens that the only way to help it is to say nothing at all," Lincoln replied, and the citizens roared with laughter. "Believing that is my present condition this evening, I must beg of you to excuse me from addressing you further." And he went indoors.

Seward, who was staying at a house around the corner from Wills's, was called forth by the serenaders, and "spoke so indistinctly that I did not hear a word of what he was saying," Hay recalled. This was not really the case; others heard Seward and recorded his fine speech. It is more likely that the liquor had impaired the secretary's hearing.

"We went back to Forney's room having picked up Nicolay and drank more whiskey. Nicolay sung his little song of the 'Three Thieves' and we then sung 'John Brown.'" The forty-six-year-old Forney, who had employed Hay at his newspaper in Washington, had a keen eye for character. He saw something in Hay that the young poet may not until now have known about himself. *In Vino Veritas:* "Hay. You are a fortunate man. You have kept yourself aloof from your office. I know an old fellow now seventy who was Private secretary to Madison. He has lived ever since on its recollection. He thought there was something solemn and memorable in it. Hay," Forney announced to the company at large, "Hay has laughed through his term." In this particular, Hay differed from Nicolay and Stoddard. Nicolay was like President James Madison's secretary Edward Coles. Stoddard—on the other hand—was not so much aloof from his office as he was disassociated from it and failed to give it due respect.

"At last we proposed that Forney should make a speech." And so Nicolay and two other revelers ran out to recruit a band to serenade the renowned publisher. "He still growled quietly and I thought he was going to do something imprudent . . . 'I am always prudent,'" said Forney stiffly, and after a few more slugs of whiskey, he went downstairs to address the large and boisterous throng.

When Forney appeared at the door, the mob cheered and shouted.

"My friends," he said, "these are the first hearty cheers I have heard tonight. You gave no such cheers to your President down the street. Do you know what you owe to that great man? You owe your country—you owe your name as American citizens." After discussing his own record as a Lincoln advocate, he went on to eulogize "the President that great, wonderful mysterious inexplicable man: who holds in his hands the reins of the republic who keeps his own counsels . . ." There were more speeches, by McVeagh and a Judge P. C. Shannon of Pittsburgh. "That speech must not be written out yet," said John Young, one of Forney's editors. "He [Forney] will see further about it when he gets sober."

It is a little known fact that the next morning, John Hay was covering the Gettysburg consecration for the *Washington Daily Chronicle,* a duty that he discharged with his usual flair and professionalism, and a commendable lack of sentimentality, pomposity, or self-importance. An occasion that seems to us virtually mythic was—to the private secretaries—one more mob scene to be negotiated and weathered without one of them or the president getting killed. On horseback, reeling from a hangover, Hay rode out with the president's party to the cemetery, having no idea he was soon to hear Mr. Lincoln's greatest speech. "Mr. Lincoln appeared in black, with the usual crape bound around his hat in memory of his little son, and with white gauntlets on his hands."

He remarked that there had never been a fairer autumn day than this. "Long before sunrise, the roads leading to Gettysburg were crowded by citizens from every quarter thronging into the village in every kind of vehicle . . . spring wagons, carts, family carriages, buggies . . . all crowded with citizens—kept pouring into town . . . while the railroad disgorged its eager crowds, while the streets ever filling, overflowed with the invading host."

About Mr. Everett's two-hour speech, Hay said only "that he did ample justice to his former celebrity, and to the impressive occasion." The Baltimore Union Glee Club sang a hymn, and Benjamin French, commissioner of public buildings, read a poem of five stanzas.

"The President," Hay wrote, "then delivered his address, which, though short, glittered with gems, evincing the gentleness and goodness of heart peculiar to him, and will receive the attention and command the admiration of all of the tens of thousands who will read it." Hay supposed, knowing Mr. Lincoln as he did, that he "sensibly felt the solemnity of the occasion, and controlled himself by an effort. This might have been fancy," Hay allows, "but it is our impression, and as such we record it." In his diary, he only remarks that "the President in a firm free way, with more grace than is his wont said his half dozen lines of consecration and the music wailed and we went home through crowded and cheering streets."

THE PRESIDENT WAS ILL. He returned from Gettysburg with a fever, and the physicians determined that he had varioloid, a mild form of smallpox. For three weeks, he kept to his bed, seeing few visitors. "At last," he told his secretaries—who had seen him endure and guarded him against an endless file of office seekers—"I have something I can give everybody." He was in good spirits despite his illness. The November elections, which the Republicans dominated, showed steady support for his administration. His public utterances, including the widely published letter to Conkling and his Gettysburg address, had struck a chord in the public; and the success of Ulysses S. Grant, William T. Sherman, and George Thomas at Lookout Mountain and Missionary Ridge had nearly rid Tennessee of rebel armies, raising hopes that the Federal troops might finally advance upon the heart of the Confederacy.

At last, the new capitol had been completed. At noon on December 2, 1863, five days before Congress convened, engineers raised the statue of Freedom to the tholos of the dome. Stoddard watched as the colossal figure of Lady Liberty was steam-hoisted from the ground to the three-hundred-foot apex in just twenty minutes. "Freedom now stands on the Dome of the Capitol of the United States," Benjamin French exulted, "may she stand there forever, not only in form, but in spirit." The president, still bedridden, was working on his State of the Union message.

In his newspaper column, Stoddard noted ironically the difference between "the effect of elevation upon men and statuary. The higher you lift the bronze or marble, the smaller it appears, while human beings, especially politicians and generals, expand before our eyes as we ... hoist them higher." The reality of the expansion is further proven "by the fact that so many of them burst like bubbles when we lift them beyond a certain point."

According to Stoddard, there had been a superstition that the dome would never be completed, and the demise of the Union would leave the building in the hands of vandals who would raze it and carry the stones away to Richmond to build mansions. Now the determination of the president and his men had laid such fears to rest. Congress convened once more, the Stars and Stripes floated above both wings of the Capitol, and the legislators awaited the president's State of the Union message.

Stoddard had once described the keen excitement of acting as the emissary of the White House, bearing the president's message, which he called his "paper latch-key" to the Senate and the House. The doors to the building seemed to open of themselves, "so prompt is the ready doorkeeper to recognize the presence of an errand from the Executive." On this particular day, December 9, 1863, it was not Stoddard but John Hay who had the honor of being formally presented to the Congress. The sergeant at arms introduced "the President's Private Secretary." The Speaker of the House, Schuyler Colfax, rapped his gavel for attention and announced, "A message from the President of the United States!" and Hay, bowing, handed over the president's scrolled speech.

As the speech was read aloud, Hay "watched the effect with great anxiety," for he knew that the ailing president had been laboring over the text for days; the final paragraphs boldly set forth the criteria for the readmission of the seceded states, as well as a Proclamation of Amnesty and Reconstruction. "Whatever may be the results on the verdict of history," Hay wrote that night, "the immediate effect of this paper is something wonderful." He had never seen such a response. "Men acted as if the Millenium had come." Charles Sumner, the Radical Republican senator from Massachusetts, "was beaming, while at the other political pole, [Senator James] Dixon & Reverdy Johnson said it was highly satisfactory." Hay's friend John Forney said, "We only wanted a leader to speak the bold word. It is done and all can follow. I shall speak in my two papers tomorrow in a way to make these Presidential aspirants squirm." One of these—who dared take exception to the message—was cabinet member Salmon Chase.

In brief, what Mr. Lincoln had determined was that any rebel—with a few high-ranking and criminal exceptions—who swore allegiance to the Constitution would be pardoned; that governments reestablished "as prescribed in rebellious states" would be recognized; that the president would permit those governments to provide for the freed slaves each in its own manner; and that Congress would have the sole authority to admit delegates of those reinstated governments. The president's carefully considered plan balanced the conflicting interests of the liberals, who wanted assurance that the governments of the South would not reinstitute slavery, and the conservatives, who desired generous terms for the returning rebels. "[Massachusetts senator] Henry Wilson came to me," Hay recalled, "and laying his broad palms on my shoulders said 'The President has struck another great blow. Tell him from me God bless him.'"

Hay would convey the blessings of Wilson, Owen Lovejoy, James Garfield, and many others to the convalescent Mr. Lincoln. "[Congressman Francis William] Kellogg of Michigan was ecstatic. He said 'The President is the only man. He is the great man of the century. There is none like him in the world. He sees more widely and more clearly than anybody.'"

ON SUNDAY EVENING, DECEMBER 13, the celebrated Shakespearean actor and comedian James Hackett arrived in Washington, and Mr. Lincoln was well enough to receive him. It was Mary Lincoln's birthday, but her time was taken up with her half sister, Emilie Helm, who was visiting for the week. Emilie's husband, Confederate general Benjamin Hardin Helm, had been killed at the Battle of Chickamauga, and now the Lincolns, at great political risk, had provided her with safe passage and sanctuary as she made her way to Lexington, Kentucky. Her presence in the White House was a secret to be kept from the public, and so John Hay passed back and forth diplomatically and discretely from the president's office, where James Hackett regaled the gentlemen, to a parlor below, where the ladies consoled each other over their recent losses.

The group in Lincoln's office included the round-faced, clean-shaven comedian, who looked younger than his sixty-three years; the swaggering General Daniel Sickles, who had lost a leg at Gettysburg; and General James Wadsworth, military governor of Washington. Hackett, now in his prime, was a pioneer in the genre of American comedy, and an incomparable mimic; his Falstaff, for decades, was considered the finest ever done. Hay recalled that "the conversation at first took a professional turn, the President showing a very intimate knowledge of those plays of Shakespeare where Falstaff figures." Why, Lincoln asked, do the productions of *Henry IV* omit one of the best scenes in the play—the one in which Falstaff and Price Hal take turns imitating the king? Hackett claimed that it made better reading than acting onstage (which future actors would disprove, too late for the president's enjoyment). "There is generally nothing," Hackett continued, "sufficiently distinctive about the actor who plays Henry [the king] to make an imitation striking."

Hay observed that Hackett was very talkative but also extremely amusing, as he told stories about Davy Crockett, Sam Houston, and other characters of a bygone era. Mr. Lincoln was quite taken with him. So the next evening the president ventured outdoors in his carriage for the first time in weeks, to watch Hackett play Falstaff in *Henry IV* at Ford's Theatre. The party included Hay, Nicolay, Lincoln's friend Leonard Swett from Illinois, and Senator James Dixon of Connecticut.

As they made their way to their seats in the flag-draped presidential box to the right of the proscenium arch, word of Mr. Lincoln's presence preceded them. The audience applauded the chief executive as he bowed before relaxing in the rocking chair reserved for him.

The drama critic for the *Washington Chronicle,* seated below, remarked that Hackett was a perfect physical representation of the fat, sly knight who laughs and rolls and swigs his sherry. "It is a great animal performance," he admits, but it lacks subtlety. "We have the rich mellow laugh; the beefy, sensual face, the mutterings and pantings; the smacking of the lips over sack; the keen, low cunning . . ."

It was always exciting to attend a play with Mr. Lincoln, who laughed heartily and thoroughly enjoyed himself, but was not above confiding, to his neighbors, his criticisms of the performance. As much as he admired Hackett's Falstaff, he told Hay and Nicolay that he thought the actor had misread a line of the scene in which Falstaff describes his fictional skirmish with the robbers: "These four came all a-front and mainly *thrust* at me." Hackett had put the emphasis on "thrust" when the president thought it should have fallen upon "me." Hay told Mr. Lincoln he thought he was wrong, and explained that "mainly" in the Elizabethan parlance, merely meant "strongly."

"The Presdt thinks the dying speech of Hotspur (archrival of the hero, Prince Hal) an unnatural and unworthy thing." All agreed upon it.

> O, Harry, thou hast robb'd me of my youth!
> I better brook the loss of brittle life
> Than those proud titles thou has won of me . . .

The men in the president's box had seen too much of real, untimely death to accept any such limelight sentimentality, even from the pen of William Shakespeare.

A FEW DAYS LATER, Nicolay and Therena went to Philadelphia to spend the Christmas holiday with Congressman William D. Kelly and his family, leaving Hay behind in Washington.

On a fair, bright Christmas day, Hay wrote, "A lonesome sort of Christmas. I breakfasted, dined, and supped alone. Went to the Theatre & saw Macbeth alone. Came home and slept alone." A man altogether accustomed to sleeping alone would not feel moved to comment upon it. After Christmas, he would begin angling for an assignment that would take him back to Florida and South Carolina, where he had enjoyed his interlude with Jean Lander the previous spring. Would she join him there? Whatever had passed between the two, the evidence suggests that the connection was now a thing of the past, a memory that would inspire love poems of exquisite longing in the year to come. No more will her name appear in his diary or correspondence.

After a violent Northeast storm on New Year's Eve, a night Hay spent drinking with Forney, a clear day welcomed the New Year. A gruff entry in his diary on New Year's Day shows the change that has come over him. "I did not attend the reception today, laboring all the morning under a great disgust." This was the annual public levee that filled the first floor of the White House every New Year's. The secretaries were expected to attend and assist in making introductions, but Hay had become weary of duties that did not directly involve the president or urgent affairs of state. He was beginning to distance himself from the more repetitious functions of the White House.

There is a direct correlation between the success of the administration and the disassociation of the secretaries from it. For a year, various critics of Mr. Lincoln's policies and military plans—Salmon Chase and Horace Greeley foremost among them—had been laboring to unseat him in the coming election. But since the State of the Union message in early December, it had become increasingly clear to Hay that not only was the Confederacy doomed, but so was the opposition to Mr. Lincoln.

The president agreed to make Hay a sort of advance agent for Reconstruction, sending him first to Point Lookout, Maryland. There was a sizable prison camp where Hay was to instruct General Gilman Marston in the use of the book of oaths and the accompanying identification blanks. The secretary returned on January 4, having succeeded at Point Lookout. On the thirteenth—after receiving his commission as assistant adjutant general with the rank of major—Hay packed his trunk, bound for a long trip to Hilton Head and Beaufort, South Carolina, and Camp Shaw and St. Augustine, Florida, bearing the book of oaths for repentant rebels.

Before leaving that Wednesday, he stopped by the president's office, announcing that he was ready to start.

"Great good luck," said Mr. Lincoln, shaking his hand warmly, "and God's blessing go with you John. How long will you stay, one month or six months," the president added, in a tone that demanded no answer, and with a look in his eye that might have made the younger man blush. Perhaps Hay's excuses for the extended trip last spring had fooled his mother, but Mr. Lincoln was not so easily deceived.

This time, Hay would be gone almost three months, working and relaxing in that tropical wonderland and recollecting—in his most heartfelt verses—a paradise lost. This time, the poet takes little care to disguise his subject, in a poem called "Lèse-Amour" (a crime against love) and actually dates the poem at the end: "Camp Shaw, Florida, 1864."

> *How well my heart remembers*
> *Beside these camp-fire embers*
> *The eyes that smiled so far away*
> *The joy that was November's.*
>
> . . . .
>
> *Now 'mid these scenes the drearest*
> *I dream of her, the dearest—*
> *Whose eyes outshine the Southern stars,*
> *So far, and yet the nearest.*
>
> *And Love, so gayly taunted,*
> *Who died, no welcome granted,*
> *Comes to me now, a pallid ghost*
> *By whom my life is haunted . . .*

FOUR DAYS AFTER THE poet's departure, the relative serenity of the White House gave way to a disagreement over some dinner invitations—not uncommon in this household where the mistress longed for more control over her parties and visitors than any first lady can enjoy.

That very day, January 17, Secretary of the Treasury Salmon Chase had declared he was available to run for president, and he had sufficient support among liberal Republicans to mount a plausible candidacy (although it would not survive the spring). Mary Lincoln was less optimistic about the future than was Mr. Lincoln or his secretaries. She had secret debts she feared might be discovered were he not elected to a second term, and believed that attacks on her character were part of a plot to unseat him in the coming year.

Long before this, Mrs. Lincoln had labeled Chase as a traitor and an enemy, along with his beautiful daughter Kate, who had produced a rival salon in their downtown mansion in support of her father's presidential aspirations. On January 14, Kate, her new husband, Senator William Sprague, and the secretary of the treasury had lured half of the Lincolns' guests away from an evening reception in the Blue Room. Now Mrs. Lincoln and her social secretary, Nicolay, were planning a state dinner for the cabinet members, the Supreme Court justices, and their wives for Thursday evening, January 21.

Mary Lincoln looked over the guest list Nicolay had drawn up, scratched out the names of Salmon Chase, Kate Chase Sprague, and William Sprague, and handed it back.

Nicolay, surprised by Mrs. Lincoln's audacity in cutting the secretary of the treasury and his illustrious family, held his tongue and took his leave of the lady. Straightway he referred "the snub" to Mr. Lincoln, who knew at once this would not do. Chase was a cabinet member, and excluding him would be an insult not only to himself but to the rest of the company; Kate Chase had acted as her father's hostess and companion since the inauguration; and Sprague was an influential senator. Knowing the problem was beyond Nicolay's power to resolve, Mr. Lincoln left his desk and headed down the central hall toward his wife's room beyond the library.

"After a short conference with the powers at the other end of the hall," Nicolay wrote to Hay, the president "came back and ordered Rhode Island [Sprague] and Ohio [the Chases] to be included in the list. Whereat there soon arose such a rampage as the House hasn't seen for a year, and I am again taboo." When Mary Lincoln threw one of her tantrums, the house staff ran for cover. She railed, and hissed at the very air and innocent furniture around her, opening doors and slamming them shut; she stormed and thrashed until she was tired. "How the thing is to end is yet as dark a problem as the Schleswig-Holstein difficulty," referring to the recent dispute between Denmark and Germany over the Elbe territories that nearly caused war in Europe. The disagreement with Mrs. Lincoln over the dinner invitations was not Nicolay's first run-in with her, but it may have been the beginning of the end of his desire to work in the Executive Mansion.

"Stod[dard] fairly cowered at the violence of the storm, and I think for the first time begins to appreciate the awful sublimities of nature. Things have subsided somewhat, but a day or two must bring them to a head."

Nicolay emerged from the "imbroglio of the Cabinet dinner with flying colors. As I wrote before," he informed Hay, "after having compelled Her S[atanic] Majesty to invite the Spragues I was taboo, and she made up her mind resolutely not to have me at the dinner." If she could have fired him, she would have. Instead, she put Stoddard in the middle, asking him if he could take over the arrangements for the dinner. But Nicolay dug in his heels. He ordered Stoddard to inform Mrs. Lincoln that the necessary information was unavailable to him; and if it *had* been, there was nothing he could do about it, as it was exclusively John Nicolay's responsibility. Stoddard relayed this message to his mistress, who expressed her dismay, "but still announced her determination," Nicolay recalled, "to run the machine without my help."

Two days later, on the afternoon of January 21, when the affair was scheduled to take place, Edward McManus came up to Nicolay's office with a message of apology from Mrs. Lincoln. She requested his presence at the dinner and his assistance, "explaining that the affair had worried her so she hadn't slept for a night or two," Nicolay wrote to Hay. "I think she has felt happier since she cast out that devil of stubbornness."

Nicolay reported that "The dinner was got through creditably." Gideon Welles said, "It was pleasant. A little stiff and awkward on the part of some of the guests, but passed off very well."

While Mrs. Lincoln had no power to dismiss Nicolay, she was in a position to make life uncomfortable for him. From the beginning of 1864 until April, there were twenty formal entertainments in the White House. In an election year, the levees, morning receptions, soirees, and state dinners—painstakingly planned and well executed—were crucial in building support for Mr. Lincoln's candidacy. Nicolay and Mrs. Lincoln continually wrangled over the arrangements and guest lists.

Therena Bates left Washington on or about February 10, Ash

Wednesday. That day, the White House stables burned, destroying the horses and carriages, including Nicolay's. One carriage he had kept at his own expense—he and Hay used it frequently for delivering Lincoln's messages to Congress.

He wrote to Therena on February 21: "I have had the blues badly several times this week. It seems as if the circumstances surrounding my position were getting worse day by day. I am beginning seriously to doubt my ability to endure it a great while longer. *Nous verrons.*" We shall see, he confides, in French, the tongue the lovers use in many of their more intimate letters. Is it possible that before leaving him in Washington, Therena had delivered an ultimatum, or given him a deadline for the wedding? It would be in keeping with the expectations of the mid-nineteenth century, when unmarried women Therena's age were written off as spinsters.

The circumstances surrounding Nicolay's position, referred to above, were first and foremost the demands of Mary Lincoln. And then, while Hay was in the South, Stoddard was growing less and less attentive to his duties. It is difficult to ascertain if this was because of his preoccupation with the gold line and stockjobbing, or if it was owing to a recurrence of the typhoid fever that had sidelined him in 1863. A cynical historian is tempted to equate typhoid fever with malfeasance in office, either dereliction of duty or inattention to it. Stoddard describes that winter as a "phantasmagoria routine, a kaleidoscope full of statesmen, generals, rascals, battles, dissipations, hard works, and at the end of it I was down with the typhoid fever. It was a pull of weeks and I got up too soon, only to go down again." While Stoddard is inexact about the dates, it appears that he took to his bed in late February and did not return to his desk until mid-April.

In the meantime, Nicolay was training substitutes to do the office work that he could not handle by himself, and that, indeed, he might not wish to continue much longer. The substitutes, who included Edward D. Neill, Gustave Matile, Nathaniel S. Howe, and later Charles H. Philbrick, provide little more than a footnote to this story; none served long enough to enjoy any great intimacy with Mr. Lincoln. But their presence as of February 1864 shows that the principal aides were—for different reasons—disengaging themselves from the executive office.

WHEN HAY RETURNED FROM South Carolina on March 24, 1864, he found Nicolay in bed at seven o'clock in the morning. It was a cold, dark day, with three inches of snow on the ground. As Nicolay dressed, they spoke of recent military developments, especially Ulysses S. Grant's rapid promotion to lieutenant general and then commander in chief, and General Halleck's fury over being reduced to a staff officer. Since Pope's defeat, Halleck had shirked responsibility while Grant had pursued victory in the field.

Nicolay wrote to Therena that Hay looked very well, had enjoyed his trip, and that "He will remain on duty here in his old position for the present." While neither man would leave the president's service before the election in November, neither cared to remain long after the inauguration in 1865, whether or not he was reelected. Their attitude had partly to do with the pressure Mrs. Lincoln had put upon them; she wanted them out of the house by the end of the year. The fact that Stoddard was losing his place made matters worse. When at last he prepared to leave Washington for a post in Arkansas, he recalled "John Hay telling me that Nicolay expressed his regret at my departure in this form: 'John! What'll we do with the Madame after Stod goes? Heaven! You and I can't manage her.'"

"She did not love him," Stoddard wrote, "and John's diplomacy had entirely failed there."

CHAPTER TEN

ERRANDS AND EXITS

Salmon Chase's leap for the presidency floundered in February of 1864, undermined by the infamous "Pomeroy Circular." This blunt anti-Lincoln instrument signed by Kansas senator Samuel Pomeroy argued that the reelection of Lincoln would damage "the cause of human liberty and the dignity and honor of the nation," and that Chase was the best qualified candidate for the presidency. It sailed so near the rocks of treason that the secretary of the treasury was compelled to repudiate it, and offer his resignation. He abandoned his candidacy on March 5.

"Chase having retired from the Presidential contest," Nicolay wrote Therena, "the tide continues to set as strongly as ever to Lincoln, and politicians therefore have but little to intrigue about." There were still malcontents in the Republican Party, and presidential hopefuls such as General Benjamin Franklin Butler—the favorite of congressional radicals on the Joint Committee on the Conduct of the War. And there was the perennial candidate of Radical Republicans, General John Charles Frémont. The public's disappointment over the unending, harrowing war, the inequitable draft, or Lincoln's conservative approach to slavery might still provide an opportunity to unseat him. So the president would do everything in his power to consolidate his support.

New York, crucial to Lincoln's success, continued to be a quagmire of political opposition. "Peace" Democrats, bitter copperheads, undercover secessionists in the government bureaus, abolitionists, and some dissatisfied Republicans were all working to undermine the administration. The president carefully chose which intrigues and grumblers to address.

On March 25, the day after John Hay returned to his office, Nicolay took a night train for Manhattan, on a political mission for Mr. Lincoln. It was what Hay later called a "rather delicate matter to manage at a distance from Washington."

Thurlow Weed, the sixty-six-year-old publisher who until recently had edited the *Albany Evening Journal,* remained a powerful force in state and national politics. Lanky, needle-nosed, and vitriolic, he was a fierce opponent of the radical antislavery wing of the Republican Party, and a close ally of William Seward—Weed's first choice for the presidency in 1860. Weed had proposed a plan of ending the war based upon early amnesty and an armistice. Now he took a keen interest in the management and personnel of the powerful New York Custom House. He complained that it was lousy with secessionists, enemies of the president, and friends of Salmon Chase, and was impatient for Lincoln to do something about it.

It is difficult to explain just how a private citizen who held no high office, wrote nothing memorable, and had even cast off his affiliation with the newspaper by which he had shaped public opinion could wield such power as did Thurlow Weed. In a thirty-year career of journalism, informal diplomacy, and lobbying—first in service of the Whig Party and later for the benefit of Republicans—Weed had made friends who were loyal to him, and enemies who feared him. Supporting successful candidates had made him a lord of patronage. He knew how to reward his friends and terrify his foes. His means did not exclude bribery, blackmail, the promulgation of rumors, or influence peddling.

For instance, he knew far more about Mary Lincoln's personal debts and padding of White House payrolls than he had any right to know, and eventually she became scared to death of him.

Lincoln wanted Thurlow Weed's support in New York in the months approaching the election. Now he heard that Weed was disgruntled. Summoning this personage to Washington would be awkward, so Lincoln sent Nicolay to Manhattan. Mr. Weed's ideas and opinions were too important to be entrusted to the post, and so were the president's inquiries. These Nicolay carried in an envelope, and when he arrived in the morning at the Astor House, the five-story Greek Revival-style hotel on lower Broadway, Mr. Weed was waiting for him in the lobby.

When they had exchanged greetings, Nicolay handed Weed the president's note.

> My dear Sir:
> I have been both pained and surprised recently at learning that you are wounded because a suggestion of yours as to the mode of conducting our national difficulty, has not been followed—pained, because I very much wish you to have no unpleasant feeling proceeding from me and surprised, because my impression is that I have seen you since the last Message issued apparently feeling very cheerful and happy. How is this?
> Yours truly,
> A. Lincoln

The pale, clean-shaven old man read the letter, and frowned. Nicolay watched him. Weed read it over again carefully.

"I don't quite understand it," he said. "I did write a letter to Judge David Davis. The Judge probably showed it to Lincoln, but I said nothing in it about anything but the Custom House."

So the president had been wrong. During this day and the next, in intense conversation with Thurlow Weed, Nicolay gathered that his great solicitude was for the New York Custom House, the organization of the cabinet, and the impact that these matters were to have upon the coming election and the fate of the Union. On March 30, 1864, Nicolay sent a long letter to the president marked *Private,* which he enclosed in an envelope addressed to John Hay to assure the utmost security. It is an extraordinary document, a perceptive summary of Weed's opinions concerning the personnel of the Custom House, Lincoln's management style, and the New Yorker's own position in the scheme of things.

Weed began by assuring Nicolay that his main concern was for the president. Hiram Barney, the collector of the port of New York, was not evil but weak; under his leadership corrupt deputies in the Custom House, including surveyor Rufus Andrews and secretary Albert Marshman Palmer, were intriguing against Mr. Lincoln. Excellent men were being turned out "for no other reason than that they take active part . . . in behalf of your [Lincoln's] renomination."

In January, Lincoln had promised Weed that he intended to make changes in the collectorship, but then had let him down. The New Yorker believed that if Lincoln lacked strength "to hold the Union men together through the next Presidential election," then the country would go to ruin. Weed wanted to strengthen Lincoln as much as possible. More important, he wanted the president to strengthen himself. [He felt] "you were being weakened," Nicolay wrote, "by the impression in the popular mind that you hold on with such tenacity to men once in office, although they prove to be incapable and unworthy." Nicolay knew there was a grain of truth in Weed's critique. "This feeling among your friends also raises the question as to whether, if re-elected, you would change your Cabinet." Weed then lambasts the cabinet—all but Seward—calling them "notoriously weak and inharmonious." Although Chase and Frémont might not succeed as rival candidates, still they could lead dangerous factions. Something decisive must be done.

Weed returned to the subject of the Custom House—a key to political influence in New York. "A change in the Custom House was imperatively needed because one bureau of it had been engaged in treasonably aiding the rebellion." He was in despair over Lincoln's procrastination in appointing a new collector, and Nicolay could see that the old "kingmaker" who had helped Lincoln get to the White House took it personally. His ambition in life, he told Nicolay, was "not to get office for himself, but to assist in putting good men in the right places." As an outsider, his strength was in advising the administration, but this was only possible if he maintained the administration's trust.

Nicolay told the president that Weed "feared he did not have your entire confidence—that you only regarded him with a certain degree of leniency; that you only regarded him as being not so great a rascal as his enemies charged him with being." The next day, Weed received a letter from the governor informing him that Mr. Lincoln had nominated one John T. Hogeboom—one of Chase's cronies—to be surveyor of customs. Meeting with Nicolay again, he expressed his astonishment. Weed had assured Lincoln's friends in New York "that when in your own good time you became ready to make changes, the new appointments would be from among your friends; but that this appointment of one of your most active and malignant enemies left him quite powerless."

We have no record of President Lincoln's response to Weed's concerns, so sensitively communicated by the secretary. Presumably Lincoln answered with the solicitude that the delicate situation required. Weed was shrewd and ruthless, and by his own report a rascal, but in this case he was more right than wrong. His criticism of the Custom House appointments and the cabinet weighed heavily upon the president during that spring. When John Cisco, the widely respected assistant treasurer of New York, announced his resignation in June, Salmon Chase nominated his friend, assistant secretary Maunsell Field, a former New York journalist and a Democrat, to replace Cisco. Because Field was unqualified, the nomination was inappropriate and dangerous in the ways that Weed had described to Nicolay.

So Lincoln opposed the appointment. Chase resigned, and the president, to Weed's delight, accepted the resignation. It was the beginning of significant change in the cabinet, just in time for the November election.

As the president's emissary in New York, Nicolay had other business in that last week of March. He met with General Carl Schurz, who defended his reputation against an accusation that he had delayed troop movements en route to Tennessee. A close friend of Lincoln, Hay, and Nicolay, Schurz had important information regarding the German-American support for Frémont in the coming election. They "are bent upon defeating you at all events," Nicolay reported.

Before packing his bags to leave on April 1, Nicolay read "the villainously unfair and untrue editorial in the Tribune of this morning," as he wrote to Hay. Horace Greeley, America's most influential publisher, had become, according to historian John C. Waugh, "a major headache for Lincoln," and now was opposing his reelection. In the offending editorial, Greeley argued that the Union Party nominating convention, scheduled for June 7, should be postponed. On that date, they were sure to choose Lincoln as their standard-bearer, and Greeley could think of no other way to interfere. He predicted that significant events—military developments in the summer—were likely to affect the mood of the electorate, and so any decision about a candidate ought to be postponed until September. This was nonsense, Nicolay believed, Greeley's last ditch effort to get Lincoln off the track. So the secretary "determined to stay till I can have another talk with Greeley and [Sydney Howard] Gay [the managing editor] and tell them a fact or two, so that if they print misrepresentations in the future they would do so knowingly." As in his defense of the president against the *Chicago Tribune* in June of 1863, Nicolay was assuming the role of press secretary, a function he understood instinctively, and could be trusted to carry out on his own recognizance.

Acting in the same capacity a few weeks later, on April 25, Nicolay wrote an editorial for the *New York Tribune* to correct a false story Greeley had published concerning one of Mrs. Lincoln's sisters, Martha Todd White. According to the *Tribune,* the president had granted Mrs. White permission to carry contraband goods south—including medicines, merchandise, and rebel uniforms with golden buttons. Nicolay's editorial of two hundred words avers upon the highest authority that "Mrs. White went south with only the ordinary pass which the President gives to those persons whom he permits to go. The President's pass did not permit Mrs. White to take with her anything but ordinary baggage, nor did she attempt to take anything more. The President's pass *did not* exempt her baggage from the usual inspection; and her baggage *did* undergo the usual inspection." The truth was that the malicious canard—which anti-Lincoln papers were eager to retail—was gotten up by the secessionist Martha White herself, miffed that her sister and brother-in-law had not made her welcome in the Executive Mansion.

LINCOLN'S FATE IN THE autumn election would indeed depend—as Greeley had prophesied—on military successes over the summer. As General Grant prepared to move the Army of the Potomac across the Rapidan River and advance upon Richmond, John Hay grew restless in his office. He let the president know that he would like to be on the front in some capacity when the campaign got under way. "The President assents to my going to the field for this campaign," Hay wrote on April 28, 1864, "if I can be spared from here." That was a big "if." Hay did not know how important his presence had become for the chief executive's equanimity. Lincoln himself would travel to military headquarters several times during the coming year, and when Jubal Early's troops attacked the Washington ramparts in July, the president would actually command troops at Fort Stevens. But he would not put Hay in the line of fire; Hay would never go to the front.

The twenty-four-year-old poet had become as important to the president as the president was to Hay, as remarkable as that seems. One of Lincoln's best friends, Owen Lovejoy, had passed away on March 25 after a long illness. Orville Browning's term in the Senate had ended, and now Lincoln's most intimate friend from Illinois still in Washington had grown so conservative that the men would go for months without speaking. The president's marriage was unraveling, as Mrs. Lincoln's mood swings became more violent, and military affairs consumed more of her husband's time. Mrs. Lincoln and Tad spent a great deal of 1864 in New York, Boston, and the White Mountains of New Hampshire. John Hay was often the only company—and the most congenial—that Lincoln had.

On April 30, two days after he expressed his desire to follow General Grant to the front, Hay spent much of the day with the president. Mary Lincoln had gone to New York on a shopping trip, taking Tad with her. Lincoln loved to read aloud, and Hay was probably his favorite audience of one. He had become so familiar with the president's style that he learned, eventually, to imitate it. That morning, he read Hay a letter to General Grant, on the eve of battle: "Not expecting to see you again before the spring campaign opens, I wish to express, in this way, my entire satisfaction with what you have done up to this time. . . . You are vigilant and self-reliant; and, pleased with this, I wish not to obtrude any constraints or restraints upon you. While I am very anxious that any great disaster . . . shall be avoided, I know these points are less likely to escape your attention than they would be mine. . . . And now with a brave Army, and a just cause, may God sustain you."

Hay pronounced this letter "an admirable one, full of kindness & dignity at once," and assured Mr. Lincoln that Grant would be very grateful for it as he launched the campaign.

This was a busy day, with half a dozen important appointments and visitors, including the painter Francis B. Carpenter, who introduced Lincoln to the suffragette Elizabeth Cady Stanton and her brother-in-law Samuel Wilkeson, Washington correspondent for the *New York Tribune*. The president wrote out an "order for pardon" of twenty-six Sioux Indians who had been imprisoned in Davenport, Iowa, for eighteen months under sentence of death, and then another order for an exchange of military prisoners.

As night fell, "the President came loafing in" to Hay and Nicolay's room and took a chair. He wanted to talk about an open letter he had written on April 4 to the editor of the *Frankfort* (Kentucky) *Commonwealth*, Albert G. Hodges, and how it had been received. The letter expresses Lincoln's personal feelings about slavery as these clashed with his oath to defend the constitution: "I am naturally antislavery. If slavery is not wrong, nothing is wrong. . . . And yet I have never understood that the Presidency conferred upon me an unrestricted right to act officially upon this judgment and feeling . . . to this day, I have done no official act in mere deference to my abstract judgment and feeling on slavery."

The Hodges letter, addressing Kentuckians who were angry over the enlistment of Negroes as soldiers, is Lincoln's most concise and eloquent defense of the Emancipation Proclamation and the use of freedmen as soldiers, seamen, and laborers. "I felt that measures, otherwise unconstitutional [Emancipation] might become lawful, by becoming indispensable to the preservation of the constitution, through the preservation of the nation. . . . I had [not] even tried to preserve the constitution, if, to save slavery or any minor matter, I should permit the wreck of government, country, and constitution all together."

It was a powerful argument that the secretaries had heard from its inception. They had seen it develop in the inhospitable world of men, guns, and dollars, since the president first lectured them in his office in May of 1861, "on whether a free and representative government had the right and power to protect and maintain itself." That had been almost three years ago to the day. Now, in the Hodges letter, Lincoln's argument had reached its apotheosis, and the secretaries were privileged to view yet another dimension of it, personal and metaphysical.

"I add a word which was not in the verbal conversation," Lincoln wrote, referring to the original discussion with the editor, of which the letter was a formal memorandum. "In telling this tale I attempt no compliment to my own sagacity. I claim not to have controlled events, but confess plainly that events have controlled me." John Hay, probably the only man in the room who had read the ancient Greek tragedians, heard the ghost of Sophocles in Lincoln's sentence, and sensed, perhaps, that it, too, would become immortal. Count Leo Tolstoy—an admirer of Lincoln—had just begun writing *War and Peace,* the sublime fictional expression of the same idea.

The president, Hay recalled, "seemed rather gratified that the *Tribune* was in the main inspired by a kindly spirit in its criticism" of the Hodges letter. Horace Greeley was unpredictable, chastising Lincoln in one breath and praising him in the next. The president was by turns annoyed and amused by the *Tribune*'s publisher. Right now, he was amused. Rising from his chair, he went to fetch an old letter from a pigeonhole in his desk. When he returned, he handed it around for the boys to read. The message was from Greeley, dated July 29, 1861, a week after the Federal defeat at the Battle of Bull Run. In it, Greeley begged the president to surrender to the Confederates if he believed them too strong to be conquered. Now Hay read it aloud with humorous emphasis, and they laughed. "This most remarkable letter still retains for me its wonderful interest as the most insane specimen of pusillanimity that I have ever read," Hay decided.

When Hay had finished the dramatic reading, Nicolay remarked that the letter would be a rare treat for Greeley's archrival James Gordon Bennett, publisher of the *New York Herald*. "Bennett would willingly give $10,000.00 for that," he said.

The president, tying a red cord around the precious letter, replied, "I need $10,000 very much but he could not have it for many times for that." Bidding the young men a good night, Lincoln took his leave of them and went off to bed.

Nicolay described that time as "another week of terrible suspense. Grant began moving last Wednesday morning . . . and we were without any information from him for two or three days." No one in the White House slept easily. By the light of an oil lamp, Hay scribbled in his diary; Nicolay stretched out on the bed. At the other end of the hall, the president's lamp was also burning as he lounged in his nightshirt, chuckling over a short story by the English writer Thomas Hood. The story, about a man who, on his wedding day, stumbles over his father-in-law's beehives was just too funny for one man to read in a large bedroom all by himself. One can laugh louder in company.

So Mr. Lincoln marked the page with his finger in the book and padded down the long hall to Hay and Nicolay's rooms, where the light was still on.

"A little after midnight I was writing," Hay recalled, "the President came into the office laughing, and with a volume of Hood's works in his hand to show Nicolay & me the little caricature 'An unfortunate Bee-ing.'" The secretaries stirred and looked over Lincoln's shoulder at the drawing. Hood, who was a clever cartoonist, illustrated his work with pictures as entertaining as the preposterous stories themselves. Here was the drawing of a man in a cutaway coat who has knocked over a beehive. His back is to us, his fists are raised toward heaven; his right knee is lifted as if by an antic dance he might shake off the bees that stream from the broken hive and cling to him. The hive is broken in half; the top lies on a table, and the bottom is turned up on the ground next to the victim's leg.

It would be difficult to imagine a better emblem of the broken Union of states, the angry citizens of the North and the South, and Lincoln's ill fortune in stumbling into the White House at this particular moment in history. Lincoln laughed until the tears came to his eyes, and his companions laughed with him.

Lincoln seemed

> utterly unconscious that he with his short shirt hanging about his long legs & setting out behind like the tail of an enormous ostrich was infinitely funnier than anything in the book he was laughing at. What a man it is! Occupied with matters of vast moment, deeply anxious about the fate of the greatest army in the world, with his own fame & future hanging on the events of the passing hour, he yet has such a wealth of simple bonhomie & good fellow ship that he gets out of bed & perambulates the house in his shirt to find us that we may share with him the fun of one of poor Hood's queer little conceits.

Apparently the president slept very little. Hay remembered other times that year when he would be awakened by the weight of someone sitting on the edge of his bed with a light and a book. It was Mr. Lincoln, whispering: "Lie still; don't get up. Would you mind if I read to you a little while?" And he would begin to read in that soft, musical voice, a passage from Shakespeare or Ecclesiastes, or one of Hood's poems:

Of all our pains, since man was curst—
I mean of body, not the mental—
To name the worst among the worst,
The dental sure is transcendental;
Some bit of masticating bone,
That ought to help to clear a shelf,
But lets its proper work alone,
And only seems to gnaw itself . . .

This, or some other piece of wisdom or nonsense, would get them to chuckling and laughing until whatever problem had troubled the president's sleep was banished. Bidding John Hay good night, he would rise from the bedside and take up the candle. "After perhaps twenty minutes or half an hour," Hay recalled, "his mind having become calm, the tall gaunt figure would rise from the edge of my bed and start for the door and on down the dark corridor. The candle carried high in his hand would light the disheveled hair as the President in flapping nightshirt, his feet padding along in carpet slippers, would disappear into the darkness."

AS GRANT'S ARMY ADVANCED in secrecy toward Virginia's Wilderness, the suspense was hard to bear. Stoddard, who had returned to his desk, wrote on May 2 that "this oppressive sense of something coming—this pause and hush before the coming of the hurricane, is really something dreadful." When the first report arrived by special messenger, at 2 a.m. on May 7, the president was gratified and then appalled. The Federal troops had made a commendable but costly attack upon Lee's army, and held their ground. "How near we have been to this thing before and failed," he told Hay. "I believe if any other General had been at the Head of the army it would now have been on this side of the Rapidan. It is the dogged pertinacity of Grant that wins." The casualties were breathtaking. Of a hundred thousand Federals engaged, 2,246 were killed and more than 12,000 wounded. Soon they would fill the city's hospitals.

"With faith, with hope, but nevertheless with deep and heartfelt anxiety, we now look forward to the end . . . ," Stoddard wrote. "Every minute, marked sadly by the death of a hero, brings us nearer to the goal." Senator James Lane, wandering into Hay's office on Friday the thirteenth, said that "the President must now chiefly guard against assassination. I pooh-poohed him," Hay wrote, "& said that while every prominent man was more or less exposed to the attacks of maniacs, no foresight could guard against them." This was an echo of the president's own rehearsed response to assassination threats. Hay seemed more concerned about the state of Lincoln's health. The next night, the president padded down the hall in his nightshirt to talk to Nicolay and Hay of how the enemy had retreated from the breastworks at Spotsylvania, and how Grant pursued them. All Hay could think of was how gaunt and hollow-eyed the president looked. "I complimented him on the amount of underpinning he still has left & he said he weighed 180 pds. Important if true."

Mr. Lincoln was stricken by the loss of his friend, General James Wadsworth, mortally wounded in the Battle of the Wilderness. Hay thought that the president had not been so deeply affected by a personal loss since Edward Baker died at Ball's Bluff three years before. Comparing Wadsworth to General John Sedgwick, who died alongside him, Lincoln said that "Sedgwick's devotion and earnestness were professional. But no man has given himself up to the war with such self-sacrificing patriotism as Genl. Wadsworth. . . . not wishing or expecting great success or distinction . . . actuated only by a sense of duty which he neither evaded nor sought to evade."

The tall figure in black that John Nicolay saw working in the office the next day, a Sunday, was not bowed in sorrow or wracked with anxiety. Grant's progress had been so encouraging that there was every reason to think he would crush the rebel army and capture Richmond. "The President is cheerful . . . and now as ever watching every report and indication, with quiet, unwavering interest," Nicolay wrote to his fiancée, struck by the difference between Mr. Lincoln's mood and his own. "I think I have been more nervous and anxious during the week past, than for a year previous, lest some unexpected and untoward accident should prevent . . ." the longed-for end of the rebellion. "If my own anxiety is so great, what must be his solicitude, after waiting through three long, weary years of doubt and disaster, for such a consummation, to see the signs of final and complete victory every day growing so bright and auspicious!"

Therena Bates, seven hundred miles away in Pittsfield, Illinois, read her fiancée's weekly letters (rarely now did he write except on Sunday) with devotion, longing, and a forlorn tolerance that would not quite give in to despair. She would be twenty-eight years old at the end of May. Why did he never remember her birthday? Recently she had written him a letter in which she unburdened herself of her concerns, that their commitment to each other, to a future together, was in doubt.

"What did you mean," he asked, obtusely, "when in your letter before the last you wrote that you thought we were slowly but surely drifting apart?" He wondered: Had she ceased to care for him, to pray and plan for their marriage, weaving and unraveling the tapestry of her future while she waited for him indefinitely, or forever? Had she accepted the advances of another man? Nicolay had told her that he did not know how long he could endure the circumstances surrounding his position . . . But now her birthday had come around again and she remained, by all measures except her interminable engagement, a spinster, a maiden lady immured in a rural village and her stubborn consecration to a man married to his adoptive country.

She could not now or ever compete with Mr. Lincoln for the attentions of John Nicolay.

WHILE IT WAS A foregone conclusion that Lincoln would be nominated president at the National Union Convention in Baltimore—a month after the Wilderness campaign—party unity was still up in the air. So was the slot for vice president. Nicolay was the president's envoy on that occasion. On June 5, he traveled on the train with Simon Cameron, the former secretary of war, still a powerful voice in politics, hoping to replace Hannibal Hamlin as vice president. In the coming days, the contrary Cameron would confound the convention every way he could while Nicolay, Lincoln's surrogate, would promote harmony among the radicals and conservatives.

The weather in Baltimore was fair and cool that Sunday. The delegates of the New York and Illinois delegations were just arriving at the Eutaw House uptown, where Nicolay also unpacked his bags. News of Grant's disastrous attack at Cold Harbor on June 3 had not yet reached the North. Even Whitelaw Reid, the war correspondent for the *Cincinnati Gazette,* knew little of it. Buttonholing Nicolay in the lobby, the brilliant anti-Lincoln journalist wanted to talk politics, wanted Lincoln's secretary to understand that the Radical Republicans had conceded the president's nomination and now what they were pushing for was a radical platform.

From hotel to hotel, from room to room, and from lobby to saloon, Nicolay made his rounds, gathering information. His most important contact was Burton C. Cook of Illinois, with whom he had "quite a long and substantial talk." Cook had planned to go to Washington and meet with the president, but now was confident he could entrust his message to Nicolay.

Late at night on June 5, the secretary wrote a memorandum which he had delivered by express mail on the seven o'clock train Monday morning. A few hours later, Hay read it aloud to the president. The points of his letter are: First, that any ambivalence on the part of the Illinois State Convention was caused by "a few plotters," but that now "the delegation will vote and act as a unit" in backing Lincoln and whatever platform and vice presidential candidate he might prefer. Second, according to Cook, "[Leonard] Swett may be untrue to Lincoln." This rumor was based on the fact that Lincoln's old friend had urged the Illinois delegation to go for Joseph Holt, judge advocate general, whom Lincoln had not considered as a running mate. Third, there might be trouble over contested seats from Missouri, where party infighting had been intense. Radical delegates from there had the right to be seated, and threatened to withdraw if the conservative delegates were also admitted. This was the typical infighting that Nicolay had the diplomatic skill to quell behind the scenes by acting with the president's approval—if Lincoln wished.

Fourth, and most important, party leaders wanted to know the president's wishes regarding the vice president's position on the ticket. Was Swett correct that "in urging Holt for V.P. he reflects the President's wishes"? There was a strong movement for Andrew Johnson, former senator of Tennessee, and there were rumors that Lincoln favored him. Everyone was curious "whether the President has any preference, either personally or on the score of policy—or whether he wishes not even to interfere by confidential indication."

In closing, Nicolay asks Hay to get Lincoln's response immediately, and send the letter "by express so it will reach me by the earliest practicable hour on tomorrow (Monday)."

When Hay finished reading the letter aloud to the president that morning, Mr. Lincoln took the pages from him. He turned them over and wrote some notes in pencil: "Swett is unquestionably all right. Mr. Holt is a good man, but I had not heard or thought of him for V.P. Can not interfere about platform—Convention must judge for itself—" He handed the letter back to Hay, instructing him to write a full letter of response to Baltimore. In the interest of haste, Hay first filled out a telegraph blank: "Your letter recd & answered, declines interfering." He then ran it over to the cipher office in the War Department so Nicolay would receive it within the hour.

Then he sat down and wrote a succinct letter fully articulating the president's notes and their discussion. "The President wishes not to interfere in the nomination even by a confidential suggestion. He also declines suggesting anything in regard to platform or the organization of the Convention. The Convention must be guided in these matters by their own views of justice and propriety." Notwithstanding the president's confidence in Swett, Swett's backing of Holt for vice president has neither Lincoln's approval nor disapproval—he "intends to be absolutely impartial in the matter."

Ever since the Baltimore convention of 1864, there has been controversy over whether or not the president secretly instigated the nomination of Johnson for vice president. One neglected source of in-

formation is William O. Stoddard, who arrived in Baltimore a day after
Nicolay. According to Stoddard's memoirs, the president had fingered
him for an appointment as marshal of a district of Arkansas, and had
advised Stoddard to get endorsements from that state and the border
states of Kentucky, Maryland, and Delaware in order to assure that the
appointment would go smoothly.

With this in mind, Stoddard boarded the train to Baltimore, and
booked a room at the Barnum Hotel downtown. Then he "had gone
to work and identified myself with the Border State delegations, as one
of the leading men of Arkansas, and we were all pulling together, for
I told them we must have the vice president named from among our
own men, in place of that unnecessary statesman Hannibal Hamlin,
of Maine, who never appeared to admire me. . . . They agreed with me
enthusiastically and I put my prospective finger upon Andrew Johnson
of Tennessee . . ."

In his autobiography, written forty-three years later, Stoddard
recollected, "I will say that I had somehow strengthened my idea
that Lincoln did not want Hamlin and that he had a leaning toward
Johnson. . . . John Hay played the diplomat in the matter." According to Stoddard, Hay indicated that it would be unseemly for either
Nicolay or himself to express the president's preference, but some
other person might. "That is precisely what I did and I could not now
be qualified as to how many delegates received, directly or indirectly,
the idea that they were instructed confidentially to comply with the
President's wishes. It was a narrow affair . . . and Andrew's nomination
was entirely due to the Arkansas and other Border State men among
whom I was sitting . . ." He insisted, years later, that Hay or Nicolay had
given him the impression—"more or less distinctly"—that Lincoln
preferred Johnson, and as he wrote to Hay in 1875, "Right or wrong, I
went in on it like a beaver."

An intriguing comment in Hay's diary of June 5, 1864, gives weight
to Stoddard's plausible story. After conversing with Ward Hill Lamon
on June 4, Hay reports that Marshal Lamon, one of the president's
oldest friends, "thinks Lincoln rather prefers Johnson or some War
Democrat [for vice president] as calculated to give more strength to the

ticket." The fact that Stoddard and Nicolay had little or no contact in Baltimore—they stayed at opposite ends of town—and that Stoddard reported neither to Hay nor to the president also lends credence to the third secretary's account. "I did hear something," Stoddard recalled years later, "which prevented me from reporting to either him [Hay] or Nicolay. It was as well for them to remain in ignorance." That way no one of them would have to lie about the president's true role in the Baltimore convention, and the nomination of Andrew Johnson.

ON A HOT WEDNESDAY afternoon, June 8, Lincoln received word of his nomination for president, and of Tennessee's military governor Andrew Johnson for vice president. That night, he attended Grover's Theatre alone.

The next day was taken up with receiving various delegations, committees, and serenaders come to congratulate him on his nomination. Addressing the National Union League in the East Room, he said that he had "not permitted myself, gentlemen, to conclude that I am the best man in the country, but I am reminded, in this convention, of a story told of an old Dutch farmer, who remarked to a companion once that 'it was not best to swap horses when crossing streams.'"

The president's calm demeanor was deceptive. He was distracted by a quarrel between his secretary of war and one of his top generals, William S. Rosecrans.

Late that night, just as Hay was preparing for bed, Mr. Lincoln came to his room. He said "that Rosecrans had been sending dispatches [from St. Louis] requesting that an officer of his staff [John P. Sanderson] might be sent to Washington to lay before the President matters of great importance in regard to a conspiracy to overthrow the government." In telegraphing Lincoln, Rosecrans was going over Stanton's head. Rosecrans detested the secretary of war, who had once court-martialed a messenger he had sent to Washington. Now Lincoln suspected "that the object of the General is to force me into a conflict with the Secretary of War and to make me overrule him in this matter."

Also, if the message was all *that* important, Lincoln did not believe Sanderson was the proper person to deliver it.

"I have concluded," said Mr. Lincoln, "to send you out there to talk it over with Rosecrans and to ascertain just what he has. I would like you to start tomorrow."

The next morning, while Hay was still in bed, the president came into his room and slipped this note into his hand:

> Major General Rosecrans
> Major John Hay, the bearer, is one of my Private
> Secretaries, to whom please communicate in writing or
> verbally, anything you would think proper to say to me.
> Yours truly,
> A. Lincoln

The trip from Washington to St. Louis in 1864 took about four days. Hay's account of his whirlwind visit to interview Rosecrans fills many pages of his diary on the day of his return, June 17, a week later.

After dining with the general and his staff at the Lindell Hotel, Rosecrans and Hay withdrew to a heavily guarded private room. Lighting up a cigar, Rosecrans offered Hay one, which the secretary politely refused. "There is a secret conspiracy on foot against the government carried forward by a society called the Order of American Knights," Hay learned. "The head of the order, styled the high-priest, is in the North, [Clement L.] Vallandigham, and in the South, Sterling Price." Vallandigham, a former Ohio congressman, had been so strident in his opposition to the war that a military commission in Cincinnati convicted him of treason. Banished to the Confederacy, he made his way to Canada.

According to Rosecrans, several hundred thousand men were plotting to overthrow the government, working in hundreds of secret societies in Illinois, Missouri, Ohio, Indiana, and Kentucky. Their members had sworn oaths to end the war and curtail the emancipation of slaves. One of their first objectives was amnesty for their leader, the copperhead Vallandigham, who was plotting to return in glory as a delegate to the Democratic convention in Chicago.

Hay was impressed. "My instructions placed me in a purely receptive attitude," he noted. He made no suggestions and did not even ask for Sanderson's report (the colonel had headed the investigation, employing the agent Harry Truman) or copies of any of the papers he had been shown. The general did not offer them. Mr. Lincoln had been correct in thinking that what Rosecrans really wanted was for Sanderson to go to Washington in person to discuss the business, bypassing Stanton. "Rosecrans is bitterly hostile to Stanton . . . & is continually seeking opportunities to thwart and humiliate him."

Returning to Washington on June 17, bedraggled and sleep deprived, Hay immediately reported to the president. The secretary was struck by Mr. Lincoln's sangfroid about the plot that so distressed Rosecrans and Sanderson, not to mention his philosophical attitude toward Vallandigham's case. While Hay was on the way to Washington, Vallandigham had been sighted in Ohio—defying his sentence. At first, the president was irritated that Rosecrans had not sent him the pertinent documents on the conspiracy via Hay, "reiterating his want of confidence in Sanderson, declining to be made a party to a quarrel between Stanton and Rosecrans . . ." Lincoln dismissed the emphasis upon secrecy, saying that any secret that had already been confided to so many officers "could scarcely be worth the keeping now," and called the whole northern section of the plot malicious and puerile.

As for Vallandigham, the significant question "for the Government to decide is whether it can afford to disregard the contempt of authority & breach of discipline displayed in Vallandigham's unauthorized return: for the rest it cannot but result in benefit to the Union cause to have so violent and indiscreet a man to go to Chicago as a firebrand to his own party. The President had some time ago seriously thought of annulling the sentence of exile," Hay wrote, but had been too busy to get around to it.

Where others saw enemies, the shrewd president saw opportunities. Vallandigham at large was a menace to his own cause; in exile or in prison, he would be an influential martyr.

NICOLAY, WITH PRIVILEGES OF seniority, had gone directly from Baltimore to Springfield on a much-needed holiday. He arrived there on June 14 to attend two weddings before going to see Therena the week of June 20. Hay, returning from St. Louis, encountered Nicolay in Springfield, and alerted him of the plot to overthrow the government. On June 20, back in Washington, Hay wrote a boozy letter to his friend describing a recent night at the opera with Lincoln, and voicing his concern over the president's cavalier attitude toward the copperheads: "The Tycoon thinks small beer of Rosey's mare's nest. *Too* small, I rather think." Hay had actually confronted Lincoln on this score, insisting that the followers of Vallandigham posed a genuine threat to the stability of the Union.

"I went last night to a Sacred Concert of profane music at Ford's [Theatre] . . . [Joseph] Hermanns & [Theodore] Habelman both sung: & they kin ef anybody kin. The Tycoon & I occupied private box & (both of us) carried on a hefty flirtation with the Monk Girls in the flies [offstage]." The Monks were chorus girls, described by Speaker of the House Schuyler Colfax as "those southern girls with their well rounded forms, lustrous hair and sparkling voices." Mrs. Lincoln was out of town. The president was kicking up his heels.

Either Nicolay could read between the lines of Hay's lighthearted letter, or the two secretaries had already agreed that the state of affairs in Missouri warranted further scrutiny. Perhaps a letter of command has been lost. In any case, a week later Nicolay was in St. Joseph, Missouri, a town just north of Kansas City and on the far side of the state from St. Louis. He was on his way to Colorado to go hunting, but not before completing an investigation of the entanglement of military and civil authorities that had created the panic in Missouri.

On June 29, 1864, Nicolay sent John Hay a long memorandum marked *Confidential:* "During my few days' sojourn here, I have been looking a little into 'the situation.' If Missouri be not 'governed too much,' it is at least governed by too many different and conflicting authorities." Nicolay has written a veritable treatise on the state government, which, at the time, was an organization of military provost

marshals appointed by General Rosecrans, regulated by Colonel Sanderson, and overseen by an independent district commander, General
C. B. Fisk. Nicolay explains how "perpetual confusion and conflict of
authority, and especially conflict of policy grows out of this state of
things."

The most stunning revelation concerned the detective, Captain
Harry Truman, who "professed to be able to ferret out a great conspiracy which had for its object the capture of Hannibal, Quincy and
other points by guerillas." He was actually "a very bad character . . .
immoral, and subsequently criminal. Gen. Fisk suspected him from
the first . . ." and ordered Truman to cease his investigation and return
to St. Louis. "Instead of obeying the order, [Truman] telegraphed to
Sanderson and Rosecrans, asking permission to 'stay in the field a week
longer,' saying it was a military necessity." They told him to go ahead.
"He went ahead and in a few days summarily shot and hung *seven* men"
in Chariton County—men unarmed and not engaged in treasonable
acts. "Of course it produced a reign of terror . . . Everybody took to
the brush, and since that time *thirteen* Union men have been murdered
in retaliation."

"I do not pretend to say who is right and who is wrong," wrote
Nicolay. "The point I make is, that the division and conflict of authority as it now exists, is powerless for good and potent for mischief."

In the same envelope, Nicolay folded another sheet marked "*Confidential:* Please lay the enclosed before the President, if he can find the
time to read it." Lincoln would certainly find the time to read it, as well
as the letter to Hay, for the senior secretary had succeeded remarkably
in delivering the intelligence the White House needed in order to re-
spond to the turmoil in Missouri.

"Sanderson's Chariton Co. Affair has a very bad look about it. . . .
Both he and Rosey seem to have been miserably duped by the man
Truman. . . . This affair really shakes my faith in the truth of the Val-
landigham conspiracy. . . ." In conclusion, Nicolay stresses his doubts
about Sanderson and complete confidence in the district commander,
Fisk. Before leaving St. Joseph for his month in the Rockies, he wrote

to Hay, "If things break loose generally so as to make my presence desirable at home, telegraph me to Fort Kearney . . ."

HAY MANAGED WELL ENOUGH that summer, with the help of assistant secretary Edward Neill. Stoddard departed for the South in July. An unreliable narrator of his own history, he is unconvincing in his explanation of his removal from the White House—where he had enjoyed considerable privileges—to the wilderness of the Ozarks.

"All my business operations," Stoddard claimed, "had been more or less interrupted by my long illness," and what he needed was fresh air. "I was no longer fit for close confinement and late hours." He said that it was his idea to go "upon a prolonged inspection of the armies in the west and south," but Little Rock, in the withering heat, is where he spent most of his time that summer, talking to generals and bureaucrats in smoke-filled rooms.

Stoddard returned in the late summer to report to the president, then left days later to go back to Arkansas where he took up his position as marshal of the Eastern District of that state. With the general election only weeks away, it was "an odd time indeed for a presidential aide to depart the White House staff," as the editor of Stoddard's autobiography observes in his introduction. The editor, Harold Holzer, adds that Stoddard left Washington over the vociferous objections of his sister Kate. In an unpublished memoir, Kate wrote: "It seemed like throwing William's life away as he was not calculated to contend with the rough times and men that awaited him in the southwest." She even persuaded New York senator Ira Harris, a family friend, to call upon the president and urge him "not to send my brother to border life . . . he was unfitted and not in the temperament to contend with . . . the difficulties that must arise at the close of such a war."

In light of Kate's testimony, William Stoddard's version of the events that year begins to break down. The timing of the appointment, as well as its remote location, strongly suggest a quiet exile or moral quarantine rather than a voluntary career move. The president was then under relentless pressure from his own party as well as from the "peace Demo-crats." He had called for half a million men to be drafted—a wildly unpopular measure; rebel troops had nearly seized Washington; Grant had blundered at Petersburg; and Lincoln had pocket vetoed a highly esteemed bill for Reconstruction because he thought it punitive. In a printed circular, senators of his own party denounced him. On August 25, Nicolay wrote to Hay, vacationing in Illinois: "Hell is to pay. The N.Y. politicians have got a stampede on that is about to swamp every-thing. Weak-kneed d—d fools like [Senator] Chas. Sumner are in the movement for a new candidate—to supplant the Tycoon."

The last thing the president needed in an election year was a stock-jobber and currency gambler running a gold line from the White House to the New York banks.

And so, Kate Stoddard wrote, "Will went. It was a bubble soon burst and left him a sick man, a very broken man, and I think his full strength never came back."

LINCOLN WOULD WIN THE election handily, notwithstanding the mis-fortunes and discouragements of the summer of 1864. Atlanta surren-dered to Sherman on September 1. Three weeks later, General Philip Sheridan drove Jubal Early's rebel army from the Shenandoah Valley. And as a concession to the radicals in his party, Lincoln removed the unpopular conservative Montgomery Blair, the postmaster general, from the cabinet. Military success, and the virtual implosion of the Democratic Party under the leadership of its standard-bearer, George McClellan, assured an overwhelming mandate for Lincoln.

The night of the election, Hay recalled, "was rainy, steamy and dark." He and the president "splashed through the side door of the War Department where a soaked and smoking sentinel was standing in his own vapor with his huddled up frame covered with a rubber cloak." They went upstairs to the cipher room. In a few minutes, dispatches came over the wire from Philadelphia, Baltimore, and Boston, all very promising. In Stanton's room, Gideon Welles and Gustavus Fox of the

Navy Department joined them. They were elated that the moderate Alexander Rice had won his congressional district in Massachusetts, Fox remarking that this had brought retribution on two of the president's enemies, radicals John Hale and Henry Winter Davis.

"You have more of that feeling of personal resentment than I," Lincoln said, with a mildness Hay recorded. "Perhaps I may have too little of it, but I never thought it paid. A man has not time to spend half his life in quarrels. If any man ceases to attack me, I never remember the past against him. . . . recently Winter Davis was growing more sensitive to his own true interests and has ceased wasting his time by attacking me. I hope for his own good he has. He has been very malicious against me but has only injured himself by it."

As the midnight hour approached, the men had tallied votes enough to call for a victory celebration. Major Thomas T. Eckert of the telegraph office provided coffee and a pan of fried oysters. The men sat around the table as the president shoveled out a portion to each.

Nicolay was not among them. He had been in Illinois for a month, reporting on military and political developments in the West, and visiting his fiancée in Pittsfield. At last, he and Therena were seriously discussing the question of what he would do after the next fourth of March, when the president was inaugurated for his second term. Although he had "not as yet reached any definite conclusion," he would presently write to her, "I am pretty well resolved not to remain here in my present relation after that time, and I think the chances are also against my remaining in Washington."

Two days later, Nicolay posted election results from Illinois to John Hay: excellent news, a twenty-five thousand majority, ten Republican congressmen, and only two copperhead Democrats. That morning, the cabinet gathered at the long table in the president's office for the first time since the administration had received its mandate. It was a time of celebration, congratulations, and lighthearted banter. Hay stood near the president as he moved to his desk near the window. Opening a drawer, Mr. Lincoln took out a paper that he had carefully folded and pasted.

Quite theatrically, by all measures, including that of his theater-going companion John Hay, who recorded the incident in his diary on November 11, the president addressed the company: "Gentlemen, do you remember last summer I asked you all to sign your names to the back of a paper of which I did not show you the inside? This is it," he announced, like a parlor magician, holding it up for all to see, as if he were about to turn it into a sparrow.

"Now, Mr. Hay," he said, turning to his assistant, "see if you can get this open without tearing it."

Hay saw that the paper had been pasted up in so peculiar a manner that it would take deft work with the knife to get it open. As he probed and sliced, the suspense in the room mounted until the page lay flat. Lincoln took it from him and read aloud.

> Executive Mansion
> Washington
> Aug. 23, 1864
>
> This morning, as for some days past, it seems
> exceedingly probable that this Administration will not
> be re-elected. Then it will be my duty to so cooperate
> with the President elect, as to save the Union between
> the election and the inauguration; as he will have
> secured his election on such ground that he cannot
> possibly save it afterwards.
>
> A. Lincoln

On the reverse the paper was endorsed with the following signatures: William H. Seward, W. P. Fessenden, Edwin M. Stanton, Gideon Welles, Edw. Bates, M. Blair, JP Usher, and the date, August 23, 1864.

On that bleak day in August, Hay had been in Illinois. Nicolay was about to write him that "the N.Y. politicians have got a stampede on that is about to swamp everything." While Nicolay had been managing Lincoln's campaign, Hay had accompanied the obstreperous Horace

Greeley to a "peace conference" in Canada in late summer that Lincoln could neither condone nor wholly ignore. The movement for a peace candidate threatened to fatally divide the Republican Party. In a characteristic gesture, Lincolnesque and magical, the president was using the divine invention of writing, *great in enabling us to converse with the dead, the absent and the unborn, at all distances of time and space*—as he had written in "Discoveries and Inventions"—to link the past and the future. He meant to demonstrate to these men the constancy of his highest principles.

"You will remember," said Mr. Lincoln, "that this was written at a time ... when as yet we had no adversary, and seemed to have no friends. ... I resolved, in case of the election of General McClellan, being certain that he would be the Candidate, that I would see him and talk matters over with him." He would have admitted to McClellan that he had superior influence while he, the president, still had the executive power; he would have beseeched the general to raise the troops so Lincoln might finish the war.

Seward could not resist commenting on this scenario. "And the General would answer you '*Yes, Yes*'; and the next day when you saw him again & pressed these views upon him he would say 'Yes—yes' & so on forever and would have done nothing at all."

And Lincoln answered, "At least I should have done my duty and have stood clear before my own conscience."

Looking around the room at the distinguished men who now made up the cabinet, Hay observed—with the eye of a statesman-to-be—who had signed the paper and who had not, who had departed and who had endured. Secretary of State Seward and Secretary of the Navy Welles were the anchors of the administration, part of the team from the start. Stanton, who had replaced Simon Cameron in January 1862, made the third pillar of the monumental structure.

Of the seven original members, five were gone: most conspicuously, the contentious secretary of the treasury, Chase—undone by his own ambition—had been replaced by William Pitt Fessenden of Maine. Montgomery Blair, the unpopular aristocratic postmaster general, gave way to William Dennison of Ohio, who had been true to Lincoln throughout Chase's Ohio-based bid for the Republican nomination. John P. Usher now occupied Caleb Blood Smith's seat as secretary of the interior (Hay's actual employer); Attorney General Bates had resigned, in weariness, hoping that Lincoln might make him chief justice (an honor that went to Chase). Now James Speed of Kentucky, the brother of Lincoln's old friend Joshua, sat in his place.

These were the men, the secretaries hoped, who would see the president through his second term of office. Hay and Nicolay had done their best for the president, and had received a unique education in return. Now it was time to move on. It would not be easy for either of these men to say good-bye to Mr. Lincoln, and leave the place that was for so long their home and the axis upon which the world turned. And neither Hay nor Nicolay could imagine that the parting would be so difficult, that the president would exit first before anyone had a chance to say good-bye.

THREE DAYS BEFORE CHRISTMAS, 1864, William Tecumseh Sherman sent this telegram to President Lincoln: "I beg to present you, as a Christmas gift, the city of Savannah . . ." Grant was at Petersburg, the "back door to Richmond," and General George Henry Thomas had routed the Confederate Army of Tennessee under General John B. Hood in the Battle of Nashville. The question was not whether Lee's Army of Northern Virginia would surrender, but when.

Taking leave of his fiancée after Thanksgiving, Nicolay had promised to write to her twice a week. Therena—for her part—kept him longing for her words. He wrote on December 18: "Why don't I deserve a letter? Charge it to the mails if they don't come along regularly, for I have written two every week, according to promise, since I have been here." The Washington winters had been hard on his constitution, and the couple had agreed that this was one important reason for him to resign. "Of course I will pay heed to the doctor's warning that my health will suffer if I stay here." He believed he would get through this season without difficulty. "I shall watch my own sanitary condition with a great deal of solicitude," he promised.

On Christmas night, 1864, a Sunday that has left no trace in the record of Hay's diary or Lincoln's general correspondence, Nicolay sat at his desk in the quiet house. He felt lonely. Christmas had lost its meaning for him, and today was a "mere holiday or day of rest from ordinary cares and labors."

He confessed to Therena, "I have been so long astray in the world—cut off from all those close and endearing associations of *home* and *kindred,* that I feel rather like a traveler in a strange land, who sees the pleasures and enjoyments of people about him, but at the same time feels that he himself has no part or right in them." He had a faint recollection "that in Germany, while yet a child, I was able to enjoy that perfect illusion which cheats care, and gives us a brief foretaste of perfect happiness." Perhaps this was "the superstition of childhood, or the subtle influences of home and kindred, I am not now able to analyze; but I do know that the feeling, whatever produced it, was left on the other side of the sea."

Such a perfect illusion certainly could not survive the trials of wartime Washington. "Still I have not lost faith in the potency of the charm, although I have learned from sad experience, that alone I have no power to evoke it." Someday, Nicolay muses, he will have a home of his own.

And then, he promises Therena, "I shall instate you wizard-in-chief, and trust to your skill to surround the Christmas Holidays with all the brilliant and delicious enchantments of the olden fairyland! Your George."

CHAPTER ELEVEN

LIGHTS IN THE SHADOW

On the evening of April 14, 1865, as Mr. and Mrs. Lincoln were taking their seats in the presidential box at Ford's Theatre, Jean Margaret Lander was making her entrance onto the stage of McVicker's Theatre in Chicago, six hundred miles away. That night she played the title role in the drama *Charlotte Corday,* the famous "angel of assassination" who murdered Jean-Paul Marat to save the French Republic from civil war.

The great actress had returned to the stage on February 6, at Niblo's Garden, New York, opening in her own translation of *Mesalliance, or Faith and Falsehood.* The critic for the *New York Herald* wrote: "Mrs. Lander is a small, beautifully formed lady, with a sweet, expressive face, and a voice as clear as a bell. She carries us back to those old, delightful days when it required brains, not brass, to be a star. . . . She does not shriek, nor scream, nor beat the air, as is the fashion . . . Neither does she affect the statuesque and depend upon her poses for her affects. In everything she is true to nature, and uses her art to conceal art most carefully. . . . She presented us last evening with so moving a picture of a suffering but innocent woman, that, at times, the whole audience were in tears . . ." Jean had rehearsed long and carefully. Her comeback was triumphant. In three weeks on Broadway, the actress played leading roles in seven plays. But *Mesalliance,* the story of the mismatched, ill-fated lovers, was the play that no one could forget.

Now she was in Chicago playing Corday. The next day, she was scheduled to perform in a piece called *The Stranger.* The show would not go on. All the theaters in America would be dark because of the terrible news about Mr. Lincoln.

AT THE MOMENT JOHN Wilkes Booth shot the president, John Hay was in his room at the White House chatting with Robert Lincoln.

Robert had just come from Virginia. He had served as General Grant's aide-de-camp during the final assault on Petersburg, and the fall of Richmond. The men had much to discuss, including Hay's recent appointment as secretary of the U.S. legation in Paris. It was Hay's custom to entertain Robert with whiskey and cheese, and at eleven o'clock, five days after Lee's surrender at Appomattox, the old friends had more reasons than ever to lift their glasses and toast good fortune.

Their merrymaking was arrested by a clamor and commotion in the street and below stairs. It was a strident sound readily distinguished from the cheers and singing and shouts of triumph that had been ringing in the capital for days. From Ford's Theatre on Tenth Street, five minutes away, "a crowd of people rushed instinctively to the White House," Hay wrote (in *Abraham Lincoln: A History*), "and, bursting through the doors, shouted the dreadful news to Robert Lincoln and Major Hay. . . . They ran downstairs. Finding a carriage at the door, they entered it to go to Tenth Street."

As the carriage rolled, someone shouted to them that Mr. Seward and other cabinet members had been murdered. This all seemed so far-fetched that Hay and Robert Lincoln doubted it could be true. "But when they got to Tenth Street and found every thoroughfare blocked by the swiftly gathering thousands," Hay recalled, "agitated by tumultuous excitement, they were prepared for the worst."

The wounded president had been carried from the theater across the street to William Peterson's rooming house. Now he lay in a small bedroom beyond the staircase. "Those who had been sent for, and many others, were gathered in the little chamber where the chief of state lay in his agony," Hay recalled. At the door, Lincoln's son was met by Dr. Robert Stone, "who with grave tenderness informed him that there was no hope."

Hay remained with the president and his family for more than eight hours. "As the dawn came," he remembered, "and the lamplight grew pale in the fresher beams, his pulse began to fail; but his face even then was scarcely more haggard than those of the sorrowing group of statesmen and generals around him. His automatic moaning, which had continued through the night, ceased; a look of unspeakable peace came upon his worn features." When Lincoln passed away, Hay was standing at the head of the narrow bed in the low room, alongside Senator Sumner, Secretary Welles, General Halleck, and Robert Lincoln, as Edwin Stanton broke the tearful silence by saying, "Now he belongs to the angels."

When Surgeon General Joseph K. Barnes formally announced the death at 7:22 a.m., April 15, all the cabinet members, three other doctors, a half dozen officers from the War Department, and a few civilians were present. The Reverend Phineas D. Gurley, kneeling, offered a prayer. Then "the widow came in from the adjoining room supported by her son and cast herself with loud outcry on the dead body."

NICOLAY HAD GONE ON a cruise to Cuba on March 28, and he would not return until April 17. On March 31, Hay had written to his brother Charles about his new position as secretary of the legation in Paris; three weeks earlier, Nicolay had been confirmed consul to the French capital. It was a happy coincidence, for the friends would leave on the same ship. "I am thoroughly sick of certain aspects of life here, which you will understand without my putting them on paper," he wrote. Mrs. Lincoln had done everything in her power to make Nicolay and Hay resign, and already had tapped her friend Noah Brooks to replace them. "I was almost ready," Hay recalled, "after taking a few months active service in the field, to go back to Warsaw and try to give the Vineyard experiment a fair trial, when the Secretary of State sent for me and offered this position abroad. It was entirely unsolicited and unexpected."

In the same letter, Hay wrote: "Meanwhile Nicolay, whose health is really in a very bad state, has gone off down the coast on a voyage to Havana, and will be gone the 'heft' of the month of April, and I am fastened here, very busy." Mr. Lincoln had asked Hay to stay until the end of April "to get him started with the reorganized office," and he had agreed. He planned to sail for France in June.

The *Santiago de Cuba,* bringing Nicolay from Havana, stopped at Cape Henry on the Chesapeake Bay on April 16 to take a new pilot aboard. It was from him that the secretary learned of the assassination. "It was so unexpected, so sudden," he wrote to Therena,

> and so horrible even to think of, much less to realize, that we *could* not believe it, and therefore remained in hope that it would prove one of the thousand groundless exaggerations which the war has brought forth during the past four years.
>
> I am so much overwhelmed by this catastrophe that I scarcely know what to think or write. Just as the valor of the Union arms had won decisive victory over the rebellion, the wise and humane and steady guidance that has carried the nation through the storms of the last four years, is taken away . . . It would seem that Providence had exacted from him the last and only additional service and sacrifice he could give his country, that of dying for her sake.

His final words to Therena written aboard the ship were to the effect that his personal plans might now be changed by this turn of events—and they had at last decided to go to Paris as husband and wife.

Debarking at the Navy Yard that afternoon, then riding up Pennsylvania Avenue in a hack, Nicolay saw the houses draped and shuttered. Men were standing idle in groups on street corners, whispering. The White House was "deeply draped in mourning, and the corpse is laid in state in the East Room where great crowds are taking their last look at the President's kind face . . . The funeral will take place tomorrow."

John Hay and Robert Lincoln greeted him upstairs. There were no words for what they felt. Robert was in charge. On the morning of April 15, with a trembling hand, he had written a telegram to his father's friend Judge David Davis, in Chicago, Illinois: "Please come at once to Washington & take charge of my father's affairs . . ." Davis, whom Lincoln had appointed to the Supreme Court, was not only a trusted family friend, but also a smart businessman who could work with Robert and Mary Lincoln. He wired back immediately that he was on his way.

Robert's main concern was for his mother and his brother Tad. Mrs. Lincoln's condition was deplorable. Returning from the Peterson house the morning of April 15, she had at first refused to enter any of the bedrooms, recoiling from one after another in terror. At last, her friend Mrs. Mary Jane Welles, wife of Gideon Welles, was able to persuade her to lie down in the tiniest guest bedroom at the end of the hall.

Mrs. Lincoln's former dressmaker and maid, Elizabeth Keckley, was summoned to relieve Mrs. Welles. Keckley found the widow tossing and turning on the bed in a darkened room, "nearly exhausted with grief." She left for a few minutes to view the president's body in a room down the hall, and when she returned she found Mrs. Lincoln "in a new paroxysm of grief. Robert was bending over his mother with tender affection, and little Tad was crouched at the foot of the bed with a world of agony in his young face. I shall never forget the scene," Mrs. Keckley wrote, "the wails of a broken heart, the unearthly shrieks, the terrible convulsions, the wild, tempestuous outbursts . . ." Tad's grief was as great, "but her terrible outbursts awed the boy into silence." He begged her to stop, and for a while she was quiet for his sake.

Too distraught to attend the funeral on the nineteenth, Mary

Lincoln remained in the darkened room. Although her friends Mrs. Welles and Elizabeth Blair Lee came to attend her, she would not allow anyone to remain long in her presence except Mrs. Keckley. The sisters in Springfield Mary had alienated would not come to her now. Commissioner French wrote that "the sudden and awful death of the President somewhat unhinged her mind, for at times she has exhibited all the symptoms of madness."

She emerged on April 21 to accompany her husband's body on a special funeral train. It would retrace the same meandering seventeen-hundred-mile journey back to Springfield that the president-elect had traveled on his way to Washington four years before. With Robert Lincoln, Ward Hill Lamon, General David Hunter, Justice David Davis, John Hay, and John Nicolay aboard, it would make the same stops. At major cities, such as Baltimore, Philadelphia, New York, Albany, Cleveland, and Chicago, the casket would be unloaded so the embalmed corpse could lie in state. There were corteges and obsequies in public buildings and squares, funeral after funeral as millions of mourners paid their respects to the fallen "Father Abraham." The train from Springfield had been gaily decorated in red, white, and blue bunting; this one was draped in black. Where cheers had greeted the smiling president-elect, now all the station stops were hushed, the people in tears.

When word of Lincoln's assassination reached William Stoddard, he was lying on a camp bed in the marshal's quarters of the dilapidated statehouse building in Little Rock, Arkansas. His duties there in keeping the peace are vaguely known. In his memoirs, he refers to dealing "in cotton operations" for which he had obtained a permit. "My profits on that line were a large hole in my pocket," he concluded. It is noteworthy that the day after Mr. Lincoln was reelected, John Hay wrote in his diary that the president had been summoned to the War Department to "consult in regard to some suggestion of [General Benjamin] Butler's, who wants to grab & incarcerate some gold gamblers. The President don't like to sully victory by any harshness." In Arkansas, Stoddard the gold gambler was out of harm's way.

There had been a long delay in getting the telegraph dispatch from Memphis to Little Rock. Three days after the president's death, on a warm morning in Arkansas, the heavy guns heralded the bad news. Awakening to the awful truth, Stoddard was shattered. Stores and offices did not open that day.

Officials, soldiers, and civilians gathered at noon in the Masonic Hall to express their grief. The president's former secretary made a speech "which was received with evidently sincere and intense interest by an intelligent body of men who saw and felt that in the murder of Abraham Lincoln the really best friend and protector of the future interests of the defeated South had been taken away. I finished my address," Stoddard recalled, "and walked away to my office, weary and sick at heart." After supper, he lay down to grieve for Lincoln. "I had not yet had time to consider how great a change this loss of my best friend was making in my own position and in my future course of life."

On April 22, Stoddard wrote to John Hay: "The terrible news was some time in reaching us. Now that the first stunning effects are over, I feel for the first time how much I loved and venerated Abraham Lincoln. I cannot write about him, even to you. I only wish to say that something of personal sympathy for you and Nicolay weighs tonight with my sorrow for the man who has done more for me than all my other friends. Men who had never seen him wept when the news came. How shall we say our sorrow,—who knew him as he really was?"

There is some question about where and when Hay and Nicolay boarded the funeral train on the twelve-day journey. It appears that they started out with the others, turned back in Philadelphia or New York, then rejoined the cortege up the line a week later en route to the burial in Springfield on May 4. On April 24, Nicolay wrote to Therena from Washington, explaining that after the funeral there five days earlier, "I felt entirely too depressed in spirits to write you a letter. Words seemed so inadequate to express my own personal sorrow at the loss of such a friend . . ."

He added, "Major Hay and I are still here arranging the papers of the office, which has kept us very busy." The task of boxing up the president's general correspondence, as well as drafts of inaugural

speeches, state of the union messages, and every memorandum and jot-
ting in Mr. Lincoln's hand was arduous and emotional. And it was most
efficiently accomplished in the few days they had without Mrs. Lincoln
and Robert in the house.

"I think that I do not yet, and probably shall not for a long while,
realize what a change his death has wrought in my own personal relations," Nicolay confided to his fiancée, "and the personal relations of
almost every one connected with the government in this city who stood
near to him . . ." In May, he was still so uncertain about the future that
he considered postponing their marriage again. "I am sorry to say that
I think I shall not be able to take you to Paris with me this time—
but this I will talk over with you while at Pittsfield. I am still trying to
get ready to sail about the first of June."

Happily, by May 30, the lovers had reached an agreement. They
would be married in Pittsfield on June 15, 1865, in the home of Therena's parents. John Hay served as bridegroom. On June 24, the three of
them sailed on the *City of London* from New York to Europe.

ONE WOULD THINK THAT the city of Paris, with its lively boulevards,
beautiful gardens and churches, theaters, museums, and opera, would
be a fitting reward for Nicolay and Hay after the terrible war years and
the trauma of the assassination. Their duties, as consul and secretary of
the legation, respectively, were mainly social and ceremonial—not at
all onerous. Hay seems to have enjoyed himself, perfecting his French,
frequenting the museums and restaurants, and observing the curious
manners of the court during the reign of Napoléon III.

Although Nicolay remained in France until 1869, two years longer
than Hay, the consul's career in the City of Light seems to have been
troubled from the first. According to his daughter Helen, who was born
in Paris in 1868, "cholera had invaded Paris." Nicolay took his wife and
the baby to Switzerland, set them up in a pension there, "then returned
to pursue his duties." The extant letters suggest that much of the time
they spent in Europe was spent apart.

Then, within a year of taking up his post, Nicolay saw that the new administration under Andrew Johnson was trying to remove him. He may have disliked the French capital, its weather and its politics (he called the city "an aggregation of *debris* rather than a fresh healthy organic structure of vital and intelligent forces") but the Paris consulate was a highly desirable, coveted post. Johnson, in political trouble from the first, would have loved to trade this plum for support. By the autumn of 1866, Nicolay was hearing reports that he would be superseded. On October 29, he received a dispatch from the State Department informing him that "representations had been made" charging him with "*negligence, inefficiency,* ignorance of the business and receipts of the Consulate, and habitual disrespect toward the President," he informed Therena. He said that the odds of maintaining his job in Paris were ten to one against.

Eventually he received a terse letter of support from the assistant secretary of state, Frederick Seward. John Hay—having returned to Washington in February of 1867—wrote to reassure him: "You are all right everywhere. That push against you came from cops [copperheads] who want your place." Nevertheless, his daughter wrote, "the charges were renewed from time to time," and included accusations that Nicolay was "an habitual drunkard, and a victim of syphilis."

Nicolay maintained his position in Paris until Ulysses S. Grant's inauguration in March of 1869. He returned to Illinois with his family in June. He would never again have a diplomatic post, although he lobbied persistently for one. During the next two years, he returned to journalism for his livelihood, writing for the *New York Times* and the *Atlantic Monthly*. With some friends, he discussed reviving the *Chicago Republican*. He actually served as the paper's editor for three months before resigning, saying that he "had neither courage nor physical strength to continue." Later he got the idea of starting a "penny newspaper" in St. Louis for the purpose of educating the broader electorate, but nothing came of this. It is fair to say that Nicolay was fixated upon the idea of writing the definitive biography of Abraham Lincoln, and was not really satisfied with any other career prospect until he could have time to devote to that end.

Nicolay's daughter says that after returning from Paris in the summer of 1869, "He was so much out of health that his main efforts, during the next three years, had to be directed toward regaining his strength. Winters were spent in Florida, summers in a northern climate." Nicolay's illness is a mysterious theme shadowing his entire biography. His daughter refers time and again to his blindness. He began to lose his eyesight in his late thirties, and by the age of fifty-five he could not see well enough to write. He dictated his great historical works, first to his wife, and, when she died suddenly in 1885, to his devoted daughter.

Never does Helen Nicolay, John Hay, or Nicolay himself mention the cause of his excruciating ill health or his blindness, or the efforts of any physician to cure him—with one exception. There is an unpublished letter of July 20, 1861, in which he tells Therena that his doctor is treating him for "bilious fever." Doctors used that now archaic term to describe a remittent fever, usually accompanied by vomiting and diarrhea.

In that long letter, Nicolay describes his symptoms in detail. He has no fever. He is "in a state, at the same time, of great *muscular* lassitude, and great nervous vigor and excitement. ... The nerves constantly crave 'action: action!' while the muscles as eloquently plead, 'rest, rest.'" Nicolay has none of the symptoms of bilious fever. And what does the doctor prescribe? Blue mass pills and calomel—both mercury compounds, the treatment of choice for syphilis—and laxatives. The doctor denies him water. The doctor's hope was that the concentration of antibacterial mercury in the body, deprived of water, combined with the laxative, might force the disease out of the patient's system. Nicolay probably had syphilis, one of the only diseases of that century that dared not speak its name. This would explain his long delay of marriage. Because of the remissions in the progress of the disease, for syphilitics there was always the hope for a cure. They sometimes lived long lives—he would reach the age of sixty-nine—and were contagious only in the early stages.

Fortune smiled upon the family in December of 1872 when Nicolay was called back to Washington. He had applied for, and was appointed to, the position of marshal of the United States Supreme Court. Overjoyed, he informed a French newsman that this was "une très jolie position." It had been a considerable advantage to him in applying that out of the nine justices, he knew six personally. Along with prestige, the job provided a comfortable office in the Capitol, a good salary, "and not too much hard work." This was perfect for the frail writer, who longed to begin research on the biography of Abraham Lincoln.

The job of marshal—also called the "Crier"—is mostly ceremonial. As the nine justices enter from the curtains to take their seats, the marshal calls, "Oyez, oyez, oyez," and announces their arrival with formulaic phrases. "All persons having business before the Honorable the Supreme Court of the United States are admonished to draw near and give attention . . ." That was the height of the marshal's responsibility. After that, Nicolay could go home to lunch. In the summer, there was a long recess when the Crier had even less to do, and his office was only a short walk along the tessellated marble paving to the Library of Congress. Apart from Lincoln's papers, that library was to be Hay and Nicolay's main reference source for the book to come.

The Nicolays purchased a cream-colored brick house at 212 B Street, S.E. (two blocks from Jean Margaret Lander), a two-minute walk from the Capitol.

JOHN HAY'S CAREER AS a diplomat, an editor, a businessman, and an author, from 1869 until his death in 1905, at sixty-seven, was so spectacular that no biography—and there have been five—has done it justice. Hay was a man doomed to extravagant success—success of a different sort from the kind he had hoped for in his youth. His careful observation of Mr. Lincoln, Seward, Chase, Stanton, and other titans of that legendary administration had prepared him for diplomacy of the highest caliber. He became a legend in his own time, first as writer of popular verses, then as a statesman.

Soon after Hay returned from France in 1867, Seward sent him as chargé d'affaires (temporary ambassador) to the U.S. legation in Vienna.

The salary was $6,000 per year. He resigned that post in August of 1868 and returned to the United States in October. For a few weeks, he took over as editor of the *Illinois Journal* in Springfield before he was appointed secretary of the legation in Madrid. He sailed to Europe in July of 1869, but gave up the position ten months later because the hours were too long and the salary ($1,800 per annum) too low. It would be nine years before he would resume his career in the foreign service.

From 1870 until 1875, Hay lived in Manhattan, where he edited and wrote for Greeley's *New York Tribune.* Stoddard, having left Arkansas, had also returned to journalism, as a reporter for the *New York Examiner*—difficult work for him because complications of malaria had ruined his hearing. Stoddard and Hay occasionally exchanged letters, but there is no evidence that they visited each other in New York.

In 1870, Stoddard married Susan Eagleson Cooper, a schoolteacher. They had five children. In the 1870s and 1880s, he ventured upon "railway, telegraphic and manufacturing enterprises," and patented a printer's frame for type. He never returned to gambling in gold or stocks; he had learned his lesson in the White House. But he was an erratic businessman who was unable to preserve his capital. Writing suited him. Never at a loss for words, he could always rely upon his pen to turn a dollar, and upon his wife to put it to good use. In his mid-thirties, he wrote a satire of Tammany Hall called *The Royal Decrees of Sanderoon.* He went on to write and publish more than a hundred books before his death at eighty-nine. The needs of his growing family made him accept a position as chief clerk of the Bureau of Engineering in New York's Dock Department during the first few years of the marriage. Yet he continued writing books: memoirs, biographies, and novels for boys. Eventually he would make his name and his living as an author. "I ought to be comfortable," he told Nicolay. "It is not exactly what they call fame, but it will do."

Meanwhile, John Hay won great fame for his poems in the dialect of rural Illinois, collected as the *Pike County Ballads,* and his book *Castillian Days,* based upon his travels in Spain. On August 27, 1873, he wrote to Nicolay, "I am engaged to be married to Miss Clara Stone of

Cleveland. . . . She is a very estimable young person, large, handsome, and good. I never found life worth while before." The daughter of the railroad magnate Amasa Stone—whose ventures included mines, banks, and iron foundries—Clara Louise Stone was also a very rich woman. They were married in February of 1874. The next year, Hay resigned from the *Tribune* and moved to Cleveland, where he began a successful business career under the guidance of his father-in-law.

Financially secure at last, Hay returned to politics during the congressional canvass of 1879, making pro-Republican speeches. As a reward, Rutherford B. Hayes appointed him assistant secretary of state. Sworn into office in November, he served for seventeen months, resigning after James Garfield was inaugurated in 1881. Disappointed that Garfield did not offer him a cabinet position, Hay retired from public life. In the 1880s, he toured Europe with his wife and four children, wrote and published (anonymously) a novel of social criticism called *The Bread-winners,* which became a best seller, and built a mansion on Lafayette Square across from the White House.

The Hays moved to the capital in 1886. It was during that decade that he and his friend Nicolay completed the monumental ten-volume biography of Lincoln that would be published in book form in 1890.

The Lincoln biography was the most significant literary effort of Hay's life. But for Nicolay—after his years with Lincoln in the White House—the biography was *the* central event in a life that was otherwise a sad tale. In the mid-1870s, he was struggling with Robert Lincoln to get the iron-bound boxes of Mr. Lincoln's papers delivered, unmolested, from Robert's home in Chicago to Washington. It was crucial, he wrote to Robert, "that I should be there at the first overhauling of the papers, as there may be many little things of which note should be taken at the moment. . . . The merest memorandum, mark, signature or figure, may have a future historical value . . . and the only good rule is to *save everything.* . . . I do not flatter myself that this is a trifling work. But I know that no one has equal advantages with myself for doing it . . ."

He begged Robert not to wait. There were so many men in the capital who must be interviewed in order to clarify points of the history, and they "are growing old, and in the course of Nature will not appear here many winters. As examples I mention Cameron, Blair, Sumner, Wade, Wilson and others . . ."

When at last Nicolay received the papers, he was called upon to defend the precious cache against Robert and other raiders when they requested this or that document in order to settle a dispute. The most famous incident concerned the question of Seward's power over Lincoln in the administration. After Seward's death, there was speculation that Lincoln had been no more than a figurehead, and that the secretary of state had been the true mastermind. In Nicolay's custody were Seward's lengthy memorandum of April 1, 1861, in which he suggests that he should direct the administration's domestic and foreign policy, as well as Lincoln's letter of reply: "If this must be done, I must do it." Nicolay's protest to Robert Lincoln is an eloquent summary of his feelings about the work in progress.

> I beg of you to no longer think of us as mere boys, but as men who have reached reasonably mature powers, who have learned something in the school of experience at least, and who believe ourselves capable of doing creditable work, when we have, what all other men have needed before us, the proper opportunity. We find such an opportunity in your father's history. He is our ideal hero. We wish to delineate the grandeur of the era in which he lived, the far-reaching significance and influence of the events he led, and to set him in history of the type, the Preserver and Liberator of the People. In support of this view we wish to present a compact, and exhaustive logical and historical *demonstration*.
>
> On the other hand both yourselves and the public naturally expect great things of us . . . and especially *new things*. If we can have the exclusive use of such leading documents as the Seward memorandum and reply . . . & c. . . . we shall be able to justify this expectation. . . . Now in proposing to give this paper to Mr. Welles you propose to take the strong link out of our chain—the key-stone out of our arch.

Nicolay won this argument and others with Robert Lincoln. During the 1870s and 1880s, Hay and Nicolay labored tirelessly to build the magnificent arch. It was a difficult time for the older man. According to his daughter, he was constantly "fighting his battle against ill health." At times, his eye trouble required him to remain in a darkened room for days at a time. He read nothing but letters and books pertaining to the history, and seldom went into society. In 1877, his only son, George Bates, died at the age of three months. In 1885, his beloved Therena, forty-nine, died after an illness of two weeks.

Helen had fond memories of the writers and their collaboration. "We kept no carriage," she wrote. "Colonel Hay probably had several, but when he wanted to confer with my father on the book, he was likely to leave them to other members of his family and take one of the horsecars that plodded at intervals along Pennsylvania Avenue from Georgetown to the Navy Yard."

Hay would get off at First Street in front of the Capitol. On the way to Nicolay's, he passed the cottage where Jean Lander still lived when she was not on tour. Perhaps he would stop by to congratulate her on her latest artistic triumph: as Marie Antoinette or Mary Stuart; as Hester Prynne in her own adaptation of *The Scarlet Letter* in 1877. Of her *Queen Elizabeth,* the critic for the *Washington Chronicle* wrote: ". . . to say that they [the audience] were spell-bound by the genius of the great actress is but a moderate expression of the emotion everywhere evinced. . . . Most beautifully were the opposite traits of character portrayed by Mrs. Lander—the kingly, fierce and masculine traits and the tender, womanly and sometimes tearful emotions. In her love passage with Essex Mrs. Lander was incomparable. There her noble, gentle and sweet character, fully expressed itself, and . . . she showed her own pure and loving soul. . . . glimpses of that noble devotion with which she loved her lamented husband, and of the lofty nature which gained for her the admiration of that noble and chivalrous man." She never remarried.

Mrs. Lander became one of the most beloved and revered actresses of the century. "A career of pre-eminent brilliance," wrote a *Philadelphia Press* contributor, "which will shine in memory long after the queenly face and form have passed from sound and sight."

It is hard to believe that Hay did not see her—at her door or in her garden—during the twenty years he worked with her neighbor Nicolay, two short blocks east. But let it pass. The lovers have left no traces, not even the appearance of the multimillionaire's carriage parked before her door. No, Hay preferred to go by horsecar, with the mechanics and the housemaids, or on foot.

Nicolay's study on the second floor of his home faced south. So, in fair weather, sunshine flooded the space, shone upon the overflowing bookshelves, the enormous desk (he had purchased his old desk from the White House), the hand-colored photograph of Mr. Lincoln and his two secretaries that hung on the wall. Hay "would come in, greet us brightly," Helen recalled, "and settle into a chair. If the session promised to be long and serious, he would relieve me of my seat across the desk from my father. . . . I would retreat to a corner and listen. Devoted to both of them, and immensely proud of the work . . . I was yet too young to realize fully the unusual privilege I enjoyed in listening to their lively talk and pungent comment." Helen, who became a renowned author and painter, wished she had taken notes. Her father used the "picturesque phrases of the frontier. John Hay had an almost uncanny faculty for suggesting much more than he actually said."

WILLIAM STODDARD WROTE SIX books about Abraham Lincoln. One of these, *Abraham Lincoln: The True Story of a Great Life,* was not at all welcomed by Nicolay and Hay. Stoddard's book was published in 1884, two years before his colleagues went to press, and it was a considerable success.

Nicolay and Hay were dismayed when Stoddard wrote to Hay that his first edition of *Abraham Lincoln* sold out sooner than he had expected because the critics had received the book kindly. Nicolay refused to receive it at all. Hay groused that Stoddard's book would "take away market value" from the one he and Nicolay were writing. So Stoddard wrote another letter, explaining that he had no intention of taking away their readers, and had actually said so in his preface. "Long ago I wrote you and Nicolay that I had a book in my mind and it was my idea, year after year, that yours would come out first. Is it too much to say that that idea died of old age? I hope you will make as full and valuable work as I have thought of your making and that it will succeed *enormously.* . . . "

Stoddard continued, "I have certainly done something in the way of advertising you. Never mind if your note nettled me a little but I certainly have not intentionally stolen a march on anybody." This was true. Stoddard had aged well. He had become a man of great generosity of spirit, one who had learned Lincoln's lesson not to waste energy on contention, particularly with friends. His good humor won out. In later years, Nicolay resumed correspondence with Stoddard and referred to him as "a very good fellow, and a man of considerable talent."

The publication of Hay and Nicolay's ten-volume *Abraham Lincoln: A History* commenced two years after Stoddard's book appeared, and was completed in 1890. When they had finished the biography, the partners began editing Lincoln's complete writings, which were published in 1894.

No one knows exactly how the writing of the great book was apportioned between the authors. "They seemed to take a mischievous delight in keeping it a secret," Helen recalled. She knew, of course, but the secret passed away with her in 1955, in that house where she lived alone for forty years after her father died. "Still respecting their wish, it can be said that they had no set schedule. Each wrote the part he felt ready at the moment to handle. They sometimes wrote alternate chapters, and again one of them might write a whole volume. . . . Every chapter was talked over and submitted to the frankest criticism, possible only between friends as thoroughly in accord as these two."

THE ECONOMIC DEPRESSION OF 1893, thirteen hundred labor strikes, and what Hay judged to be the unprincipled leadership of the administrations under Benjamin Harrison and Grover Cleveland roused Hay from his book-lined study. The rise of the free-silver, populist presidential candidate William Jennings Bryan sounded an alarm. After finishing the Lincoln biography, a sense of duty prompted John Hay to return to political life in his mid-fifties.

He believed that if men like himself did not return to government, the Republic that Lincoln had given his life to preserve would give way to anarchy. In Governor William McKinley of Ohio, a hard-money Republican, Hay saw possibilities. Working with the methodical business tycoon and political boss Mark Hanna, Hay helped McKinley to weather a personal financial embarrassment and win the presidency in 1896.

McKinley appointed Hay ambassador to England in 1897; he and his family arrived in London in April. It was a happy time in his life. His success there came of finding ways that the two nations could work together to resolve difficulties involving third-party nations—Spain during the war over Cuba, China's inaccessibility to trade—after two centuries of Anglo-American conflicts and tensions. In August of 1898, Hay was appointed secretary of state. Before the end of his first year in office, he negotiated the peace after the Spanish-American War.

In 1899, Hay sent notes to Great Britain, France, Germany, Italy, Russia, and Japan, advising them that all nations have equal rights in trade and business development with China. In March of 1900, he announced that this "Open Door Policy" proposal had been approved. It is the visionary act of diplomacy for which he is most remembered. But in the first years of the twentieth century, the secretary of state also negotiated several complex treaties with Great Britain, Columbia, and Panama that cleared the way for the construction of the Panama Canal.

President McKinley died of an assassin's bullet on September 14, 1901. When Theodore Roosevelt was sworn into office, Hay became—by the presidential succession act of 1886—a heartbeat away from the presidency. "Shortly after this," Helen Nicolay recalls, "Colonel Hay came to see my father, who had grown much weaker." She told him she thought it would be hazardous to tell the frail man of McKinley's death. "Colonel Hay's hand flew to the band of crape he wore on his arm. 'I must take this off before I go up to him!' he exclaimed and would have torn it from his sleeve. I had to tell him that my father could not see it—that he was already more in the other world than in this."

Slowly Hay went up the stairs. Helen waited below for a little while. Hay came down even more slowly, "his face stricken with grief. He never saw his old friend again . . ." When Nicolay passed away a few days later, on September 26, 1901, Hay was abroad, and could not return in time for the funeral.

Under Roosevelt, Hay remained secretary of state, and he would continue to bring honor to that high office until he died. His diplomacy was crucial to settling the U.S.-Canadian dispute over the Alaskan boundary in 1903, and in negotiating numerous reciprocity agreements with France, Germany, Cuba, and other nations. All told, his name came to be associated with more than fifty treaties before his death of a pulmonary embolism in 1905. He had suffered for many years from heart trouble and uremia. It was said that the revered and diligent statesman had to die—at the age of sixty-seven—in order to convince the world that he was truly ill.

Three weeks before his death, Hay wrote in his diary:

I dreamed last night that I was in Washington and that I went to the White House to report to the President who turned out to be Mr. Lincoln. He was very kind and considerate, and sympathetic about my illness. He said there was little work of importance on hand. He gave me two unimportant letters to answer. I was pleased that this slight order was within my power to obey. I was not in the least surprised at Lincoln's presence in the White House. But the whole impression of the dream was one of overpowering melancholy.

ACKNOWLEDGMENTS

Thanks to my agent, Neil Olson, and my editor, Elisabeth Kallick Dyssegaard, for their enthusiasm for this project from its inception, and for their advice on the manuscript as it evolved.

I could not have written this book—in less than a decade—without reference to the published writings of John Hay, John Nicolay, and William Stoddard edited so brilliantly by Michael Burlingame. My bibliography lists six indispensable texts edited by Mr. Burlingame. In addition to his published contribution, Mr. Burlingame personally offered significant advice and guidance as my research progressed.

Once again, I want to thank the staff at the Library of Congress for their assistance, especially Dr. John Sellers, Civil War Specialist of the Manuscript Division, Jeffrey M. Flannery and Bruce Kirby in the Manuscript Division, and librarians Travis Wesley and Gary Johnson in the Newspaper and Current Periodical Room. My research for this book was an outgrowth of the study that commenced a decade ago with my work on Abraham Lincoln and Walt Whitman, and continued more recently with my research concerning Abraham Lincoln's marriage. In all those years the staff at the Library has been a constant and friendly source of information.

I commend the manuscript curators at the John Hay Library at Brown University for their attention and patience during my days in Providence, Rhode Island, especially Holly Snyder, head of the Manuscript Division, and librarians Ann Morgan Dodge, Patricia Sirois, Andrew Moul, and Ann Patrick. It was necessary to have hands-on experience of John Hay's original diaries and manuscripts, and Ms. Snyder and the staff there made that possible.

I am grateful to Nancy Martin of the Manuscript Division of the University of Rochester Library, who sent me copies of William Stoddard's letters from the Martin Brewer Anderson Papers and the Seward Collection, and to Aislinn Sotelo of UCLA's Charles E. Young Research Library Department of Special Collections for sending me letters written by Jean Margaret Lander. And thanks to David Bergman for reading and commenting on the final draft of the manuscript.

Rosemary Knower read and edited the manuscript from the first draft to the last, and as ever, I am in her debt for her many suggestions and wise advice concerning matters of fact as well as the progress of the narrative.

BIBLIOGRAPHY

SOURCES

Abbreviations and Short Titles Employed in the Notes

BROOKS: Noah Brooks, *Washington in Lincoln's Time.* New York: Rinehart, 1958; reprint of 1895 edition.

BROWNING: Orville Browning, *The Diary of Orville Hickman Browning.* Ed. Theodore C. Pease and James G. Randall. 2 vols. Springfield: Illinois State Historical Library, 1925–33. Unpublished supplements courtesy of ISHL.

CW: Abraham Lincoln, *Collected Works of Abraham Lincoln.* Ed. Roy P. Basler. 8 vols. New Brunswick, N.J.: Rutgers University Press, 1953.

DAY BY DAY: Earl Schenck Miers, ed., *Lincoln Day by Day: A Chronology, 1809–1865.* 3 vols. Washington, D.C.: Lincoln Sesquicentennial Commission, 1960.

DENNETT: Tyler Dennett, *John Hay: From Poetry to Politics.* 2 vols. New York: Dodd, Mead, 1933.

DISPATCHES: William O. Stoddard, *Dispatches from Lincoln's White House: The Anonymous Civil War Journalism of Presidential Secretary William O. Stoddard.* Ed. Michael Burlingame. Lincoln: University of Nebraska Press, 2002.

DLC: Document in the Library of Congress.

DRPB: Document in the Hay Library, Brown University, Providence, R.I.

FRENCH: Benjamin Brown French, *Witness to the Young Republic: A Yankee's Journal, 1828–1870.* Ed. Donald B. Cole and John J. McDonough. Hanover, N.H.: University Press of New England, 1989.

HAY DIARY: John Hay, *Inside Lincoln's White House: The Complete Civil War Diary of John Hay.* Ed. Michael Burlingame and John R. Turner Ettlinger. Carbondale: Southern Illinois University Press, 1997.

HAY LETTERS: John Hay, *At Lincoln's Side: John Hay's Civil War Correspondence and Selected Writings.* Ed. Michael Burlingame. Carbondale: Southern Illinois University Press, 2000.

ISHL: Illinois State Historical Library, Springfield.

KUSHNER: Howard I. Kushner and Anne Hummel Sherrill, *John Milton Hay: The Union of Poetry and Politics.* Boston: Twayne Publishers, 1977.

LINCOLN'S JOURNALIST: John Hay, *Lincoln's Journalist: John Hay's Anonymous Writings for the Press, 1860–1864.* Ed. Michael Burlingame. Carbondale: Southern Illinois University Press, 1998.

LINCOLN'S SECRETARY: Helen Nicolay, *Lincoln's Secretary: A Life of John Nicolay.* New York: Longman, Green, 1949.

NICOLAY: John G. Nicolay, *With Lincoln in the White House.* Ed. Michael Burlingame. Carbondale: Southern Illinois University Press, 2000.

NICOLAY AND HAY: John G. Nicolay and John Hay, *Abraham Lincoln: A History.* 10 vols. New York: Century Company, 1886–90.

POEMS: John Hay, *The Complete Poetical Works of John Hay.* Boston: Houghton Mifflin, 1916.

RANDALL: Ruth Painter Randall, *Colonel Elmer Ellsworth.* Boston: Little, Brown, 1960.

RPB: John Hay Library, Brown University, Providence, R.I.

STODDARD MEMOIRS: William O. Stoddard, *Inside the White House in War Times.* Ed. Michael Burlingame. Lincoln: University of Nebraska Press, 2000.

STODDARD'S LIFE: William O. Stoddard, *Lincoln's White House Secretary: The Adventurous Life of William O. Stoddard.* Ed. Harold Holzer. Carbondale: Southern Illinois University Press, 2007.

THAYER: William Roscoe Thayer, *The Life and Letters of John Hay.* 2 vols. Boston: Houghton Mifflin, 1915.

CHAPTER NOTES

All but a few sources of the quotations in this book are listed in the bibliography above, and most sources are apparent from the context of the quoted material. For example, John Hay kept a diary during the war. It was edited and published in 1997. Hay also wrote letters and newspaper columns, most of which are dated and in print. Quoted information from Hay, with a few exceptions, is from one of those published sources, and I have tried to distinguish among letters, journalism, and diary entries in the text. Quotes from Lincoln's letters and speeches are from the *Collected Works,* edited by Roy Basler. All are dated.

Nicolay wrote regularly to his fiancée, and many of those letters were collected in *With Lincoln in the White House,* cited above. Nicolay letters that are *not* included in that edition, and passages that have been deleted from published letters, can be found in the John George Nicolay collection at the Library of Congress. The sources of William Stoddard's dateline journalism, like Hay's, are easily located. But his autobiographical impressions are undated, so I have annotated them.

The informal notes below will assist readers in locating important sources of quotes when the source is not clear from its context. I have tried to avoid annotating the obvious.

1 ∽ ILLINOIS PRELUDE

The main source of information on Ellsworth, and quotes from his letters, is RANDALL. Hay's comments on Ellsworth are from HAY LETTERS, pp. 144–45. The main source of information on Nicolay's life, apart from his own writings, is LINCOLN'S SECRETARY. The story of Howells and Hatch comes from that source, p. 34. The milking machine joke is traditional, like others attributed to Lincon; vide *Phunny Phellows* (Chicago: Rhodes & McClure, 1889), p. 242. Hay's early youth is told by DENNETT, and in A. S. Chapman's, "The Boyhood of John Hay," published by the *Century Magazine*, vol. 78, pp. 444–54. As there is no biography of Jean Margaret Davenport [Lander], I have relied on the Frederick West Lander collection at the Library of Congress (which contains her incoming letters and scrapbooks), Joy Leland's *Frederick West Lander* (Reno: Desert Research Institute, 1993), *Brown's History of the American Stage, Annals of the New York Stage*, and standard encyclopedias of American biography. All prewar letters of John Hay are courtesy of the RPB. Anna Ridgely's description of Hay is from "Springfield, Illinois in 1860 . . . ," an unpublished memoir, DRPB. Hay's quote on first meeting Lincoln is in the introduction of HAY LETTERS, p. xvi. Lincoln's comment "Let Hay come" is from DENNETT, p. 87.

2 ∽ WASHINGTON, 1861

The Republican leader who criticized Nicolay on page 20 was Herman Kreismann. The quote is from NICOLAY, p. xvii. Hay's comment "I'm the keeper of the President's conscience" is from F. A. Mitchell, quoted by Burlingame in the introduction to HAY DIARY, p. xiii. Stoddard tells the story of his first visit to the White House in STODDARD MEMOIRS, p. 216. His description of Nicolay is in ibid., p. 317. The quotes on page 30 concerning Lincoln's "confinement" are from *Abraham Lincoln: The Observations of John G. Nicolay and John Hay*, ed. Michael Burlingame (Carbondale: Southern Illinois University Press, 2007), p. 34; comments to Robert Wilson are in ibid., p. 34. Hay's comments on Ellsworth are from a biographical sketch of the soldier in HAY LETTERS, pp. 141–51. All other information on Ellsworth is from RANDALL.

3 ⬭ WAR

Stoddard's conversation with Lincoln (pages 44–45) is in STODDARD'S LIFE, pp. 220–22. Jefferson's story is told in *The Autobiography of Joseph Jefferson* (New York: Century Company, 1890), p. 27. Stoddard tells of Ellsworth and the broken window in STODDARD MEMOIRS, p. 164, and STODDARD'S LIFE, p. 228.

4 ⬭ GRAVE RESPONSIBILITIES

Lincoln's response to Ellsworth's death is in RANDALL, p. 262. Stoddard's comment on Douglas's death (page 66) is from STODDARD MEMOIRS, p. 164. Reference for details of the war's progress is E. B. Long, *The Civil War Day by Day* (New York: Doubleday, 1971). Stoddard's comment "We live a strange life here . . ." is from DISPATCHES, p. 27. Information about Baker comes from Harry C. Blair and Rebecca Tarshis, *Colonel Edward D. Baker* (Portland: Oregon Historical Society, 1960). Lander to Hay, December 31, 1861, is courtesy of RPB. Stoddard on Mrs. Lincoln is from STODDARD MEMOIRS, p. 33. For Stoddard re. the mail, vide STODDARD'S LIFE, pp. 242–45. Re. Mrs.Lincoln's mail, vide STODDARD MEMOIRS, pp. 17–18. Incident of Stoddard and the pardon comes from STODDARD'S LIFE, p. 245.

5 ⬭ TEAMWORK

The Lincolns' conversation concerning state dinners is in Elizabeth Keckley, *Behind the Scenes* (New York: Penguin, 2005; reprint of 1868 edition), p. 43. Stoddard's anecdotes on the ball tickets are in STODDARD'S LIFE, pp. 260–61. Recollections of the dancing and French tutor are in ibid., p. 235. Nicolay on Mrs. Eames is from NICOLAY, pp. 45–46. Stoddard on gambling fever is from STODDARD MEMOIRS, p. 36, and STODDARD'S LIFE, p. 273. Letters from Stoddard to Anderson are courtesy of the University of Rochester Library.

6 ∳ THE TYCOON AND LITTLE MAC

McClellan's quotes are from Mark E. Neeley Jr., *The Abraham Lincoln Encyclopedia* (New York: Da Capo, 1982), p. 199. Lincoln's quote on contention is from NICOLAY AND HAY, vol. 1, p. 222. Stoddard's recollection of visiting McClellan is in STODDARD MEMOIRS, pp. 63–65. Lincoln's fury regarding the canalboats is in NICOLAY, p. 72. Lincoln's comment on the Penninsular Campaign (page 113) is cited by Burlingame in ibid., p. 221. Stoddard's account of Hay's joke is in STODDARD MEMOIRS, pp. 95–96. Lincoln's quote "McClellan's bodyguard" is from DAY BY DAY, p. 143. His quip about McClellan's horses is from Neeley, *Abraham Lincoln Encyclopedia*, p. 201. The "stationary engine" quote may be found in John S. Bowman, *Who Was Who in the Civil War* (North Dighton, Mass.: JG Press, 1998) p. 143.

7 ∳ FROM HELL TO PARADISE

Descriptions of the weather and events in Washington on December 7 are from the *Washington Chronicle,* December 8, 1862. Mrs. Frederick Lander to Hay, December 27, 1862, is courtesy of RPB. Stoddard's description of the drinking life is from STODDARD'S LIFE, p. 259. The reporter who noted that Lincoln looked "haggard" was from *Frank Leslie's Illustrated Newspaper,* February 28, 1863. Quote from Seth Rogers is courtesy of the collection of James S. Rogers, available at www.unf.edu/floridahistoryonline. Essential sources for this chapter are the Hay scrapbooks, Hay MSS, DLC, which contain columns from the *New York Herald Tribune* dated May 22, 26, 27, and 28, describing the picnics and ceremonies in Beaufort and Hilton Head. Higginson's quote is from *Letters and Journals of Thomas Wentworth Higginson, 1846–1906,* ed. Mary Thatcher Higginson (Boston: Houghton Mifflin, 1921), pp. 201–2.

8 ∳ BLOOD AND GOLD

For "What will the country say?" vide BROOKS, p. 61. Stoddard on Lincoln's pacing is in STODDARD MEMOIRS, pp. 114–16. For Stoddard on the July 4 celebration, vide ibid., pp. 117ff; for French on the event, vide FRENCH, p. 425. Stoddard's comment on the gold market is STODDARD'S

LIFE, p. 313. His remarks on his illness and the draft riots are from Ibid. pp. 314–16. Information on the observatory is from *Philp's Washington Described,* ed. William D. Haley (New York: Rudd & Carlton, 1861), pp. 156–58. The conversation over the Conkling letter is indexed in both of Stoddard's autobiographical works. The target practice and the McManus joke are recounted in STODDARD MEMOIRS, pp. 22–25, and the Durant incident on p. 37. Information on the scandal and Stoddard's gold line comes from Michael Burlingame's introduction to STODDARD MEMOIRS, pp. xvi–xvii, articles in the *Washington Star* of March 12, 1878, and the *New York Evening Post* of March 11, 1878, and letters from Stoddard to Hay in RPB. Stoddard publicly denied the accusations.

9 ⬯ THE TIDE TURNS

All Helen Nicolay quotes are from LINCOLN'S SECRETARY. Her comment on the Washington visit is on p. 192, and the length of the engagement on p. 239. The journalist who commented upon Lincoln and Booth was George Alfred Townsend in the *New York World,* quoted in notes to HAY DIARY, p. 325. The *New York Times* article on Mrs. Lander appeared on August 14, 1863. The Wadsworth Papers are DLC. Hay's news column on the Gettysburg consecration was published in the *Washington Daily Chronicle,* November 21, 1863. Stoddard's description of his 1864 illness is in STODDARD'S LIFE, p. 317. His anecdote at the chapter's end is in ibid., p. 339.

10 ⬯ ERRANDS AND EXITS

On Horace Greeley, vide John C. Waugh, *Reelecting Lincoln* (New York: Crown, 1997), pp. 134ff. Thomas Hood's poem "A True Story" may be found in its entirety in *The Choice Works of Thomas Hood* (Boston: DeWolfe, Fiske, n.d.), p. 211. The quote "Lie still . . . into the darkness" is recounted by Elihu Root, and quoted in the footnotes to HAY DIARY. Stoddard's involvement in Johnson's nomination is indexed in both of his autobiographical works. He tells the story of his departure for Arkansas in STODDARD'S LIFE, p. 325. Kate's memoir is quoted in the introduction to ibid., p. 8. The famous Sherman quote may be found in CW, vol. 8, pp. 181–82.

11 ℅ LIGHTS IN THE SHADOW

Jean Lander's performance in Chicago is cited in the *Chicago Tribune,* April 14, 1865. Robert Lincoln's telegram to Davis is quoted in Ruth Painter Randall, *Lincoln's Sons* (Boston: Little, Brown, 1955), p. 164–65. Mrs. Keckley's observations of Mrs. Lincoln are in *Behind the Scenes,* pp. 82–85. Stoddard's notes on Lincoln's death are in STODDARD'S LIFE, pp. 344–46. His letter to Hay of April 22 is DRPB. Most information and quotes concerning Nicolay, as well as his letters from 1866 to 1891, are from LINCOLN'S SECRETARY, pp. 239ff. The information on Stoddard's later years comes from STODDARD'S LIFE, specifically Harold Holzer's excellent introduction, and the postscript by his granddaughter Eleanor Stoddard. (The quotes about the secretaries' competing books are from Holzer's introduction.) The reviews of Mrs. Lander's comeback are in the pamphlet by T. B. Hugh, *Biographical Sketch of Mrs. F.W. Lander* (Philadelphia: Lander Histrionic Company, 1867), pp. 7–10. Hay's diary entry of June 13, 1905, is published in THAYER, vol. 2, p. 405.

INDEX